ABOUT MY SKETCHES

They represent a record of experiences I shared with other young men during our years of military service. Camp life, training, maneuvers, week end passes and finally combat. The combat cameraman records scenes as the happen and a artist paint what he sees before him. My sketches are created after the event of things I've seen or of which I have knowledge.

The burning castle is an example. That event occurred about seven miles from where I was. The Germans had broken thru the defense lines of the 28th division and were rapidly approaching Clervaux and the burning castle. The street was jammed with soldiers & vehicles falling back toward Bastonge. Add to that civilians joining the exodus. In the flickering glare & shadows cast by the flames there was certainly fear and panic in the air.

I thought I'd like to paint that scene, but I was not there or had any idea what the castle looked like. Many years after the war I found a picture of the burned ruins of the castle in an old National Geographic. Using that as a base I created the scene as I imagined it. I had to improvise the foreground and vehicles. I did not have the skill to capture the feeling of panic and fear. The painting portrays an event during the battle of the Bulge.

The sketches in this book vary in quality for several reasons. Those done in ink or watercolor have printed nicely. Most pencil sketches have faired poorly. All have been subjected to heat, dampness and careless handling. Some even damaged by fire. Considering they are over sixty years old, I am satisfied they printed at all.

Order this book online at www.trafford.com
or email orders@trafford.com

Most Trafford titles are also available at major online book retailers.

Print information available on the last page.

ISBN: 978-1-4120-9674-4 (sc)
ISBN: 978-1-4269-9007-6 (e)

Trafford rev. 05/06/2021

Trafford www.trafford.com
PUBLISHING®
North America & international
toll-free: 844-688-6899 (USA & Canada)
fax: 812 355 4082

SKETCHES AND MEMOIRS FROM WWII

M.H. "Bill" Kunselman

ACKNOWLEDGEMENTS

For their time, computer skills

And help preparing my original

Work for publication

Rose Miller and Daughter Kimberly

Phillip Thompson

Rick Phillips

Dennis Burchfield

Shannan Greenhouse

Thanks to my mother Lea Maurice Kunselman

for saving my letters

Love to my wife Lois Elaine Kunselman my Pride & Joy

AUTHOR

DRAFTSMAN-DESIGNER-ARCHTECT

MARRIED 65 YEARS-4 CHILDREN-8 GRANDCHILDREN

IV

SKETCHES & MEMOIRS
FROM WORLD WAR II

by

Maurice (Bill) Kunselman

CHAPTERS

MAPS

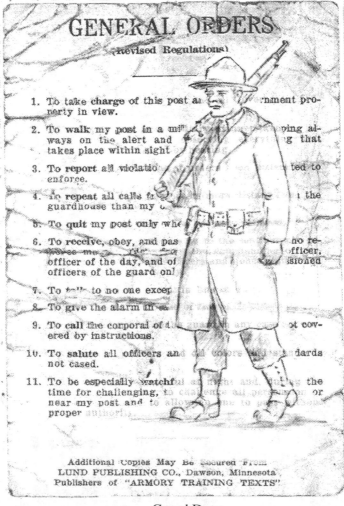

GENERAL ORDERS
(Revised Regulations)

1. To take charge of this post an ... nment property in view.

2. To walk my post in a mi... ...ying always on the alert and ... ...g that takes place within sight ...

3. To report all violatio... ...ted to enforce.

4. To repeat all calls fr... ...the guardhouse than my ...

5. To quit my post only whe...

6. To receive, obey, and pas... ...no re... ...officer, officer of the day, and of... ...sioned officers of the guard onl...

7. To t... to no one excep...

8. To give the alarm ...

9. To call the corporal of ... ...ot covered by instructions.

10. To salute all officers and ... ...dards not cased.

11. To be especially watchf... ...the time for challenging, ...or near my post and to allo... proper ...

Additional Copies May Be Secured From
LUND PUBLISHING CO., Dawson, Minnesota
Publishers of "ARMORY TRAINING TEXTS"

Guard Duty

VI

PENNSYLVANIA

JANUARY-AUGUST 1944

28th Div.

PENNSYLVANIA

The years after I graduated from high school in 1939 were troubled years. A growing threat of war in Europe as Hitler's Nazi German gobbled up one country after another and Mussolini's legions rattled the saber in Africa. We watched on newsreel the awesome mass of storm troopers shouting "Zeig Heil" as Hitler raved his hatred and demands. We saw pictures of 8 & 9 year-old Italian children training with wooden rifles and bayonets. Then there were the Life magazines coverage of savage Japanese bombing of civilians and cruel bayoneting of prisoners in China. It all looked pretty grim and foreboding to us with a standing army of only 125,000.

In September 1939, war broke out in Europe, but a strange war as Hitler's army carried out its blitzkrieg offensive that totally destroyed the large Polish army in a matter of weeks while the armies of France and England stood passively by. Could France and England stand against this formidable tripartite of Germany, Russia and Italy? In the Far East, Japan became increasingly belligerent toward the western powers. In spite of all the signs we felt insulated from world events by our two oceans. It was still seven days to Europe and two weeks to the Far East. The day of the jet and intercontinental missiles was undreamed of. We were more concerned with the lingering effects of the great depression than with foreign wars. Yet submarine warfare raging and powerful German battleships raiding in the Atlantic stirred some concern. At home, the audacity of the German Bund waving the Nazi banner sparked violence with the American Legion.

The French sat in false security in their Maginot Line as Hitler completed the conquest of Norway in April 1940, opposed only by the British navy and a small expeditionary force. Then the quiet on the western front was shattered as Holland, Belgium and France fell before the lightning blitzkrieg attack. The magnificent evacuation of the British army at Dunkirk stirred us; forgetting it was the aftermath of total defeat, not victory. No one expected her to withstand the next assault for even her lifeline to the empire was threatened as Mussolini's legions entered the war like jackals wanting their part of the carcass. Events shocked us and we began to wonder how safe we were with the rest of the world falling under the power of fanatical dictators dedicated to world conquest.

Roosevelt recognized that if the free world were to survive, America would have to become involved. First as the arsenal of democracy, later as a full war partner. Dunkirk had saved Britain's army, but stripped her of her arms. Lend-lease became a new terminology as we began converting our industrial power to war production. Then steps were taken to strengthen our navy and build an army and air force. A tremendous task for a nation that was virtually defenseless. Selective service (draft) was started and the National Guard was called up for a years training. It was against this background that Howard Lewis and I decided to join the local National Guard unit both for the adventure and to get our years service out of the way. Meanwhile the air blitz raged over London and England as Churchill marshaled the British will to survive.

We joined Co. B, 1st Battalion. Of the 112th Inf. Regiment in January of 1941. The Armory was located on Diamond Park in Meadville, Pa. and there we began our basic training for a few weeks prior to leaving for camp. Of course, we were rookies at the mercy of every non-com in the company. My chief concern was to get past the final physical exam, as I knew my eyes would never pass. The day of the exam, Capt Bowen assigned me to help keep records for the eye test, giving me an opportunity to memorize the first four lines on the chart. Later, when my turn came I passed the test but if they had changed the chart, my duplicity would have been revealed. I wasn't very smart though. If I had failed the test I could have spent the war at home with the girls.

1

It was a cold crisp night in February with snow on the ground when the company formed up in front of the armory. Then with the American Legion drum and bugle corps leading the way, we marched the four blocks down to the Erie RR station at the foot of Chestnut Street. There we had time to say goodbye to those who had braved the cold to see us off. The troop train already had picked the companies from Greenville and Grove City. We loaded up and stowed our gear best we could on the racks or under the seats as the train pulled out. At Corry the rest of our battalion joined us, then we rolled east thru the changing scene of moonlit snow covered hills and darkened forest. At Salamanca the train switched to the Lackawanna tracks, twisting southeast thru the Appalachians toward eastern Pennsylvania.

We arrived at a bleak windblown siding near Indiantown Gap at some ungodly hour of the morning and trucks took us into camp. It was a depressing sight with stark rows of darkened barracks and snow-covered piles of construction materials and equipment. The camp was still under construction. Finally after a series of stops and starts we were deposited by a group of cold empty buildings that was to be our home. It was my luck to draw guard duty first thing. My spirit was at low ebb as I tramped my post amid the unfamiliar surroundings in the pre-dawn darkness. The temperature was in the 20's with a brisk wind blowing and somewhere an unlatched door kept slamming. The rest of the day would be busy as the company settled in. Steel cots, mattresses and footlockers hauled in and set up in the barracks. Supplies drawn and stowed in the supply room and the mess hall made operational. Finally when taps sounded and lights went out it dawned on us that this communal living, regulated by schedules and authority was going to be a way of life for a long time. A lot of us were homesick as we crawled into our bunks.

The 28th Division was Pennsylvania's National Guard commanded by Major General Martin. Its shoulder patch was a red keystone. Organized on the lines of the WW-I square division, it consisted of the 55th Brigade Composed by the by the 109th and 110th infantry regiments and the 56 Brigade composed by the 111th and 112th Infantry regiments from western Penna. Each brigade had two artillery battalions equipped with WW-I French 75's.

In addition there was one medium artillery battalion of 155 howitzers, a troop of mechanized cavalry equipped with armored cars and light tanks, an engineer battalion plus quartermaster, communications, ordnance and chemical units and the less than popular MP Company.

This type of division was designed for the static type of trench warfare of World War I. Later the army would reorganize these divisions to make them more mobile for the open type of warfare evidenced in Europe. The brigades were eliminated and one regiment of infantry and one battalion of artillery removed. Thus from every three divisions, one new division was gained. The square division became the triangular division composed of three regimental combat teams. I should note that many of our higher officers were veterans of WW-I.

Indiantown Gap Military Reservation was designed for the old square division. There were two brigade areas subdivided into regimental and battalion areas. There were separate areas for quartermaster and special units. It covered a big area. Battalion areas were arranged in the form of a quadrangle with the barracks facing inwards and enclosing a large open space.

Typical of National Guard units, we were probably at about 60 percent of combat strength. Soon after getting settled in we began receiving draftees to bring us up to full strength. This was an interesting experience to suddenly find these boys from New England, New York and especially Brooklyn amongst us. Their manner of speaking ,accents, abrasiveness. It was suddenly a different world as this flood of foreigners invaded our provincialism.

We quickly fell into routine. The bugle blared reveille; seeming to say "I Can't Get Them Up! I Can't Get Them In The Morning!" Then the lights would go on and the sergeant would yell, "Roll out – Grab your socks," empathized with colorful phrases I wouldn't dare print. The mad rush for the showers and washbasins, then hurriedly dress in time for roll call formation. After that some calisthenics as daylight started to break. Returning to the barracks for a few minutes to make beds and get our places shipshape before mess call for breakfast. We ate well as a rule despite our gripes. One item frequently on the menu was Philadelphia Scrapple, a mush like mixture pressed into a flat like cake and fried. Never did know what it consisted of.

After breakfast a few minutes to get our equipment and fall in for the days training. Joining the rest of the battalion we marched past regimental HQ and the staff on our way to the training fields. There, it was a full day of close order drill, manual of arms, weapons instruction, bayonet practice and more calisthenics. It was cold in February and March. The squad leader occasionally picked a man to drill the squad for practice. One day I was reluctantly trying my hand at it. Right Shoulder Arms! Column of Twos to Right – March! To the Rear – March; by the Right Flank – March! Everything seemed to be going pretty well. Then to my horror I saw I had the squad headed straight for General Martin and his staff, who had ridden up on horses to observe the training. My mind froze and I couldn't think even to say "Squad Halt". They marched right into the group of officers and horse, resulting in a confused melee. The men thought it was a great joke on me, but there was some a—chewing over that calamity including the platoon sergeants for letting this rookie drill the squad. I ended up on the platoon sergeant's black list and did latrine duty and KP for the following week. Never did get another chance to drill the squad. My stomach still tightens up when I think of that scene.

It was always a relief to get back to the warm barracks in the late afternoon. The 1st Sgt checked the barracks while we were gone and if anything didn't meet his satisfaction we'd soon hear about it. The 1st Sgt was God as far as we were concerned. It might get us extra guard duty, some special detail or loss of a weekend pass. Normally a man free of extra duty would spend the evening cleaning his equipment and then spend the rest of the time till taps, playing cards, reading or writing. However, ours was not a normal situation, being in a new raw camp. So we spent our evenings, especially as the spring thaw started, building sidewalks and roads until dark and later. There were details to haul slate in the weapons carrier from the nearby coalmines. Then details to shovel, wheelbarrow, spread and crush the slate as we tried to keep one jump ahead of the mud around us. At times we worked right thru the weekend because there were battalion details, regimental details and division details to man as well as our own company efforts.

My buddy Howard Lewis was fortunate in having some typing experience and the 1st Sgt grabbed him for company clerk. That kept him in a nice warm office while the rest of us shivered out on the training fields or sweated on the slate details. I couldn't help but envy his good fortune, as I was to endure the miseries of a common infantry private for a while longer. At the time I saw no hope in the future.

There was no relaxation on Saturday mornings. Barracks inspection was followed by a division parade. If our barracks passed inspection a certain quota got passes. If it failed the whole barracks could be restricted to camp. Woe to the individual (or individuals) who caused their barracks to be restricted. Their life would be made pretty miserable. We'd begin by scrubbing the whole barracks including the latrine, cleaning the windows, dusting the shelves, etc. Then we would police the grounds outside. Each barracks had to supply a detail to clean the supply room, mess hall and office.

After that, we had to arrange our own area. Bed made up tight as a drumhead, boots shined, material on shelves just right, clothing hung properly, footlockers packed correctly, rifle cleaned, brass buttons polished and so on. Believe me it was a busy time. Then waiting until the ominous order "Attention" aas the company commander approached our floor. We each stood rigidly by the foot of our bunks as the inspecting party – the Capt, the 1st Sgt with his notebook and the barracks Sgt inspected each man and his area. The Capt wore white gloves which he ran over every thing. A smudge on them or something out of order and the 1st Sgt made a note in his book. One would get a clue as to how he made out by the look on the barracks Sgt's face as they passed on to the next guy. After they had finished and passed on we'd receive the order "At Ease". Then we berated anyone who obviously had goofed or took stock of our chances to have passed. We didn't have much time to brood though, as we had to get ready to fall in for the division review parade.

We marched out to the parade grounds by regiments and then formed up in brigades. It was quite a sight to see 15,000 men in solid blocks, guidens fluttering, flags flying. Sometimes we stood at attention so long that on a hot day men would fall over in a faint. We learned to keep our knees flexed just a little to avoid that. When all the units were in place and the formalities over, the division band lead off and battalion sized formations wheeled out and passed in review before the division staff and guests. I'm afraid the ranks didn't exactly look like West Point cadets at first. More than likely we looked like a herd of cattle but as the weeks went by practice made us presentable if not perfect. It takes quite a while for a division to pass in review. 16 battalions of infantry, 4 battalions of artillery plus all the special units. Our regiment, being the highest numbered was among the last to move out, so that meant we stood at attention the longest. Finally back at our area as we were dismissed, we rush to the bulletin boards to see how we made out in the mornings inspection. If OK, then we still and another hurdle to cross because if we goofed in the division review, we could end up doing close order drill all Saturday afternoon.

When I was lucky enough to get a pass I usually went into Lebanon or Bethlehem and occasionally Harrisburg. Another nice place was Hershey, a unique town. The smell of chocolate eventually got to you though. Otherwise one spent the weekend in camp. Always a blackjack game going in the barracks and there was a big camp recreation center and theaters. Pay day came once a month. The captain with the payroll sat at a table outside the office and we'd line up according to roster. Approaching the table as our name was called; we would salute, receive our 21 dollars and sign the paybook. It was a day of high stakes gambling and the winners would have a big nite in town, while the losers mourned in camp playing penny ante. Of course there were money lenders too with the going rate 2 for 1. That was a good business. Don't know why I was not smart enough to get into that. It sure was a lot more profitable than gambling. One thing, if you were broke in the army at least you still had 3 meals a day and a place to sleep.

With spring, our training progressed to include 20 mile hikes to Mount Gretna with full field packs. That was on weekends so we didn't miss any training which wasn't too popular with us. With rifle, gas mask and all the other accouterments each man was carrying about a eighty pound load. We soon learned the importance of properly packing and wearing all this stuff. If not, then web straps would quickly chafe raw spots. Our feet were most vulnerable until they toughened up. Blisters would rub raw and each step became pure misery. Foot care became an obsession and an extra pair of dry socks a must. I disciplined myself to close my mind to everything but lifting one foot at a time and placing it forward. There were times I thought I'd never make the next hill, but managed to do it taking pride in not being one of those who dropped out. I should mention that was 20 miles out and 20 miles back.

The first time a lot of fellows dropped out, to come hobbling into our camp area after the rest of us had set up our puptests and were nursing our blisters in preparation for the return march the next day. It always seemed to rain on those over night marches which taught us to ditch around our tents well if we didn't want to wake up in a puddle of water. The smell of wet wool became a natural scent in our surroundings. We came to associate the name Mount Gretna with fatigue, discomfort and pain.

An epidemic of pneumonia and influenza hit the camp in early spring and I was one of those who ended up in the overflowing base hospital. My case was a light one and I only spent a week and a half there. A lot of fellows around me though were in bad shape and I had to watch the doctors insert large needles between their ribs into the lungs and pump out quantities of puss and liquid. That was before sulfa became available. I think it was the thought of those needles that helped me recover and get out of there, and I stayed out of hospitals the rest of my time in service.

A lot of time was spent on weapons training. Taking the different weapons apart and reassembling. The Springfield rifle, 45 cal. Pistol, Browning automatic rifle (BAR) and the machine gun. Setting the sights for distance and wind drift. Practicing the proper posture to fire a rifle was most uncomfortable as the arm had to be entwined thru the heavy leather strap as a steadying brace for the barrel. When you had your self contorted to the point of tears, then the instructor thought you might be close to achieving the proper position. It was a relief when our time on the range arrived and we could put to test all this dry practice. We were equipped with the Springfield 30-06 bolt action, clip fed rifle. A fine gun which continued to be used as a snipers rifle after we received the new heavier Garand.

The ranges were at the base of Blue Mountain, the eastern most range of the Appalachians. The mountain formed a backdrop for the long line of targets. The firing lines were on long mounds running parallel to the line of target pits. The bulls-eye looked awfully small. They divided us up so that half worked the targets while the other half completed their prescribed firing from the standing, kneeling and prone positions. Then we changed places in the afternoon and they fired while we went to the pits. The Springfield has a pretty good kick and is held tight to the shoulder; otherwise it gives you a bruising wallop. After you fire a prescribed number of rounds, the big target boards are retracted into a pit where the target crew notes the hits and misses. Then they patch the target and raise it for the next round of firing. Of course, we on the firing line anxiously await the scoring. They mark the hits with a colored disk on a handle which is held up on the face of the target. Your instructor marks the score in your record book. Any misses, the target crew indicates with a red flag, which we call Maggie's Drawers, in front of the target. Always embarrassing to see that flag waving in front of your target, and I got a few.

In spite of safety efforts, injuries occurred. The fellow next to me had an unusual accident. The retaining clip on the firing pin broke allowing the bolt to fly back and hit him under the eye. Lucky it wasn't in the eye. When we come off the firing line, one fellow failed to obey instructions to open the bolt of his rifle. Somehow it still had a live round in it and when he let the rifle butt hit the ground, it discharged. The bullet hit the underside of his helmet and deflected alongside his head. They took him off on a stretcher. His instructor should have checked and prevented that accident. They are pretty careful about accounting for live ammunition. When finishing a session of firing, we have to pick up our empty casings and they had better agree with the number of live rounds we were issued. That way it is pretty difficult for anyone to take live ammunition back to the barracks.

This firing was a welcome change from the routine, but you were under pressure to get at least a qualifying score. I was satisfied to qualify as marksman as I was no Sgt. York. That bull-eye looks awfully small and elusive to hold on the end of your sight.

Now it was our turn in the target pits. They were about eight feet deep and concrete floored. The framework and slides for the four foot square canvas target holders extended five or six feet above the pit parapet. Looking at the targets, one wondered how anybody could miss them. There was a field phone by which we received instructions as when to raise or lower the targets. It was rather scary the first time the shooting started with the bullets thumping thru the targets and ricocheting up the slope behind us. We fell into the routine of target tending. About the middle of the afternoon we heard a plop behind us and were startled to see that a four foot black snake had fallen into the pit. Our first impulse was to vacate the pit but we realized that we'd probably get our heads blown off. Instead after some scrabbling we dispatched the reptile with the wooden marker disk. Some of the other pit crews had similar experiences with reptiles, rabbits and a groundhog coming into the pits. We figured that the bullets bouncing around on the slope behind us had disturbed them and they were just trying to get away from the noise and danger. That night we had a good session cleaning our rifles.

There also was the obstacle course. This consisted of running, then crawling under some barbed wire; after that, scaling a wall and jumping a mud filled ditch and attacking several straw dummies with the bayonet. The straw dummy was tied to a vertical stake with a hinged pole projecting upwards at a 45 degree angle. You had to charge the dummy, parry the hinged pole, then deliver a thrust or butt stroke and charge on to the next one. Rather simple, but if you didn't adjust your stride to your stroke, you could mess it up. Later on, the obstacles would get more difficult.

The gas mask was bulky and a nuisance to carry and worse to wear as it was hot, difficult to breathe with or see out of. However after the terrible gas attacks of WW-I it was standard equipment as both sides had ample supplies of poison gases. Some of dad's friends had been gassed during the war and they just wasted away; complete cripples. In addition practicing to function with a gas mask we also were taught to recognize it. They put us in an airtight room, then released small quantities of mustard, lewisite and phosgene gases. We had to tuck a finger under the rubber face piece and lift it so we could sniff and learn to recognize the different poison gases. After carrying the darn thing around for nearly four years, when I did get into combat I threw away the canister and mask. Used the pouch to carry rations in which seemed a much more practical use.

Another thing was the live grenade range. Here, you learned the army way to pitch a hand grenade, holding the grenade and handle, first pull the pin, then bring it back alongside your ear and project it forward. No roundhouse swing like an outfielder throwing a baseball. After being shown how, they gave you a live grenade and said "Go up to that pit and see if you can throw it over the wall." Kind of shakes you up as you think, what if I fumble and it rolls back in the pit with me. Five seconds isn't very long. True, there is a hole in the center of the pit to kick the grenade into in case you goof, but how quick is quick? By the time you pull the pin and draw it back by your ear it's easy to feel a little nervous and it seems an awkward way to throw anything. At any rate I heaved and dropped to the floor of the pit hoping I wouldn't hear the damn thing roll back in with me. When it went off, I jumped a foot. And so another milestone was past in the martial art. There were cases where a guy pulls the pin and then freezes. He can't throw and he can't let go. That's where the instructor has to step in and gently relieves the soldier of it.

All wasn't work though, and we had our horseplay. Unfortunately when there is horse play there usually is a victim. One prank was the hotfoot. The victim of this was somebody dozing and preferably someone smaller than yourself. Breaking off a match head, it was tucked into the joint between the sole and top of the shoe and then ignited. In a moment the victim leaps up with a shout, stamping his foot and trying to get out of his shoe. It works even better if the shoe is wet as the heat generates steam and you can imagine the hopping and howling. You had to keep alert though because your buddy would pull that stunt on you as quickly as the next guy.

Our beds had flat springs and sometimes we'd go to a lot of trouble to pull a trick on someone who had a weekend pass. We knew he'd come in late Sunday night after the lights were out and that he'd probably be drunk. We would take all the little coil springs out that attached the flat springs to the bed frame and replace them with string. With the bed made up, it looked perfectly normal. We pretended to be all asleep when he'd come fumbling in grumbling with a hangover and anxious to hit the sack. When he did, the strings broke and the mattress hit the floor with a bang. Of course this generated some horrible language as he dragged himself up over the metal bed frame, probably skinning his shins in the process. In spite of his threats, with thirty guys in on the joke there wasn't much he could do about it. Frustrated he slept on the floor.

Then there was the old canteen trick. It would only work when a new fellow joined the company. We'd wait until one of those 20 mile marches. When our victim had all his equipment ready and was sacked out for a few minutes rest before the call to fall out, we'd get his canteen. Dumping the water out, a empty balloon was tucked down the neck and filled with water then tied off. Shaking the canteen, the knot could be worked out of sight then the canteen was returned to its canvas pouch. At our first rest stop after a hot hours marching, we all flopped out in whatever shade we could find. The first thing reached for was our canteens. Of course all of us in on the joke watched this fellow. A look of amazement would cross his face as he tipped the canteen to his lips and nothing came out. He'd shake the canteen and try it looked like water. By this time others not in on the joke took interest in his dilemma and we helped with such remarks as, "Maybe it's frozen," though it was 90 degrees in the shade. Finally one of them would get smart enough to hold it upside down and poke a stick inside. That broke the balloon, releasing the water and our prank was revealed as the remnants of the balloon sagged out. We had other tricks up our sleeve, but I will cover them later on in my story.

I detested KP duty and did my best to stay off that. Regardless, I got my share. When you finished such mundane jobs as peeling spuds, mopping, cleaning tables and pots and pans; the cooks always had another. Like scrubbing garbage cans, but the worse was cleaning the grease trap. Fortunately this was only done about every two weeks. If you did it once, that was once too often. The grease trap was a cast iron rectangular tank with a heavy bolted lid located in an inaccessible place under the sinks. They heavy lid had to be unbolted and dragged out, then the baffles cleaned and the grease dipped and scrapped out of the tank. When you were finished the cook expected it to be clean enough to drink out of. Nasty job but all part of the life of a private.

One day we were doing squad exercises: practicing the different formations of a squad such as advancing in extended order, or forming a skirmish line on one flank or the other from a column, or leapfrog forward displacement. It took a lot of running and flopping on the ground. On one of these maneuvers as we lay in the weeds awaiting the next command one of the fellows observed a blacksnake ahead of us.

It had its head held up among the weeds watching us. We figured the next time we ran forward we'd overrun him. However such was not the case as when we'd jump up and advance another thirty yards the snake would disappear. Then pretty soon somebody would spot him again up ahead watching us. Well, we worked our way clear across that field and he moved when we moved and stop when we did. It became sort of a game to see who would spot him first every time we hit the dirt to form a skirmish line. The game ended when we reached the far side of the field and started working our way back. I guess he decided he had enough and just continued into the woods. He had added a little excitement to the otherwise exhausting routine.

During the summer we lost some of our men for cadres slated to form new divisions as the army expanded and new camps opened up across the country, especially in the south. These men were replaced by draftees and some of our men moved up to fill the vacated con-com positions. Most popular call was for volunteers for the new airborne units and for the mushrooming Air Force. Many seized that opportunity to move from the mud to the wild blue yonder but only a few passed the rigid requirements. I didn't' bother, knowing my eyes would never pass the air corp test. Those who were accepted were considered lucky indeed for the chance to become pilots or air crew members in an exciting arm of the service. This is the way the army grew; by diving and subdividing the experience, men then filling the voids with draftees or volunteers who in turn would become trained and experience. The process accelerated with time.

In late July a big forest fire developed in the mountains west of us. By day large clouds of smoke boiled up into the sky and at night the red glow held our attention. Each day it was obvious it was spreading and getting closer. We were put on alert for possible forest fire duty. We looked forward to this for the novelty of it but it wasn't until the sixth day of the fire that we finally got called out. By this time the fire was dying down. Hauled to some remote spot on a fire blackened mountain we were given picks and shovels. Forming a line we followed the trail of the fire, putting out smoldering remnants by throwing dirt on them or pulling down burning charred trunks where possible. The novelty soon wore off in the heat, grit and ashes. The heat in the ground came right up thru your boots. All we covered was a small area of the fire. By the time we finished that night we no longer looked like white troops and were more than ready to get back to camp and some cool refreshing showers.

There was a serious accident one day due to horseplay. It was Saturday morning and everybody was busy scrubbing the floors and cleaning in preparation for inspection. At the front of the barracks there was a small wooden platform and fire escape ladder down to the ground. Two of the fellows were wrestling around on the platform when one of them lost his grip and fell. Unfortunately our company guidon was directly below, its base supported in a pipe driven into the ground. The guidon is a small flag with white crossed rifles, the letter "B" and numeral 112 on a blue background. The flag is attached to a stout hickory pole capped with a chrome spade shaped tip. Falling on this, the

6

spear sank deeply into his buttock as the pole bent and snapped under his weight. Obviously in excruciating pain, instead of lying there, he jumped up and started running across the dusty quadrangle with the broken end of the pole dragging behind. He had to be caught and held down until a jeep was brought up and along with the pole he was loaded into it and hauled to the hospital. The doctor must have shook his head when he saw that one. If it hadn't been so serious, the whole episode was quite comical as he ran across the quadrangle trailing about six feet if hickory pole behind him. I don't know if he ever returned to duty with the company as I transferred to Headquarters company shortly afterwards.

I jumped at an opportunity to transfer to Headquarters Company where I was assigned to the wire section. Working with those boys installing field telephone lines was a lot more gratifying than toting a rifle all day. The telephone was the infantry's basic communication, other than hand signals. Radio filled the gap when we were on the move or until the telephone lines were operable. Our responsibility was to establish and maintain a telephone network with our battalions and tie in to our division and artillery lines, when we were in the field. The telephone wire was laid from trucks, light hand drawn reel carriages where possible or reverted to the heavy task of hand reels where the terrain was rough. Since a combat outfit is frequently on the move, we spent as much time retrieving wire as laying it. To help retrieve we had a power winch mounted on a weapons carrier but a lot of that work was still done with hand cranked reels.

The wire was laid on the ground as quick as possible to the battalion command posts to get communications established. Then we'd retrace the lines and get them up off the ground. It was strung from trees as much as possible, otherwise we'd have to use improvised poles or take advantage of a fence line, etc. We had to be especially careful to support the lines substantially and high enough where they crossed roads for safety. Low hanging wires are a death rap for dispatch riders (cycles) or occupants of open vehicles like jeeps. All of this required a lot of climbing and the use of leg spikes which were strapped to the inside of your legs. They worked fine on telephone poles but often ripped out of the bark on trees, in particular the heavy bark on pines. When they did, you either fell or skinned up the inside of your legs and arms, so one quickly learned to take a little care to sink the spikes in as solid as possible. There was no end to the work because after one set of lines was run to each battalion, we started running alternate lines for redundancy. In combat wires are cut by shellfire, vehicles and enemy patrols so you hope one line will remain in service while others are repaired. Of course, it isn't just laying wire as telephones and switchboards have to be hooked up and lines tagged. About the time you think the work is done, the regiment gets orders to move and it is a reverse scramble getting all the wire back on the ground and reeling it up.

In camp, I spent part of each day at division communications school. They taught all the different means of military communications. Signal flags, telegraph and Morse code, telephone, radio, encoding and decoding. I did pretty well at everything except the radio. I detested those SCRs as they were very sensitive to establish and hold contact with another station. Some seemed to have the knack but I didn't. Even if you were successful establishing contact, the transmission was so full of static squeals and howls that I couldn't understand half that was said. Because of these difficulties, I wasn't too happy when I was assigned to the regimental radio section. I had a rough time and it was only the friendly help of Sgt Barron and Bob Reithmiller that pulled me thru those difficult times. When the opportunity came later to transfer to the S=2 Section I viewed it as a divine blessing.

During June, the division moved to A. P. Hill military reservation in Virginia for regimental and brigade size maneuvers. I had plenty of practice laying wire, climb trees as well as operating a radio. Previously our training had pretty well been limited to company and battalion sized exercises so this was intended to broaden our training and experience to operate as a larger unit. We made mistakes and hopefully we learned from them. It also was the longest time we had spent living in the field and roughing it. I had one weekend pass and took a quick look at Baltimore, then moved on to Washington. It was a packed, bustling town. You couldn't take five steps without having to salute some officer. It was a contrast of people obviously well off and with things to do, or bums who lay around every park, most of them drunk. That nite, I couldn't get a room anyplace. Well that's not really true because a little colored boy tugged my sleeve and said I could sleep with his sister for two bucks. I decided he didn't mean all nite so I passed up that golden opportunity and ended up sleeping with the bums in one of the parks. They seemed to be perfectly comfortable covered with their newspapers, but I was chilled to the bone. After finding a place to wash up in the morning, I recuperated some and spent the rest of the day sightseeing. It really wasn't much of a weekend, but of course when I got back to our bivouac area in the thickets of A. P. Hill I told my buddies what a good time it had been.

The S-2 (Intelligence) Section is responsible to collect, analyze and record enemy information. This information is collected from various sources such as prisoners, patrols, study of serial photos, captured material and some come down from higher headquarters (G-2). The reconnaissance squad was part of S-2. Working with maps and things was much more to my liking. Sgt. Stephenson was head non-com and we got along well. We practiced a lot at patrolling, map reading and use of the compass. I was able to put my talent for drawing to use in making sketches of terrain features not observable on maps or aerial photos. In preparing to attack an enemy position it is important to have accurate knowledge of the lay of the land beforehand. Part of our work was to maintain a map showing the disposition of enemy forces and identification of strong points, mine fields, barbed wire entanglements, etc.

Since coming to Headquarters Company I had advanced to private 1st class (PFC) with a 4th grade specialist rating. It was a pretty fancy insignia consisting of the 1st class stripe with four rockers underneath. I only mention it because specialist ratings were shortly replaced with technician non-com ratings which look like a sgt or corporal stripe with a "T" below. Most fellows in the service never saw those other stripes. They were almost as impressive as a master sgts stripes. In any event I soon advanced to corporal. I was quite content here and life was certainly much more pleasant than in a rifle company. At least being a little closer to the source, one had a better grasp of what was going on; in a rifle company usually all you heard was rumors. However, while I consider myself lucky to be in HQ Co, I still respect the rifle companies. After all they are the most important unit in the regiment and if life is a little rougher, they still take pride in their company whether it's B or G Co. If you don't think so, just make some disparaging remark and you'll have a brawl on your hands.

One group I should mention are the dispatch riders. This was the day before the jeep and motorcycles were used for this work. To us, the dispatch riders seemed to have a lot of freedom, always on the go on their Harley Davidson. Eyes covered with goggles faces often begrimed with dust or mud, they cut sort of a romantic figure. It also was a dangerous job and especially so at nite when only dim blackout lights were used on vehicles. On maneuvers they often slammed into a truck or tree. Others had accidents too, our weapons carrier with the winch turned over during a field exercise killing one man and badly injuring several others.

Rumor became official around the middle of August that we would be moving south to take part in the Carolina Maneuvers. Earlier, the Louisiana Maneuvers had received a lot of publicity because of their size and extent, but the Carolina Maneuvers were slated to be the largest ever held in this country. So we were busy packing and getting everything shipshape for the move. Most of us had never been south of the Mason Dixon line so we looked forward with excitement to seeing a different part of the country as well as taking part in these large scale operations.

FARE WELLS AS WE LOADED ON THE TROOPTRAIN IN

DISMAL VIEW FROM Co. B OFFICE

RIFLE TRAINING

THE RIFLE RANGE

10

20 MILE HIKE TO MOUNT GRETNA

IT ALWAYS SEEMED TO RAIN

HAPPY LOAD WITH A WEEKEND PASS

THE OLD HOTFOOT TRICK

10 MINUTE BREAK

HI HO THE FIELD ARTILLERY

SATURDAY DANCE AT CAMP RECREATION CENTER
Girls were hauled in by truck from the surrounding towns.

CAROLINAS

AUG-DEC 1941

GENERAL GRANT TANK

MANEUVERS

In late August our regiment loaded up in quartermaster trucks for the long haul to North Carolina (around 500 miles). Advance parties from the division had gone down earlier to select campsites. Most of the work of setting up camp would be done when we got down there. Its no simple matter to move a division considering the logistics. Probably 1600 vehicles spaced 10 to 15 seconds apart would take 7 hours to pass one point. However it would be impossible to have one long column of vehicles like that blocking normal civilian traffic. Instead, the 1600 vehicles are broken down into sections of 20 - 30 each allowing maybe 10 to 15 minutes between groups. That would allow space for normal traffic too. However that spacing makes the convoy much, much longer and it takes nearly 20 hours to pass one point. To ease further the congestion on the roads, the division move was spread over a week and only during daylight hours.

The day our regiment moved we made it down near Harrisonburg, VA. The next day we continued down the Shenandoah Valley to Roanoke, then left the valley to head for Greensboro, N.C. Remember this was before interstates so speed was limited by the traffic on two lane roads and we passed thru every hamlet and town on the way. People lined the street and crossroads, many waving as we passed thru. Large military convoys were still an unusual event in 1941. MPs or police stopped traffic and waved us on thru. We would have been happier if we had stopped at the traffic lights so we could banter with the girls, but no such luck. It was early evening when we pulled into a nice park area close to Greensboro for our second night. Many had arrived before us and it would be dark before the last of our convoy pulled into the area. An army truck isn't the most comfortable conveyance to travel that distance and it felt good to get out and stretch and set up our pup tents for the night. We like what we had seen of the south so far; nice country, towns and obviously friendly people, even if we were Yankees. A lot of people drove out to see our camp area and milled about talking with us. Some even took soldiers back into town where they were fed and shown around. I wasn't one of the lucky ones. The field kitchens had been at the front of the convoy so they were already set up and preparing a hot meal.

Broke camp and loaded up early the next morning, passed thru Southern Pines which really impressed us as a particularly nice town. This was Piedmont country, sandy soil, graceful tall long leafed southern pines. It was here that we were rammed by the truck behind us. I guess the driver was watching some of the ever present girls by the side of the street. We saw it coming and had time to brace ourselves before the impact. The fellows in the other truck were shaken up and bruised. After just a brief stop to see that our truck was OK we continued on. A convoy has to keep moving. The other truck remained with its smashed front and steaming radiator. An army wrecker somewhere toward the end of the column would eventually pick it up. At least they had time now to talk with the girls. We passed thru Rockingham and turned west toward Wadesboro. Our base camp was located somewhere between the two towns and near the meandering lazy Pee Dee River. The rest of the day was spent locating our company area, setting up pyramidal tents, digging garbage pits, latrines and all the other jobs it takes to make a camp habitable. Digging in the sandy soil was a big improvement over Penna clay. Also set up headquarters area and established basic communications with the battalions. We were more than ready to hit the sack when the soft sound of taps brought our day to a close. It was a beautiful warm night, the stars seemed so much bigger and brighter than at home. We had really been too busy to look around and see what our new home amounted to, but this was the southland and we looked forward to morning.

Maneuvers didn't start right away as many more outfits in addition to ours had to move in and get their base camps set up. This was our first opportunity to view all the different kinds of organizations that make up an army. The heavy artillery, anti aircraft, heavy ordnance, cavalry, tank units, field hospitals, bridge engineers - an endless array that filled the fields and pine woods in the surrounding area. The 26th (Yankee) division from New England moved in not far from us. Although they were to e our partner in II Corp, we continually heckled each other. These base camps were only for use between maneuvers, each of which might last up to two weeks. During the course of a maneuver we lived in the field and slept where ever and however night found us. While waiting for the 1st maneuver to begin, they kept us busy because idle men easily turn to trouble.

We were the Blue Army (mostly infantry) and would oppose the Red Army (mostly armor). I guess the maneuvers were intended to show that the panzers of Germany could be stopped by infantry with anti tank guns. For that purpose they gave us hundreds of dummy anti tank guns made with a two-inch steel pipe barrel mounted on two-wheel carriage. The U. S. by now was producing the real thing but they were being shipped to England and hoping half of them wouldn't be sunk on the way. The maneuver area covered a pretty good chunk of North and South Carolina, extending on both sides of the Pee Dee River. Sgt. Stevenson and I were inundated with an awesome pile of aerial photomaps of the area. There were a thousand different sheets. Out of that we had to sort and find the sheets covering a particular maneuver and distribute copies down to the battalions. Overlays had to be made assigning battalion areas, identify supply points, medical evacuation stations and anything else pertinent to our operations. Later we would have to issue attack or withdrawal orders with maps showing our positions and known enemy dispositions. A special pencil was used to prepare a master, which then was transferred to a gelatin sheet. Copies were made by placing a sheet of paper on the gelatin sheet and rolling it, a rather crude method but simple and practical for use under primitive conditions.

The further down the totem pole one is, the less he understands what is going on during maneuvers. We did a lot of marching and setting up positions only to receive orders to move again. Umpires rode around in jeeps flying a little flag and they'd decide whether we could stay where we were, advance or had to retreat. Sort of like a big chess game and we were the pawns. Smoke bombs were set off to stimulate artillery fire and blanks were fired to add noise. We saw tanks and halftracks stirring up dust several times. We thrashed our way thru brush and waded creeks, always apprehensive that we'd tread on a moccasin. We spent a lot of the time searching ourselves for ticks, which infested the piney woods. After it was all over somebody would have to tell us whether we won or lost. Army held a critique to tell the Corp and Div commanders what was done wrong or right. Then the divisions held a critique to tell the regimental commanders what they had done right or wrong. And so the reaming filtered down to battalion and company levels. We got caught up in this as we had to prepare large-scale maps drawn on brown wrapping paper with grease pencils to show the various troop movements during the exercise.

Sometimes there was a week between individual maneuvers while plans and preparations were being made. During these times, if we could get passes we had the opportunity to visit local towns. Wadesboro, Monroe, I even got to Raleigh one time. Otherwise we had our regular duties and personal chores to attend to like washing clothes and writing letters. I enjoyed just walking around the local area. Cotton fields and cotton bales were a new sight. We watched workers picking cotton. I think it was what the machines missed. A lot of them were girls and they were always willing to talk to us, but the straw boss soon expressed his displeasure and chased them back to works.

The tumblebug was a critter I had never seen. Well named, they tumble about as their legs work and shape what appears to be a piece of dirt into a perfectly round sphere. Pickup up one of these half inch diameter balls to examine, the stench made me quickly drop it. I decided they were really nasty bugs. They should be called dung bugs. There was another bug around that was far more dangerous and that was the black widow spider. Several of the fellows were bitten and they ended up in the hospital. Henceforth we were careful about picking up old boards or reaching into dark places. We killed a number of them.

When you get several hundred thousand soldiers and equipment moving around an area, accidents happen. I will mention several. One day a bomber came over us at tree top level with a pursuit hot on his tail. The pursuit pulled up and tried to do a vertical loop so he could drop back down behind the bomber for another attack run. However he didn't have enough speed and stalled right at the top of his loop. He dropped like a rock crashing nose first on the far side of a knoll from us. A huge fireball mushroomed up into the sky. We ran over but of course there was nothing we could do as the plane had dug a crater in the sandy soil. It was an air cobra which had a heavy air cooled Allison engine behind the pilot so it pulverized him -.too bad. Another night, we were on the move to a new location. It was just about dark when we came to a long spindly looking bridge crossing a small stream and depression. It was a plank bridge about 150 feet long and no railing. The underpinning didn't look substantial enough to support our vehicles. It was decided to bivouac in the woods until morning and then look for a place to ford the stream. I hadn't been asleep very long when the darnedest clattering and crunching awakened me with a start. At first I thought a tank was crashing thru the woods in the darkness and that's unnerving, but by then everything was dead silent. We listened and heard cries from the direction of the bridge. We worked our way out of the woods and down to the bridge by the dim light from our blackout flashlights.

16

First thing we saw was the radiator of a big diamond T prime mover projecting above the abutment of the bridge. Closer examination revealed the bridge was gone and down in the debris of shattered planks and timbers lay a big 155 howitzer. The truck and gun had taken the whole bridge down; the truck almost making it to our side. We spent most of the night crawling down among the debris on the bank or waist deep in the stream extracting injured men and dragging them up by the road. They had been riding in the back of the truck, which also was carrying a load of sandbags for simulated ammunition. Some of those fellows were hurt pretty bad and our medics treated them best they could. Meanwhile our radio people had managed to make a request from ambulances. When they finally arrived, it was on the far side of the bridge so the victims had to be hauled (on stretchers this time) back across the stream and up the far bank - a rough job in the dark. It appeared the driver had taken a wrong turn and speeding along thinking he was following the rest of his convoy, was on the rickety bridge before he knew it. It went down like a pack of cards.

We had injuries and several deaths from the blackout conditions. Vehicles were equipped with a dim light called cat's-eyes. It cast no light, but gave a bluish phosphorescent glow that could be seen quite a distance once one got his night vision. However it was impossible to judge distance or whether they were moving or stopped. This resulted in a lot of rear end collisions. As I mentioned before, this was particularly disastrous to motorcycle dispatch riders whose job required speed.

A phenomenon we had never seen before was foxfire. First time we thought it was the blackout lights of a truck parked in the woods. Investigating, we were surprised to find it emanated from the surface of a fallen tree trunk. It was phosphorescence fungus.

Still up to our (un) practical jokes, the fact that the fungus had fooled us into thinking it was the dim lights of a vehicle gave us an idea. Collecting a handful we placed it in the middle of the sandy back road and went back among the brush to wait and see what happened. Pretty soon we heard a truck slowly feeling its way along the dark road. It stopped about a hundred feet from the glowing foxfire and sat there for a while. Then the driver got out and walked up to see what was holding up traffic. When he saw it was something on the ground instead of a parked truck, he cautiously explored it with the tip of his boot before cursing and scattering the pile with a good kick. Now there were a score of little glowing lights instead of one. We pulled this trick several times with pretty good success. It was strange stuff. This thing of wandering around in the woods had its problems, like poison ivy, Quite a few of us were afflicted with it at one time or another. Something we called Virginia creeper was another nuisance. It was a woody vine and anchored itself into the lower limbs of trees. Running into one (day or night) was like running into a barbed wire fence.

Our Blue Army commander was Lt. Gen Lear who had acquired the nickname "Yoo Hoo" from some innocent episode involving a group of girls. In any event whenever the troops would spot his staff car with it three star flag they would begin waving and yelling "Yoo Hoo". I don't think any soldiers close to his car did this, just the ones far enough to figure they could get away with it. Apparently he took the kidding pretty well, thinking it didn't hurt the morale among the troops to let them kid their commander a little. Actually, under the surface he probably was seething. I also heard of the tough, fancy dan tank general on the other side by the name of Patton - didn't realize at the time that he would become one of our most famous men. Maneuvers came and went as we moved thru September and October. We had some rain, but mostly the weather was nice up till now. What we'd call Indian summer up north. When it did rain, at least the sandy loam was a lot better than the mud we would have had up north.

Mail call was sporadic and always an important event in the life of a soldier. It was always a disappointment to come away empty handed. I had a girl who lived in Punxsutawney, Penna and we corresponded regularly. She sealed her letters with luscious kisses on both sides of the envelope. The mailman would hold the letter for all to see and cry "Guess Who". A chorus of voices shouted; V - E - L -M – A from Punx – sa – taw – ny. Then handing the letter to the first outstretched hand it would pass thru man more before reaching me. All in good fun . I did meet a nice family by the name of Stanback and went to their home every chance I got. Enjoyed the good home cooked meals. It sort of became a home away from home for me. They wrote my parents and this started an exchange of letters that continued until long after the war between them. Yet in all those years they never visited each other.

There was a place near Rockingham called the marl pits. Marl is a substance used for fertilizer but I'm not sure what it consists of. It was a pretty extensive mining area, relatively barren. The residue from the mining left the ground whitish in color and numerous blue lakes or ponds dotted the area. Whenever we had a chance we would take the trucks over there and wash them, then spend the rest of the day bathing and swimming. The glare of the sun on the water and white pebbly ground was almost blinding. There were clumps of vegetation along the edges of the lakes apparently frequented by water moccasins. Our activity chased them out into the water where they circled out beyond where we splashed and swam. We'd keep an eye out for them, but they never bothered us. After dark in the moonlight we often saw the "v" shaped trail their head left on the water. Like most wild things I guess they prefer to keep away from humans if given the chance.

The following is a letter I wrote in November 1941, describing my experiences in Maneuver No. 4:

11/12/41: In the morning troops marched out at usual at 7:30 am. It was very cold and the water buckets had frozen during the night. Soldiers were beginning to wonder if "the sunny south" is as sunny as it's supposed to be. Our HQ Company had an anti tank warning problem and practiced setting up command and observation posts. Returned to camp at noon and learned we would move out again sometime after 6pm. Sgt. Stevenson and myself worked all afternoon preparing the maps and aerial photos we would use in a hundred and sixteen sheets per map so it was confusing getting everything in order. After supper it got cold very rapidly and by the time trucks had been loaded with troops and supplies, winter overcoats were gratefully donned. We moved to a position about a half-mile north of the Pee Dee River on Route 109. We settled down for a cold night in the pinewoods under a clear starry sky.

11/13/41: Remained in the same area. We spent some time putting map sheets together. Improved our sleeping area as it appeared we would be here several nights.

Anti aircraft units and artillery moved in adjacent to us. Otherwise we are just taking it easy and trying to keep warm as no open fire allowed.

11/15/41: I guess all the troops are in position now and we are given details of this maneuver. The Pee Dee is the boundary between the Reds and the Blues. Hostilities will begin tomorrow. This will be a test between infantry versus mechanized forces. Our side (Blues) consists of the I, II and VI Corps while the reds are the IV Corp and the I Armored Corp. The enemy's aircraft outnumber ours 4 to 1. The II Corp is to cross the river and drive a spearhead south into enemy territory and it is hoped the opposing mechanized forces will try an encircling movement. As they do, our I and VI Corps will try a double envelopment of the armored forces. Some enemy has been reported north of us. Our regiment, the 112th is to lead the attack as plans are now. All day there has been heavy aerial reconnaissance over our particular area. At HQ we are busy preparing battle orders and overlays to direct the disposition of our troops and designate objectives for tomorrow. Tonight under cover of darkness our units move up close to the heavily guarded bridge on Route 109. If this bridge is destroyed by enemy action then the 44th Engineers to construct pontoon bridges or supply assault boats to cross the wide river.

11/16/41: Action started early this morning as a platoon of B Co crossed the fog shrouded Pee Dee at 7:30 followed by the rest of the 1st Battalion. The 2nd Battalion had nearly completed crossing when nine medium bombers swept over at a hundred feet and bombed the bridge. Scores of planes have been over the area and the anti aircraft guns have been busy. The view of this raiding squadron sweeping overhead was a beautiful sight, considering the dropped flour sacks instead of real bombs. Meanwhile the engineers were throwing across pontoon bridges upstream and downstream of the bridge. Companies of infantry are also crossing in assault boats. Both Gen Martin and Stackpole were present to observe the action. By 12 o'clock the engineers had repaired the bridge sufficiently to allow the remainder of the 112th, vehicles, anti tank guns and the 109th Field Artillery to cross.

Large squadrons of planes have been at the area continually and small mechanized forces have been encountered forward. Having completed the crossing, our forces resumed the southwestward advance until stopped by a small tank attack at 3pm, five miles north of Wadesboro. Anti tank guns dispersed it with small losses. The tanks charged out of the woods with sirens screaming to warn troops out of their path.

At five o'clock the columns were again halted by a tank attack about three miles north of Wadesboro. This time it was a deadlock and we set up our command post. Just after dark, tanks circled to our rear and attacked our CP from the north. For fifteen minutes the night was filled with the roar and flash of 37mm gunfire and the rattle and clanking of tanks as they tried to crack our anti tank defenses. Finally the tanks receded back into the darkness having failed in their attack. Action now was limited to the shadowy forms of our scout cars creeping cautiously along country roads seeking to locate the enemy. We too (S-2 Section) sent out two patrols, one north and the other south. By morning we had quite a bit of information about the enemies positions. It indicated the entire 1st Armored Division was in front of us. During the night our anti tank forces were reinforced and by morning hoped to be strong enough the resume our advance.

11/17/41: At dawn our planned attack was delayed when a strong tank assault was made by the Red forces. Enemy aircraft supported this attack which lasted all morning without breaking our defenses. By noon the enemy had again withdrawn and we started our advance without resistance. We moved our command post forward to a position about three miles northwest of Wadesboro in the edge of a woods. Our three battalions were connected by thin lines of communications and enemy action in the form of small units was active in the entire area. At 2:24 pm I went up to the road, a distance of about 200 yards, to conceal the guide sign identifying regimental CP. I had just concealed the sign when the largest mechanized attack yet, occurred. Armored halftracks followed by tanks roared out of the woods and down the road. I threw myself into the grass and the first armored cars passed by, but one did spot me as I tried vainly to imitate a worm. The umpire declared me a casualty; a ruling I could not protest as there was a 50cal and two 30cal machine guns less than twenty fee t away looking me in the eye.

The Reds observed the tracks leading to our CP and several halftracks charged across the field toward it. It was not long till the umpires declared the command post destroyed. Thus the 112th had its first serious tangle with armored forces and came out second best. The enemy gained valuable information from our maps which by error were not destroyed. We were all declared out of action until midnight. A certain number were listed as casualties and the medics practiced on them, after which they were sent to the rear. The rest of us sat on a railroad embankment and watched the Reds continue their attacks. We saw scores of armored vehicles towing small howitzers besides their own heavy armament move up the road in a cloud of dust. Tanks crashed out of the woods a quarter mile away and move in groups of two or three thru the area while scout cars mopped up the area taken in the swift advance. However our battalions though surrounded held the ground they were on.

11/18/41: Long before daylight this morning we sent a patrol into Wadesboro. They reported by radio that few Red troops were in town at the time. At dawn our 2nd battalion was sent in and street fighting took place as the enemy reluctantly withdrew. The town was shelled by the enemy who later counterattacked with infantry and tanks, driving us out in turn. As our men fell back along Route 109 they pinched off a Red artillery battalion and took many prisoners. Shortly after noon we were reinforced by the 3rd battalion, 11th Inf which had made a long cross-country march. So again Wadesboro changed hands as in turn we counterattack the Reds. This time they could not drive us out. A group of foreign officers observed this attack and I imagine they figured it would still be a long time before we would be ready for real combat. After three days the regiment had taken its first objective. Tomorrow it would try to take the second objective, White Store southwest of Wadesboro between route 52 and 74. During the night troops displaced to their jump off locations and trucks brought up ammunition and supplies. We worked by Coleman lanterns preparing orders and map overlays.

Breakfast was before daylight and shortly afterwards an artillery barrage was laid on the enemy's positions followed by our attack. Our advance was cautious after the lesson they gave us yesterday with their tanks. Armored cars, light tanks and horse troops of the 104th Cavalry lead the way, followed by the infantry. Air activity was light. By 4:30pm we occupied our objective, White Store but our advance came to a halt on the far side of the town. Two bridges over the stream were destroyed and the Reds had taken a stand in the woods on the far side. Our command post was moved forward and the battalions were given instructions to send combat and reconnaissance patrols out during the night. Late at night orders were received from brigade to make a foray on Highway 151 between Pageland and Monroe. This was off to our right (west).

11/20/41:The advance got underway nicely the next morning as our troops crossed the stream on footbridges put in by the engineers during the night. Vehicles forded the stream at several points. We advanced about three or four miles before encountering resistance. The S-2 officer, Sgt and myself went up to the scene of action. It was evident the Reds planned to make a determined stand here as they brought up guns and armored cars. Leaving the Sgt there, we started back to report conditions to the command post. However the 22nd Tank Regiment and launched a counterattack and had cut our column in two between our forward position and white Store.; Unfortunately we drove into this breach in our lines and after a lively chase by a halftrack and one of those new jeeps we were captured. A few seconds later a brigade radio car with a Major drove unsuspectingly into the enemy's hands too. As we were waiting to be sent back to a prisoner collecting station we observed the 2nd Armored Div striking toward white Store to cut our column again. Things looked bad for the 28th division. By a ruse, we got rid of the guard on the captured radio car long enough to send this vital information to division headquarters. Finally arriving at the collecting station we were tagged and questioned and then fed. We had hash, beans and pineapple which probably was better than the troops in the field had.

From this collecting station we were sent to IV Corp prisoner of war enclosure at Chester, S. C. On the trip we passed hundreds of light and medium tanks including some of the Hugh M-3s that have a 75mm gun mounted in a side sponson. It amazed me that our slow non-mechanized outfit could put up such a show against this armored might. I decided the umpires were bending the rules to make us look good. At one point a column of light tanks (10 Tons) were preparing to deploy across an open field. Again we saw a group of foreign officers observing. When we reached the big prisoner enclosure we were separated from our open staff car and most of our equipment. We had our rank, name and serial number listed. After mess, we were issued two blankets and as all of the available tents had been occupied, we spread our blankets in an open field in the rain. Thus we unfortunates who had arrived too late for a tent spent a thoroughly miserable night.

11/21/41:At four o'clock in the morning the Sgt of the guard blew his whistle and shouted "Chow Time". That's one time I didn't mind getting up early as there was no profit laying in a puddle of water. Throwing off the wet blankets and cursing the weather and the Carolinas, we grabbed our mess gear and ran for a choice place in the line. After breakfast of grits and soggy eggs we turned in the wet blankets and formed in prisoner companies for a short march to a waterlogged field where we loaded up on captured trucks for the trip to the prisoner exchange point near Albemarle, N. C. When we unloaded at the exchange point we saw ourselves for the first time as a group in the daylight, a motley looking bunch at best, unshaven, dirty, a mixture of dress - denims, woolens, some with overcoats, others in jackets or nothing but a wet shirt. We resembled nothing better than the pictures of decrepit looking groups of prisoners in the European war.

At this point Red prisoners and captured vehicles were exchanged for Blues. We were allowed to go to our own vehicles, if we had any, so I was glad to get back to our staff car which had all my equipment. Then began another long ride to the replacement center at Fort Bragg, N. C. We arrived there about 5:00pm and once again had to go thru the troublesome procedure of being registered according to rank and military occupation classification (M.O.S. number). After that we were assigned to barracks in the camp and though some of us had to sleep on the floor for lack of enough beds, at least there were showers, water to shave and a heated building. Tomorrow we will probably be sent to the front as replacements, wherever we may be needed but at least we had a chance to clean up and get a good nights sleep.

The prisoner enclosure, exchange and replacement center were operated as one might expect in actual combat so as to acquaint us with the treatment and questioning we might expect. In any event we prisoners have traveled nearly 300 miles thru South and North Carolina since being captured. In spite of the poor accommodations it has been a splendid sightseeing tour. However most of the fellows were anxious to get back to their outfits. A soldier I guess is never satisfied.

At this point the letter ended and I must have mailed it home. As it turned out I rejoined my own outfit, but many others found themselves shipped off to strange units as replacements. The maneuvers continued until nearly the end of November. The fighting see- sawed back and forth along the border but the mobility and fire power of the Reds proved too much for our Corps to successfully carryout the planned double envelopment of the enemy. By the time it had ended we had been in the field over two weeks and the weather had been pretty cold and wet. My letter indicates all we did was ride or march around. That wasn't exactly the case as we often had to dig foxholes and build sandbagged emplacements whenever we established a position. When we moved, these had to be filled and the land returned to its original condition. Likewise with any fences we cut or damaged. After maneuvers were over the engineers, with bulldozers and grading equipment, had to cover the whole area leveling off rutted fields, repairing damaged roads and bridges, like the one destroyed by the artillery truck and howitzer. I'm sure the farmers submitted claims for any damage.

If the purpose of the maneuvers were to prove that infantry could successfully advance against a strong armored force, they certainly didn't convince the average G.I. We might successfully defend ourselves against such an enemy but if we moved out of our defenses he would quickly cut us up. I think these exercises showed that the antitank gun was a defensive weapon and that a strong combination of tanks and infantry was needed for attack. The static trench warfare of WW I was a thing of the past. Subsequently our cumbersome two brigade infantry divisions were designed into ones with three regimental combat teams and more mobility.

Maneuvers ended about the end of November, but it takes a lot of time to move a quarter of a million men out of an area. We were scheduled to move back to Indiantown Gap about December 7 and we were ready. We had enough of this outside living. Many mornings there was a skim of ice on the water when we went to wash and shave. We used the time to clean equipment and pack it in preparation for the move. I did get a chance to see the Stanbacks and thank them for their hospitality. After breakfast on the 7th we took down the large tents, folded them and stacked them at the head of the company street. Quartermaster would pick them up later. Then we policed the area, filling in the latrines, garbage pits and marking them. When everything had been returned pretty well to normal we loaded on trucks and started our trek back north.

It was a chilly day. The trucks had canvas covers but we kept the canvas closure at the rear rolled up so we could see out. It was about the middle of the afternoon that we noticed larger crowds along the road and they seemed to be shouting some thing at us. However, with the wind beating at the canvas we couldn't understand what they said. During a rest stop an officer in a jeep stopped and said there was news on the radio reporting Pearl Harbor bombed. He said at one point people had painted the information on the highway. Of course, looking out the back of the truck we couldn't have read it anyway.

As we continued north we discussed this momentous news, deciding it must be a mistake. The Philippines might have been bombed but how could they bomb Pearl Harbor? That was in Hawaii and our great naval base which was supposed to be impregnable. In any event something must have happened somewhere that was going to effect us. That night we camped on the slopes of a mountain cove somewhere in Virginia. Our campfires twinkled in a great semicircle. I thought how this scene must have been repeated many times eighty years ago as the campfires of the Union and Confederate armies twinkled in the darkness of these same mountains. The division sound truck with its big speakers was set up in the valley and that night we listened as Walter Winchell described the disastrous attack and sinking of our fleet. It was a fitting setting with thousands of men huddled around fires against the chilly darkness and listening to the words that meant war.

We kidded the dejected thirty year old men who thought they were getting out when we got back to Pennsylvania. We are all in for the duration now Boys! That one year service stuff got blown away at Pearl. It's a new ball game. As we continued up into Pennsylvania the next day we had plenty to think about. If the japs could move into our backyard (Hawaii) what was going to stop them from landing in California next. Certainly not the fleet that was laying on the bottom of the harbor. How would we match up to them when the time came? There was anger and a new sense of patriotism and a desire to strike back for this sneak attack. The crowds in the streets of the towns we passed through were larger than on Sunday and many were waving American Flags and cheering and we responded with thumbs up.

ROAD GUIDE ON THE WAY TO NORTH CAROLINA

HEAVY ARTILLERY PRIME MOVER

IT TOOK THE WHOLE BRIDGE DOWN

GEN. STUART LIGHT TANK

M-3 TD'S APPROACHING BRIDGE
Note AA Gun Emplacement

REFUELING AN M-8 ARMORED CAR

60mm MORTAR

COMMUNICATIONS SECTION

HOT WORK CONSTRUCTING AN ABATIS

CLEANING UP – WHEN WE WERE LUCKY TO FIND A STREAM

HOT DICE

WE PLAYED BLACK JACK TILL THE CANDLES RAN OUT

(Chard edge left by fire.)

27

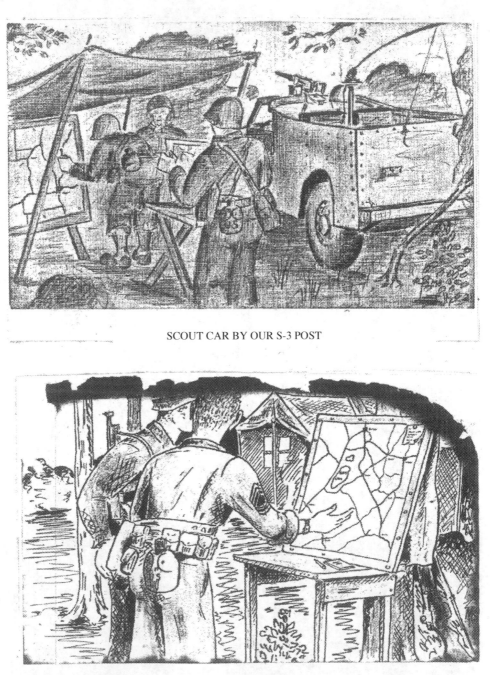

SCOUT CAR BY OUR S-3 POST

S-3 MAP BOARD

SHADE TREE MECHANIC

WE SLEPT CLOSE TO OUR VEHICLES

LOUISIANA

Half –Track Command Car

CAMP BEAUREGARDE

The week following our return to Indian Town Gap was fraught with anticipation. But anticipation of what, I don't really know. Rumors were thicker than flies in August and every rumor was supposed to be straight from the horse's mouth. We were restricted to camp, prepared to move on a moments notice. After Pearl Harbor everyone was fearful an invasion of the west coast was imminent. Eventually the restriction to camp was eased and I managed to get a weekend pass. Spent it at my uncle Harry in nearby Westchester where he was county superintendent of highways at the time. We listened to the war news on the radio. The first landings on Luzon in the Philippines and the bombing of the naval base at Cavite near Manila. The power of the Japanese navy seemed supreme as their aircraft sunk the two big British battleships Repulse and Prince of Wales off Malaya. It was a dark hour for our country.

Out of the confusion of rumors, the one that the division was being shipped to the Pacific was most persistent. When we finally received official orders to prepare to move to Louisiana it seemed to confirm the rumor. The move would be made by truck and rail. Furloughs were opened up and most of us had an opportunity for what might e a last visit home in a long time. To save time I took a plane over the snow covered Allegheny's. It was a DC-3 and a very bumpy ride. To add to our discomfort, the heating system failed and we huddled in blankets provided by the stewardess. Not a very favorable introduction to commercial aviation. My parents met me at the airport and we drove the ninety miles north to Meadville over snow covered roads.

I considered myself lucky to be assigned to make the trip with the motor convoy rather than by rail. It was a cold day in January when we pulled out of camp and headed south again. Made it to Fort Bragg the first night but no warm barracks this time. We spent the night out on the barren artillery range. No snow on the ground but it was cold. We managed to find a little wood to build a fire to sleep around. This was before zippered sleeping bags became standard army issue. We had our two wool blankets but anyone who has ever tried to sleep out with blankets knows that some part of your anatomy is always exposed. Fortunately we had thrown some quilted cotton comforters into the trucks and with these over the blankets and our feet toward the fire it wasn't too bad. Sometime in the early morning I was awakened by the guard shaking me and shouting something. As I got up I was amazed to see only a small fragment of my comforter remained and it was rapidly smoldering away. Apparently a spark from the fire, which was now dead, ignited the comforter which instead of blazing, slowly burned away. The wool blankets never caught fire, lucky for me. No wonder I had been snug and warm. The rest of the night was quite miserable with just the two blankets. Especially as it started snowing and by morning several inches of fluffy snow covered everything. I even tried sleeping in the truck, but the cold steel was worse than the ground.

Next day we continued southwest across Georgia and into Alabama bundled up in our overcoats. We thought it would be shirtsleeve weather this far south. Instead we dourly observed the skim ice in the roadside ditches as we passed. Open army trucks don't offer much protection against the wind and cold. I began to envy the ones who were making the trip by rail. We continued on by Jackson, Mississippi and camped the second night on the old battlefield at Vicksburg overlooking the river. Very nicely kept grounds. The lines of the old trenches and revetments were grass covered and not nearly so cold as Fort Bragg. Here our convoy would split up, some continuing west into Louisiana to Camp Livingston in the northern part of the state. Ours, the 112th regiment vehicles, would head southwest to Camp Beauregard near the Red river and Alexander. Camp Livingston was still under construction and unable to house all of the division. We were not favorably impressed with our first view of Camp Beauregard, nor did a closer examination improve our first impression. It was the remnants of an old World War I camp quickly resurrected for this war. The few permanent structures it contained were crude with sawdust filled wall cavities for insulation. The siding was cooked, warped and devoid of paint from the hot Louisiana sun. The bottom edges were scalloped from the depredations of termites and wet rot. The low one story buildings housed regimental and company offices, supply rooms, mess facilities and carpool garages. The rest of the camp was pyramidal squad tents set on wood platforms. Each had a small pot bellied stove for heat. Not first class, but still an improvement over the dirt floor unheated tents of our base camp in the Carolinas.

No paved streets, so when it rained we had mud. The areas around the buildings and mess halls had duckboards (wooden sidewalks) which helped some. Of course the saw dust filled walls of the buildings were havens for cockroaches. Some big enough to fight you for your food. Rodents too burrowed in these walls and I suppose there were snakes that preyed on them. Our training continued as Carolina maneuvers had revealed many areas in which we needed improvement. The fact that we were now at war put a different aspect on our training too. It was foggy and cold in the mornings as we marched out and heavy woolens felt good. By noon we were suffering from the heat. Different country from the Carolinas. Lots of pine woods, thickets and marshes here. There were advantages and disadvantages in being separated so far from the rest of the division. The fact that we were so close to Alexander though made up for the disadvantages. Camp Livingstone was out in the boondocks.

Alexander was on the west side of the Red river. With Camp Polk to the west, Camp Livingstone north and numerous small installations like ours scattered about, the town was crowded with uniforms. A short time before we came down there had been a race riot in which a couple of MPs and a score of Negro soldiers had been killed. The tensions from that had pretty well worn off by the time we first had passes to visit the town. I met a girl at the U.S.O. and soon found myself invited to her home. Also bought my first car there, or rather a buddy and I bought it. It was a 1932 Chevy convertible coupe with rumble seat. Sharp looking but it didn't run worth a darn. Paid $70 for it. I think we pushed it further than we ever drove it. Couldn't trust it for the fifteen mile trip to camp so we usually left it at the girl's house. When it ran, it was great and attracted girls like a magnet. At other times it dropped down to about six girl-power, that is six girls pushing and two riding.

I will not spend a lot of time describing training as it was in general just a continuation of what I've described before. The terrain was more rugged with swamps, brown water bayous and half flooded forests. Except in the pine woods or cultivated areas, one had to hack his way through tangled vegetation. There were gnats and bugs, but nothing like it would be when hotter weather arrived. We put in a full days schedule but being close to town, evening passes were available and every other week, one could get a weekend pass. Of course, one was lucky if he could afford two weekend passes a month. They didn't overpay us.

One day they gave a bunch of us yellow fever shots and we figured that confirmed the rumor that we soon would be on our way to the Pacific. As it turned out, they stopped giving the shots because some complications developed among the men that received them. It never bothered me but they kept a close check on us for a while. Whenever I received a physical during the rest of my time in service, I noted when the medical officer noted that shot on my record book; he seemed to give me a more rigorous examination than the others. I guess we were guinea pigs but no one ever told me so.

Perhaps they stopped giving the yellow fever shots when it was decided to ship another Infantry division to the south Pacific instead of us. I guess we were lucky because they were thrown into the jungle fighting on New Guinea and tropical diseases inflicted more casualties than the Japs. Many of those diseases little understood or unknown by our medical people.

Like most GIs, we were always hoping to find a town where there weren't any. A cab driver said he knew an area like that down in Cajun country a little over an house drive south. For fifteen dollars he'd drive us down on Friday night and pick us up on Sunday evening. Split four ways that wasn't bad, so we discovered Ville Platte and started spending every weekend we could down there. Other towns in the area were Eunice and Opelousas. This was Evangeline country, unspoiled and the few GIs around were mostly local boys. Plenty of girls, most with French names like LeFleur, Gasperacy, Vidrine. The main social spot was the Casino that ran wide open twenty-four hours a day I think, including Sundays. Gambling, dancing and drinking. We lead a depraved life; Rathskeller, McInish, Stevenson, Mates and me.

These Cajuns were hot tempered and I almost got cut up one night for just talking to a girl from Opelousas. Her date was a short swarthy Cajun GI and he came at me with a knife. I was glad others restrained him. Strangely though I never saw this girl again (Deese LeDoux) we corresponded regularly for years. In fact after the war she sent me a picture of her wedding. I guess she had a crush on me. In strange situations sometimes strange friendships are made.

31

One night a group of us, including girls, hitched a ride to Eunice. We never got there because a pig ran out in front of the car and the driver lost control when he hit it. The car skidded from one side of the road to the other and then started rolling. I guess there were nine of us packed in like sardines. One second I was on the bottom of the pile, my face pressed against the glass hoping it wouldn't shatter and the next second I'd be on top and going down again. Finally the car came to a rending screeching stop and in the silence that followed I listened to the tinkling of glass falling on the pavement.

Slowly as the shock of the experience wore off, bodies started moving as we tried to determine if anyone was hurt. It took some time to orient ourselves, manage to get a door open and extricate everybody as the car was lying on its side. One girl had cuts and a broken arm; the rest of us only minor cuts and bruises. Cars we tried to flag down wisely sped past until a couple of us stood in the middle of the road and literally forced a car to stop. Leaving the rest of the girls and driver there, we got in the car with the injured girl and he took us to a nearby town where there was a clinic. At two AM it was closed but we aroused the doctor who lived in the same building. Briefly explaining there had been an accident we turned the girl over to him and got out of there before he could get our names. I'm not very proud of our actions but we just didn't want to get involved. I may as well make a full confession and admit we didn't go back to the ones we left at the wreck either.

I don't think we were really as bad as this sounds; or at least I hope not. We behave ourselves at the private home where we rented rooms. Of course after our Friday and Saturday night excesses we were pretty subdued during the day. In any event the people allowed their daughters to associate with us and we even went on picnics several times. The girls were not allowed to go to the casino or honky tonks though.

One day we were walking along an elevated road with marshy wooded land on each side. A lean rangy pig that roam wild in the area was rooting for acorns at the foot of the embankment. For lack of anything better to do I pitched a couple of stones at him. He stopped rooting and gave me a baleful glare before resuming his activities. I made the mistake of throwing another rock at him and he charged up the bank. I turned and ran, hearing his pounding hoofs and squealing behind me as well as the laughter of my companions. Mentally I could picture his tusks slashing at my legs. Puffing like a steam engine, I glanced behind and was relieved to see he had stopped his pursuit. He stood his ground a moment then shrugged his shoulders and walked leisurely down the bank to resume his rooting. He had made his point and I never threw another rock at a Cajun pig. These were good days and we enjoyed our weekends in Ville Platte. The cabby true to his word always picked us up on Sunday night for the return trip. The one thing I missed down there was a good cup of coffee. I never could get use to chicory.

I had mentioned we lived in pyramidal tents set up on wooden platforms and heated with a small pot bellied stove. The stove pipe extended up along the center pole and passed thru a hole in the top of the tent. There were several sections of pipe above the tent to prevent sparks igniting the canvas. Ours gave us particular trouble as the slightest breeze would topple the pipe and one of us would have to gingerly crawl up the tent and replace it. A tough job as a tent isn't very stable. One night the pipe toppled off and sparks ignited the canvas. It doesn't burn or flare up. It just smolders as a thin red glowing line and ate away the canvas, leaving the center pole and ropes. You can imagine our surprise to wake up in the morning with an open sky above us.

I seem to keep coming back to the subject of snakes, but remember with us tramping around in the brush and marshlands it was a subject constantly one our minds. Occasionally we'd see a heavy bodied moccasin that had been run over by a vehicle and live one was the last thing we wanted to step on. There were other kinds too, like the colorful coral snake and we killed one of those in the pine woods. A check of its color pattern affirmed it was the extremely venomous variety. One of the fellows skinned it for the colorful hide. A job I certainly wouldn't have done.

The regiment was sent to Camp Polk which was west of Alexandria and we camped in pup tents on the artillery range. There we continued our training with the added benefit of overhead artillery fire. The range was on flat semi-marshy land spotted with hummocks of slightly higher ground. We pitched our tents on these drier elevations. Of course the mosquitoes were terrible. We were told the only defense was to hammer their stingers flat with a boot when they stuck them thru the tent wall. Then there was the story about the guy who hammered so many of them flat, that when they all flapped their wings, they flew away with his tent. During the night, moccasins would crawl up on these hummocks and we had to be careful when we got up in the morning. A number of them were killed around the tents during our stay. It wasn't a very pleasant feeling to worry about finding one of the things sharing the tent with you but to my knowledge this never occurred.

One day we came across a mother armadillo with a litter of half grown young. We had a great time trying to catch one of them. The mother was frantic and furious. When we'd get one of the little ones cornered, she came charging out of the brush and we'd scatter out of her way. We finally wore her down and caught one of the babies. After examining it and taking some pictures we let it go. The shell, instead of being hard, was soft and pliable. We were glad to leave that marshland and get back to the relative comforts of Beauregard.

Our area in Camp Livingston was finally completed and we received orders to move there to join the rest of the division. The army never makes it easy as we had to take the tents down, fold and store them. The stoves were taken apart, cleaned and carried to one of the old buildings, and then the heavy wood platforms carried to the head of the company streets and stacked. It was with rather mixed emotions that we left this rather primitive camp. It would be nice to be in a new camp with PX and recreational facilities. On the other hand we would miss the convenience of Beauregard's proximity to Alexandria and Ville Platte. We could have used a car at Livingston, but the trouble prone roadster had been abandoned to its fate some time ago.

We were surprised that Livingston didn't have two story barracks like Indiantown. Instead, it had pyramidal tents like Beauregard except in addition to wood floors they had framed side with screened openings. The tents really just served as a covering over a frame. All in all a much neater place with paved streets and graveled walks. We certainly missed our forays to Ville Platte. In time we met some girls in the area but this wasn't Cajun country and not much exciting to do. I guess I would have been tempted to throw a rock at a pig just to stir up some action, but the only ones I saw were domesticated and laying the shade under the houses. Most of the houses in this area were built on post supports and open underneath. Anyone reading this would think we were a bunch of bums. Really, the fellows I ran around with were a nice bunch. Actually the girls we met set the tone of our relationship. If they didn't drink or go to dancehalls, we respected that. On the other hand, if they did then we went along with that too. Sometimes we'd be invited to a girls home and that was a nice change from camp discipline or barrooms. We were all homesick to some extent. All in all I can't think of many actions I would be ashamed of. I'm amazed as I look thru my address book at how many girls I met wherever I went. Many of course were just the most casual of relationships. It was a time of upheaval and uncertainty as to the future. It wouldn't be realistic to omit mentioning these girls in my story.

Rathskeller and I went to New Orleans by train one weekend. We were lucky to find a dingy hotel room close to the French Quarter. The town was crowded and rooms scarce. The first place we headed for was Bourbon Street and in the course of the night visited some pretty sleazy places. After all the lectures we had on venereal diseases I was afraid to even drink out of some of the glasses. Some of the characters around the crowded bars looked like the dregs of humanity. Eventually I went into a tattoo artist pad with a bunch of guys and allowed myself to be talked into one. Glad I was conservative and held it to initials and blood type. Some of the boys would be sorry when they sobered up and saw what they had stenciled on them. Later on, I remember a fellow from Arkansas who fell in love with a girl and he went to a lot of pain and trouble trying to get a tattoo removed from his belly before he would ask her to marry him. Rathskeller and I were content to do a little bit of plain sightseeing the next day before returning to camp well bushed from the weekend.

I made it back to Meadville on furlough along with several other boys from Company B. Quite a trip with the coal fired locomotives of that day. Crowded, hot, soot filtered into the cars. When you had a chance to wash your face, the paper towel came away black. The Southern took us to St. Louis where we had a long layover for the train to Chicago. We quickly discovered there were plenty of bars around the station and the time passed quickly. In fact some of us almost missed our connection. The Erie RR station is some distance from the main terminal in Chicago. As we walked it we agreed the Windy City is well named as wind and trash buffeted us the whole way. Once on the Erie it was clear sailing home.

While home that time, I saw a sight that impressed me. One of our local boys had completed his training as a B-17 pilot and on his way to war he detoured and flew over Meadville. After circling the town, he came down to treetop level and roared right up Mill Run Valley over the football field and disappeared into the east. From where I was standing on North Street it almost seemed as if I could have reached our and touched the plane. It looked exciting and I wished I were one of them instead of in the infantry.

During this period in Louisiana changes in uniform and equipment came. The semi-automatic garande rifle and popular carbine replaced the Springfield rifle. I did well with the carbine and scored expert with it when we got on the range. Our dishpan World War I helmets were exchanged for the pot shaped helmut and phenolic helmut liner. Typical of American military procurement, no consideration was given to appearance. It came in one size. A fathead looked like he was squeezed into it while a skinny guy looked like a turtle peering out from under its shell. I was surprised when I got overseas and learned the Germans were more considerate and made their helmuts in several sizes. Various new articles of clothing were introduced; not that did anything for our appearance. Even such mundane items as the new mess kits and canteen cups were pressed phenolic fiber and not very appetizing in appearance. Those of us with the old original aluminum gear tried to hang onto it. I don't really know why because it probably wasn't as sanitary and the aluminum cups got so hot you'd scald your lips on them even after the coffee inside was lukewarm.

I had to eventually give up my cherished aluminum cup. We were on a field exercise and I had a cup of coffee before hitting the sack, and I didn't bother to wash my cup. Next morning before daylight it was chilly and I headed for the kitchen tent for a cup of coffee to warm up. The cooks get up before the rest of us. The first sip not only tasted smelled terrible but it felt as if it was full of grounds. Shining my flashlight into the cup I saw it was full of boiled ants. During the night they had found the residual sugar in the bottom of the unwashed cup. That aluminum absorbed the odor when the hot coffee cooked them and no amount of scouring would remove it.

Groups of men were still pulled out of the regiment to fill the needs of cadres as the army continued its rapid expansion. One day in April (1942) I was called to HQ company office and Capt Griffin informed me there was an urgent request for a man with my MOS (job classification). He didn't know anymore than what the request stated. The work would involve map making for the Tank Destroyer School at Camp Hood, Texas. I was surprised and pleased to know that somebody might want me. In the army, anything that breaks the routine is a welcome change. The old adage, "The grass always looks greener on the other side of the fence", held true here. I had never heard of Tank Destroyers; must be some new organization being formed and its usually good to get in on the ground floor. Texas sounded interesting too. Without hesitation I said "I'll take it!" It took a couple of days to check in my company equipment, get transfer orders, and travel papers. In the meantime I bade farewell to the many friends I had in the regiment. HQ Company had been good to me. When I joined the army, I never dreamed I would rise to the exalted rank of buck sergeant. I regretted the fact I probably would never see the girls in Ville Platte or Alexandria again, but that was the army. It is difficult to leave the security of established friends and organization and head into an unknown situation. As I got on the train with my pack and duffle bags, second thoughts raised apprehensions that perhaps I made a bad decision.

NOTE

I will take a few lines to bring world events up to date. Last January with a large share of our fleet sunk at Pearl Harbor and the Philippines invaded, things looked pretty dark. The fears of an invasion of the west coast or Hawaii never materialized, but things didn't get better during the next five months. McArthur withdrew his men into a trap on Bataan. Corregidor long hailed as our Gibraltar of the Pacific, fell. It was a shock when even Singapore couldn't be held. Everywhere the Japs surged forward; Indonesia, Malaya, even spilling into the Indian Ocean. Meanwhile German submarines cruised at will along our east coast and the Caribbean. The fires at sea from sinking tankers lighted many of our coastal cities. In Africa the British fought to save the Suez Canal after the fall of their bastion at Tobruk. In Russia, the Germans were again on the move with spring after surviving the terrible cold winter. The Battle of the Coral Sea in May stopped the Japanese advance in that area but we lost one of our precious carriers. It was the first major naval battle fought where the opposing ships never saw each other. I guess the fact that the Japanese had not scored a quick knockout after Pearl Harbor heartened us and we really never thought that we could lose the war. At the same time, the enemy's successes left no doubt in our minds that it was going to be a long hard struggle to victory. Many felt the road to victory began with the glorious naval victory at Midway Island, when the Japanese invasion fleet was turned away in June. We lost the Yorktown, but they lost their four best carriers and irreplaceable air crews.

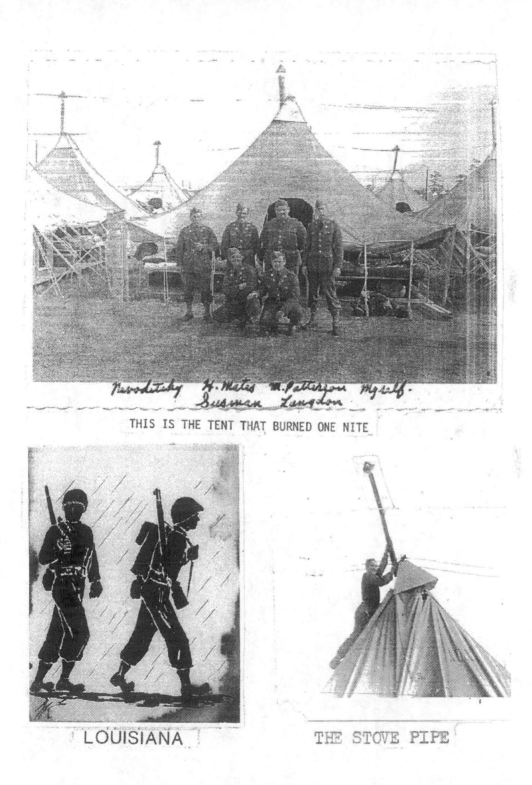

Newditsky H. Metes M. Patterson Myself.
Susman Langdon

THIS IS THE TENT THAT BURNED ONE NITE

LOUISIANA

THE STOVE PIPE

I WAS TOO BUSY TO DO
MUCH SKETCHING IN
LOUISIANA

(Too busy to do any sketching in Louisiana)

TEXAS

JUN 1942 – APR. 1943

Tank Destroyers

CAMP HOOD

It was a leisurely train ride west thru Louisiana and the pine lands of east Texas, then came the fast flat lands of the coastal plain as we approached Houston. The green fields extended flat as a billiard table to the horizon and they shimmered in the hot bright glare of the sun. I was surprised at the size of the city as the train slowly wound its way in thru crowded Mexican urban areas. Several places we seemed to be traveling right on the street. Sitting by an open window one could whiff the odors from street side fruit and vegetable markets as well as some odors not so pleasant. Changed trains in Houston and headed northwest up the Brazos. The land soon turned brown and burned looking. Eventually arrived at my destination, Temple, Texas.

I liked what I saw. The main feature that stood out was the modern, tall city hall building surrounded by green lawns and shrubs in the center of town. Clean and crisp after traveling most of the afternoon thru a brown landscape. Quite a few GIs on the streets and after some inquiries I located the Tank Destroyer HQs in an old two story building downtown. I thought to myself, this is going to be great, working right in town. Walking into the building was a welcome relief from the heat of the day and with a sigh I deposited my pack and duffle bag. Reporting to the duty officer, I noted he wore the collar insignia of the Coast Artillery. An arm of the service I had not run into before.

He directed me to the S-3 officer, Lt. Col Booth. He was a Texan; a large man with wind weathered features, sun bleached hair and bushy white eyebrows. He made me feel at ease with him right away, the kind of a fellow who doesn't stand on formalities too strongly. He showed me where I would work on the 2nd floor and briefed me on the nature of the work. Camp Hood was under construction about twenty-five miles west of Temple near a place called Killen. It had a large reservation (about 200 sq. miles) and would be the training area for the new tank destroyer branch of the army. Our job was to prepare maps of the camp and reservation area. At the time it was a pretty remote area of marginal cattle land. I would be chief draftsman and a Cpl Gould would assist me. I had done a lot of drawing and sketching but other than map reading, had no experience at map making. This would be challenging.

HQ Company was scattered all over town in rented buildings. I was assigned to a small group occupying some rented store space on a side street close to downtown. The cots were equipped with mosquito netting which I quickly found was a necessary nuisance. Because of our scattered situation, discipline as I had known it in an infantry regiment was non-existent here. No reveille, no bed check.

There was a lot of work to do in a short time, so it meant long hours. We had to prepare three maps: a large scale map of the camp area showing buildings and streets; a medium scale map of the reservation area showing roads, streams, hills and divided into zones for training assignments; then there was a small scale road map covering an area about a hundred miles square for the use of convoys with heavy armored vehicles. Weight carrying capacity of bridges and other pertinent data had to be noted. Each map was to be printed in three colors, so a plate for each color had to be made. Nine plates altogether. The work on the camp area and road map required no field work as the data was available from survey notes, civil and architectural plans and Department of Highway records, but the reservation map was a different story.

We had a good set of serial photos. Studying these thru a simple optical device gave a three dimensional effect by which one could recognize the various features of the landscape: hills, gulches, woods, streams, roads. However it was a matter of interpretation and sometimes shadows that were thought to define a ridge could just as easily define a canyon, a rather important difference to a person using the map. Photo interpretation had to be verified

37

by field inspection. During the afternoons and evenings we worked in the office roughing out a new sector of the map from information gleaned from the aerial photos. This required orienting the photos in correct relation to each other as well as to some benchmark or landmark.

Early the next morning we headed out to the reservation area by jeep to verify, correct and add details by direct observation. We used the compass and occasionally a transient to establish direction and reference points for our hand sketches. Pretty crude map making, but necessary in order to meet our deadline. I remember the first morning we headed out for Killeen and the reservation area, Col Booth, the driver, and me. we passed a sign that said "DIP" and I wondered what in the heck a dip was. The answer was quickly evident as the road dipped sharply down into a dry streambed and back out again. A small culvert carried the normal flow of water under the roadbed, but when a gully washer hit the road might be under anywhere from six inches of water to six feet of water, something worth remembering when driving along in a storm. Even after a storm and the water has subsided, stones and debris can be left littering the road. Killeen looked like any crowded, dirty boomtown. I think even the outhouses had been conscripted for living quarters.

This Texas land was new to me. A group of stony ridges with stunted looking trees dominated the southern and northern part of the reservation. In between the land was rolling and cut up by streambeds running in deep gullies. Mostly scrub brush with trees and vegetation clinging around the meandering banks of the stagnant gravelly streambeds. Lines that we thought were roads on the serial photos often turned out to be trails negotiable only by goats or four wheel drive vehicles. Potholes and rocks jarred our backs. At the time I never gave it a thought, but it must have been pretty rough on the Colonel as he was not a young man. Occasionally we'd see the bleached skull of a cow or goat. The only other signs of life during the day were the buzzards hovering on the heat currents or the suspected glimpse of a snake scurrying in the shadow of a rock. During the course of our travels we killed several rattlesnakes and I cut the rattles off as souvenirs.

Easing down into a sunken streambed one time, we spotted a flock of buzzards on a gravel bar. Apparently they had just gorged themselves on some carrion and were too heavy to fly. At any rate they paid no attention to us as we watched them. a disgusting sight as they regurgitated the rotten food at the edge of the water, then proceeded to re-eat it. A process they repeated. Apparently this is the way they digest it. My thoughts slipped back to the buzzards in the battle field scenes in Gone with the Wind. By mid afternoon we were usually dehydrated and warn out by the heat and dust. We'd head back to Temple and spend the rest of the day transferring our observed data onto the map drawings and prepare work for the next day.

July and August slipped by quickly, it was nice to have the run of the town every evening, yet there wasn't that much to do. So one usually ended up sitting in a bar drinking beer and seeking companionship. Met a few girls but these were just casual friendships. There was one beauty, a Mexican-American girl who worked at Walgreens, jet black hair and eyes with a sparkle. Unfortunately the new lieutenants with shiny gold bars monopolized her time.

One hears all kinds of stories about Texas: mosquitoes so tough they wear spurs on their boots cockroaches that arm wrestle you for the food on your plate. One night I really saw one of these Texas stories come true, it was crickets - millions of big black ones. Where they came from I'll never know but all at once they were there. At first I tried to avoid stepping on them but soon the gutters and sidewalks were black with them. Walking became difficult on the crushed bodies and the live ones clung to your pant legs. Back at our storeroom quarters we tried packing blankets around the windows and doors to keep them out. Giving up, we crawled into the bunks and pulled the mosquito netting snug but even that didn't stop them. Next morning crushed bodies lay among the blankets. The next day they disappeared as mysteriously as they had come, leaving a mess to be cleaned up with brooms and hoses.

All good things come to an end. We finished the maps and they were sent to Austin for printing. Our quarters in Camp Hood were finished and we bade our crude but convenient arrangements in town a sad farewell. Recognizing that I would be isolated at camp, I shopped around for a car. I found a 1929 Model A for fifty dollars. Looked like good transportation except the tires were worn out. This was a time of rationing and tires, especially 21 inch tires for a model A, were nonexistent. One had to scrounge around for old casings and patch them with big boots. Gas was rationed too, so I had to get a ration card. Regardless of the nuisance, the old car served me well.

The first friend it made for me was Sgt Major Thomas. He was what one would expect a peacetime, regular army Sgt Major to look like. Big, rough, and a beer belly, wise in army ways and an alcoholic. To get too close was to risk a hangover. Once you got through his thick veneer he was a nice guy, but he had to have his booze. Camp Hood was right in the middle of a dry area and the nearest package store was about forty miles away down toward Austin. So once a week I'd use most of my precious ration cards to drive him down there. He'd stock up with half pints which we'd conceal between the springs of the rear seat so we could sneak them past the guard post. Usually one of the tires would blow out a boot on that trip. That was one reason we drove down at night, to avoid the heat of the day. On a hot day probably all the tires would have blown out. In return he helped me out in many ways. Sgt Thomas had a girlfriend just the opposite of him. She was, probably in her forties like him. Tall, slender, staid; I would picture her more at home sitting in a parlor sipping a lemonade than as a government secretary in an army camp. I guess she was his guardian angel, always fussing about his drinking but mothering him like an old hen. I enjoyed their company. Sgt Thomas died in 1944 of jaundice.

Eventually a dedication day was set for Camp Hood. I had the color guard for the ceremony. The brass wanted to do it up right and a huge flag was shipped down from Washington for the occasion. It was supposed to be the largest flag available and folded up it looked the size of a duffle bag and must have weighed sixty pounds. I groaned when I saw it wondering if I could hold that bulky weight on my forearms and control it as its folds were drawn up the flagpole. Cecil Hodges was on the color guard with me and two others. For a flag that size we could have used two more.

We were all a little nervous with all the high rank around us. The chief guest was a grandson of General Hood (Civil War General) and he looked old enough to be the General himself. The flag is folded in shape of a triangle and held in a way that it flips toward the bearer as its folds are drawn out so it can be controlled. My nervous buddies placed in on my arms reversed from its normal position. I saw disaster looming as it was going to flip away from me and probably hit the ground. I tried to get their attention and change it, but they were frozen at attention and immune to my desperate hisses. As the band burst forth with the Star Spangled Banner, they attached the lanyard to the grommets of the flag and started hoisting. I managed to control the outward flipping of the flag as about twenty feet of it unfolded, then it snarled itself and rose out of my arms. I held my breath hoping it would stay tangled until it was high enough to clear the ground.

It didn't! All at once bellows of red, white and blue folds started dropping toward us. Forgetting all dignity we scrambled to catch the flag before it hit the ground. It was at that moment the news media snapped their photographs which appeared in papers all over the country. You can believe I was on the carpet for that fiasco. It didn't matter who gave me the flag improperly, I was in charge of the guard and it was my responsibility. I was lucky I didn't end up a private again.

Tank Destroyers were thought to be the answer to the German blitzkrieg which so far had swept everything before it. Flood the battlefield with anti-tank weapons and stop the tanks. It would take time to get our war production up and produce tanks and crews in the number required. To fill the gap it was quicker to produce a weapon from existing equipment. A 75mm gun was mounted on a half track and became our first mobile anti-tank weapon. Dozens of battalions would be created, equipped with these gun carriages, and trained at Camp Hood. The gun itself had a 15 degree traverse side-to-side, beyond that the halftrack itself had to be moved to follow a target. The gun had been modified but still was not the high velocity weapon needed to knock out the newer tanks. It really was out classed by the time the first battalion had completed its training.

Of course, we didn't know this and the M-3 looked pretty impressive to us. The new battalions began their training with enthusiasm and wore the orange and black panther shoulder patch with pride. Early every morning reverberated with the roar of motors and clanking of treads as the companies moved out to training areas and gunnery ranges. Clouds of dust traced the movements of units as they churned up the dry Texas landscape. The sharp bark of guns continued thru the day as crews strove to become proficient with their weapon. Quickness and accuracy was the key to survival on the battlefield. In the evenings, the weapons and vehicles had to be cleaned and serviced in preparation for the next day.

Tanks were not a plentiful item in 1942, but we had a company of light tanks and several of the old General Grants to add realism to the training. The Grant was our heavy tank. It had a 75mm cannon mounted in a sponson on the right side. It too had a limited traverse and the tank basically had to be moved to aim it. Above this it had a turret with a 37mm gun and another small turret with a machine gun, a tall ponderous looking machine with a riveted hull. Too tall to conceal, too awkward with its main armament and when hit the rivets would sheer inside the hull. Rommel's victory in Africa in June had left the British decimated in tanks. To meet their desperate need, our armored forces were stripped of the General Grants and many of our light tanks which were shipped to North Africa.

Getting the tanks safely to Egypt at a time that submarines were a scourge on the seas is an interesting story. According to my information, three convoys were sent. One had the precious tanks, the other two were decoys. Submarines intercepted the two decoys but the one with the tanks took the long route around the southern tip of Africa and delivered its cargo in time for the battle of El Alamein. In this battle, General Montgomery dealt the Africa Corp a decisive defeat. The British called them flaming coffins from their tendency to burn when hit, but they served their purpose in a time of desperate need.

With the exit of the Grants, the new Shermans with a high velocity 75 mounted in a turret were coming off the production lines and became our main battle tank. During this period we saw a number of new prototype tanks and anti-tank vehicles. I was impressed by an electric drive tank-like gun carriage with a 76mm high velocity gun. Very smooth to drive and quick to respond but if it ever reached production it must have been in limited numbers. Some of the designs were weird like the cannon mounted on a low profile carriage which looked like a "go-cart". Another was a long 105mm cannon mounted on a tank chassis. Eventually the M-10 evolved as our 2nd generation weapon. This utilized a standard tank carriage with sloped armor plating instead of a cast hull. It had a 3" M7 H.V. gun mounted in an open top turret. Its 360 degree traverse was a big improvement over the M-3. However the M-3 halftrack would remain our basic weapon until it met its demise in North Africa.

Envisioning the mass use of tank destroyers on the battlefield, two Brigade HQs were formed for tactical command over groups of TD battalions. Since my intentions (foolishly or otherwise) always had been to get overseas, I managed to transfer to the 2nd TD Brigade as S-3 Operations Sgt. HC Company was composed largely of Arkansas National Guard Boys. A rough bunch and I say this with affection. George Weaver was 1st Sgt. Some of the other names that come quickly to mind are Ben Gordes, Keg Brean, Stanfield, Cecil Hodges. The Model A helped nurture some of these friendships as it provided transportation to Dallas whenever we could get a weekend pass.

It was a 150 mile trip which was a long trip with poor tires I had accumulated some spare wheels and patched tires which we tied on the roof, five guys more than filled the interior of a Model A. when a tire would blow, I'd pull over to the side of the road. If it was a rear tire, those four big boys would hold the car up while I changed. That saved time bothering with the jack. The road took us up thru Waco and somewhere past Hillsboro we'd watch for our first glimpse of the neon lighted Pegasus (horse) on top of the tallest building Dallas. It was a landmark that could be seen quite a distance in that rolling country. In Dallas I'd deposit all our blown tires at a gas station with instructions we needed them fixed by Sunday afternoon for the return trip. Sometimes we stuck together as a group, at other times we'd split according to our situation. Together or individually we had a good time in that town and managed to get back together Sunday for the long drive back to camp. The return trip was usually pretty quiet as I was the only one who had to stay awake, but usually wishing I could sleep too.

Brigade commander was Brig. General Gordon, Executive officer was Col Mattox, and Major Damron was Adjutant. We started taking part in field exercised with the TD battalions under our command. As we moved into late fall and winter, Texas dust changed to Texas gumbo which had a texture and tenacity of thick molasses. The weather also went thru drastic changes in a matter of hours.

It could be raining cats and dogs and a half hour later you'd be steam baked dry by the sun. about the time we'd shed down to shirtsleeves a cold wind howled down out of the north dropping temperatures to freezing if it was a nice warm day in the winter, it was prudent to carry a raincoat and an over coat because you probably would need both before the day was over. In that Texas gumbo, churned up by tank treads, our wheeled vehicles would sink in up to the hubs. Then unless we could get a halftrack to tow us out, it was a matter of wading into the stuff and pushing or piling limbs and brush under the wheels. Each step was a struggle as suction tried to pull your boots off and the boots themselves became big clumps of mud. It was times like these that one wished he was in the Air Force. On these field problems we ran into a new varmint not previously encounter and that was the scorpion. They were noted for crawling into your boots at night so we quickly got into the habit of tapping and shaking our boots out in the morning before pulling them on.

We envied the 1st Brigade when they were shipped out. We assumed they were headed for the invasion North Africa. Later in February 1943, they and their battalions of M-3s would be overrun and destroyed in Kasserine Pass (Tunisia) by the 10th and 15th Panzer divisions. Other American units, including the 1st division also were roughly handled by the battle wise German units. Inexperience, inferior equipment (M-3s) and defective ammunition contributed to the disaster. Desperate gunners saw their shell hit the target, only to bounce off and skitter across the landscape without detonating. Later a frantic search for good fuses turned up a supply of old WW I French 75mm fuses in Syria. These were shipped to Cairo where the metric threads were re-machined to fit our shell. This solved the defective ammunition problem but far too late for our forces at Kasserine. Pictures I saw later showed the barren landscape littered with the burned twisted hulls of our M-3s. Not very reassuring but of course we didn't think that could happen to us. People have asked me, "How can a soldier advance across an open field knowing the enemy is out there determined to kill him?" part of it of course is discipline and in addition his mind will not allow him to consider anything terrible will happen to him. One takes the attitude that it always happens to the other guy. Sometimes too, it takes the threat of a bayonet in the hands of an officer or sergeant to inspire a reluctant soldier to leave the security of a ditch and become a hero.

Tank destroyers first big confrontation with panzers certainly was a disaster and a great deal of time was spent at Camp Hood studying that battle. Both to determine what went wrong and what we could learn to prevent another such setback. We cleared a barracks floor and used it to draw large scale maps on brown wrapping paper of the Kasserine, Sbeitla, Thala battle area. These strips were pasted together to form a large twenty-by-thirty sheet on which troop dispositions and movements were show (both ours and the enemy's). the conclusion was that the defeat resulted from inexperience at the field and command levels plus overmatched equipment. I think at this point confidence dropped in the ability of lightly armored forces stopping tanks. Opinion started shifting to the idea that it takes a tank to stop a tank.

I enjoyed basic artillery training. Learning how to align (or lay) a field piece from established reference points for indirect fire. That is to hit a target many miles away that you couldn't see. Calculating the time of flight, powder increments required, and fuse length. Of course, this was just basics and we didn't get to do any actual firing. Directing artillery or mortar fire gave a real sense of power at your fingertips. Observing a target, one would plot its map coordinates relative to some ground feature, then call for a ranging shot. This was usually a smoke round so it could be spotted. Noting where it hit in relation to the target, it was then a matter of calling corrective instruction back to the battery and maybe by the third try you were right on the target. The observer uses field glasses that have vertical and horizontal scales etched on the lens for estimating distance.

We also had a number of Piper Cub artillery spotter planes. I had an opportunity to go up in one of those and it was a great experience at first with the ground spread out like a relief map below. However looking down and trying to plot the location of a target while the plane circled and bounced in the updrafts was impossible. The unaccustomed motion soon made me sick as a dog and I was grateful for the plastic bag they had given me. I thought I was going to die before we reached the ground again. Sgt Thomas said I was green as a cucumber when I staggered out of the plane. I wasn't cut out to be either a flyer or a sailor.

To break the monotony of a weekend in camp, several of us went over to the motor pool to see if we could borrow a couple of motorcycles. Figured we'd have fun learning to ride them on the truck park. I quickly found it wasn't as easy as riding a bicycle. The unfamiliar controls like the handle bar accelerator, clutch and brake made it difficult and after several spills on the gravel I decided I'd live a lot longer if I stayed off those things. A couple of the other fellows did pretty well after a little practice. Several weeks later there was a accident that convinced me that I had made the right decision. A fellow was sitting on a cycle up on its stand in the motor pool garage. He was revving up the motor and practicing shifting gears, when it lurched off the stand. When the wheel hit the floor it projected the cycle and rider right thru the garage wall between two wall studs. Unfortunately there was a two by six cross member about five feet above the floor and this flattened the top of his skull, killing him. If it had been a foot higher he would undoubtedly have survived going thru the wall. The military (except combat) was no different from civilian hazards in that vehicular accidents caused most of our fatalities.

When the army gave its new I.Q. test at Camp Hood, I lucked out and scored a 127. that was the second highest score among the ten thousand who took the test which probably doesn't say much for our intellectual level. In any event I became sort of a celebrity overnight and during the ensuing weeks several tempting opportunities were offered me. One was to attend the University of Illinois and pursue the subject of my choice; second was the offer to send me to any officer candidate school I chose. To attend college, I would have to take a reduction to buck Sgt as that was the highest rank allowed. When one considers all the lonely girls attending colleges in those days, I can't imagine my stupidity in rejecting that offer. I was seriously considering Engineers or Air Force Administration officer candidate schools when General Gordon called me in and congratulated me on my score. He said, "you have several wonderful opportunities here and I don't want to adversely influence you, but there is a third choice. This is confidential, but the Brigade will soon be going overseas. I'd like to have you go with us. Your job rates a Master Sgt rank and if you choose to stay with us I will move you up to that rank as quickly as possible. Now give this serious thought and let me know as soon as possible". Right there I proved those intelligence tests are meaningless if you don't have any common sense, because I said with a flair of patriotism, "I'll stick with the Brigade!"

The general was as good as his word and in a week I was raised to Tech Sgt and a couple of months later to Master Sgt, a pretty respectable rank. I may not have foresight, but I do have hindsight and it makes me sick to think I turned down either college or Air Corp Administration. With the expanding air force, I probably would have made a career of that and retired the ripe old age of 39.

Well, we didn't get orders for overseas. Instead we were slated for Tennessee maneuvers with orders to move to Camp Forrest. I received permission to drive my old Model A up there. Took Keg Brean along with me for company. We loaded the car with our stuff and all the old wheels and tires and headed east. Made it to Ruston, La. the first night. Looked up a couple of girls I knew from my Camp Livingston days. From there we drove to Birmingham, Ala. and got a hotel room. The day had been rough on tires, so the first thing I did was find a gas station that promised to have them ready sometime the next morning. Unfortunately there was a party going on across the hall and of course we joined it. When I looked at Keg the next morning, I knew we weren't going to get an early start. Not that I was in much better condition.

Between sleep and black coffee I managed to go out about noon to get the tires. They showed me that five of them were beyond redemption but at my urging they managed to get two of them to hold air. For how long was hard to tell. It was evening by the time we pulled out on our last leg to Camp Forrest. Far behind schedule and we probably would have to drive all night. It was cool and was going to get a lot colder before the night was thru. The engine wasn't running right and throwing clouds of fumes into the car. Cold or not we had to open all the windows to avoid suffocating. It seemed everything was uphill and the engine was missing so bad all it could do was crawl up the grades. In the valleys we felt our way through fog and when we stopped for a blowout we hoped the engine would restart. Hardly saw any other traffic or even many signs of habitation. At one place we seemed to follow along the top of a mountain for hours. It was some trip and Keg hanging his head out the window and complaining every mile of the way didn't help.

About dawn we finally found Camp Forrest and located our new barracks. None too soon as we had used up all our spares and one of the tires had developed a big bulge on the inside that was thumping against the frame each time it came around. Just as I parked the car, it gave a final cough, belched and died. We were both blue with cold and with shattering teeth we staggered into the welcome warmth of the barracks only to hear reveille sound and the barracks Sgt yell, "Roll em out! Hit the deck!" WHAT A WELCOME TO TENNESSEE.

NOTE:

War events from July 1942 to April 1943. During the summer of 42 German armies continued to overrun vast areas of Russia and we wondered if she would collapse. Leningrad and Moscow continued to hold out and with the advent of winter the tide changed with the Russian winter offensive. An entire German army was surrounded and destroyed at Stalingrad. In the Pacific Guadalcanal in the Solomans was captured by our forces after seven months of desperate fighting including a dozen costly naval engagements. After the battle of Santa Cruz, the badly damaged Enterprise was the only carrier we had left in the Pacific. The Jap advance toward Australia finally bogged down in the jungles of New Guinea. The powerful raid across the English Channel by Canadian troops was repulsed with appalling losses and certainly set back any thought of a second front for a while.

Submarines continued to take a heavy toll from the convoys. Wolf packs of twenty to forty submarines fell on the hapless ships with impunity. Our losses exceeded our production. In Africa the fortunes of war changed again as Rommel, the desert Fox with victory in his grasp, was dealt total defeat in the battle of El Alemein that raged for ten days. He began his long retreat through Libya and to Tunisia. In November the surprise amphibious assault on French North Africa met with success from Dakar to Algiers. This was mainly an American show. The advance of these forces east into Tunisia was slowed by winter weather and supply difficulties. In February 1943 these green troops were dealt a series of defeats. However after quickly regaining their balance these troops were pressing the western defenses of Tunisia while the British 8th Army stood poised at the southern gate. The final campaign to drive the Germans and Italians out of Africa was about to begin.

M-10 TANK DESTROYER

STAFF CAR & TEXAS GUMBO

COL. KING

LT. CAVANAUGH

GEN. GORDOR

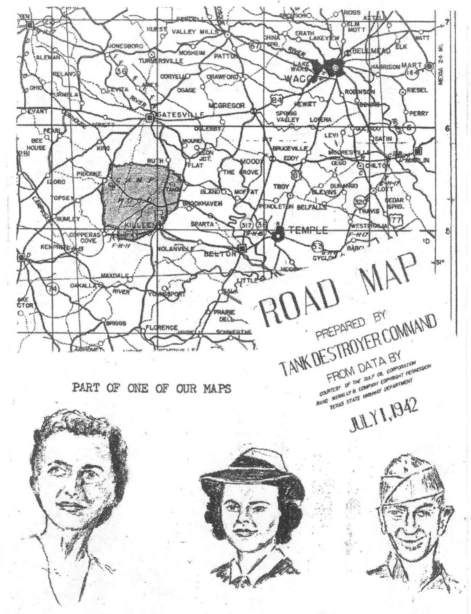

PART OF ONE OF OUR MAPS

ROAD MAP

PREPARED BY
TANK DESTROYER COMMAND

FROM DATA BY
COURTESY OF THE GULF OIL CORPORATION
RAND McNALLY & COMPANY COPYRIGHT PERMISSION
TEXAS STATE HIGHWAY DEPARTMENT

JULY 1, 1942

FACES

LOOKING OUT OVER COWHOUSE CREEK

OBSERVER DIRECTING ARTILLERY FIRE

M-3 TANK DESTROYER

LOOKING NORTH ACROSS RESERVATION

TENNESSEE

MANEUVERS

Tennessee was beautiful in the spring. Dogwood and redbud cast their blush over the landscape. The biggest impact was the green crowding in all about, certainly a welcome change from the wide open brown spaces of Texas. During the month or so that we spent at Camp Forrest there was ample time to get acquainted with the towns around it. Shelbyville, Tullahoma, Winchester. I didn't regret the time I spent in Texas, but it was good to be back among the forested hills. In many ways Tennessee reminded me of western Pennsylvania.

We began to wonder if we ever were going to be shipped overseas and hoped Tennessee was the final stop before a Port of Embarkation. This was to be a series of maneuvers pitting infantry and tank destroyers against armored forces. Camp Campbell and Fort Knox was the staging area for the armored forces while Camps Forrest and Breckenridge were our staging area. The maneuver area itself was in middle Tennessee, and about fifty miles square from Lebanon east to Cookeville and from Carthage on the Cumberland south to McMinnville.

Our brigade would have at least a half dozen TD battalions under its command. Most of these were equipped with the M-3 half track and 75mm gun but some would be equipped with the 3-inch towed gun or the M-10 tank like gun carriage. The next weeks were busy as we established liaison and command with the units assigned us as well as getting acquainted with maps and air photos of the maneuver area. There was a lot of preparation work to be done. Establishing ordnance support, logistics such as rations, fuel and ammunition dumps, air support, prisoner of war enclosures, medical facilities, etc. a mound of paper work. The assembly areas had to be selected and assigned and convoy movements planned and coordinated. Our six or seven battalions with supporting units amounted to a lot of vehicles and we were only a small part of the units moving into the area.

So we spent the summer on these war games on the Cumberland Plateau and its rugged western slopes. It might be called plateau, but most of it seemed to be just plain mountains with gorges and limestone cliffs. In 1943, backwoods in Tennessee looked pretty primitive. It was a dry summer and by July the pretty streams that usually flowed over the shelf rock dried up leaving only green scum covered pools here and there. The engineers pumped our water out of these into portable canvas tanks. Of course this water had to be heavily laced with chlorine to make it drinkable. Well, I should say safe to drink because in our opinion it was never fit to drink. Sometimes it was so thick with chemicals that some claimed it was easier to eat with a spoon than drink. In spite of odor and taste, the lister bag hanging from its tripod drew us like flies, to slake our thirst and wash the dust out of our throats. Occasionally we'd find a mountain spring or farm well where we could fill our canteens with sweet water. It was worth walking quite a distance for a good drink of water.

Between the tanks of the Red army and the treads of our tank destroyers the dirt roads were reduced to a talcum like dust. Convoys moved in dust clouds that could be seen miles away. The trees on each side of the roads were covered with thick layers of dust that showered down on anyone brushing them. of course we were usually covered in dust too, that our sweat turned into streaks of mud. It wasn't a very comfortable time since the drought didn't permit a lot of water to wash with. Everything was covered with clinging dust; the vehicles, our equipment, even our food tasted gritty.

During the summer we learned by our mistakes (and successes) how to manage and use our tank destroyers for best effect. The towed battalions were usually emplaced as far forward as possible to cover roads and terrain favorable for a tank assault. Since these guns were not very mobile, they depended on surprise to successfully hold a position. If tanks broke the line it was difficult to extricate the guns. Therefore great care and secrecy was used in emplacing them as their forward position made them vulnerable to detection and destruction. Usually they were moved up at night or under the cover of morning fog to previously prepared and camouflaged positions. Daylight movement to and from these positions were restricted to deny the enemy any clue as to the guns location.

The self propelled battalions were rushed to the scene of an enemy attack to contain it. With their mobility they could fight and fall back until the momentum of an enemy breakthrough was absorbed and finally stopped. In a running fight like that, the tank destroyers in the forefront engaged the enemy tanks they withdrew to new positions under the covering fire of those behind them. Another tactic was to advance to a previously selected position in the path of an enemy attach and set up an ambush. In any case, mobility was the key to survival because if one remained too long in any one position it was destroyed by tank or artillery fire.

As a headquarters, intelligence and communication was the main thing. Anticipating the enemy's actions and placing our units in best position to counter them, learning to work effectively with our air and artillery liaison people. Regardless of how realistic they try to make maneuvers, there is no substitute for actual combat. That is the final classroom.

By August, little localized thunderstorms materialized out of the blue to bring some relief from the heat. When the raindrops first hit, they raised little puffs of dust from the dry ground which soon ran with liquid streams of mud. In Pennsylvania when it rained, it rained everywhere. Here the storms seemed selective. We often would be sitting in the sun and dust with a blue sky all around us while a mile across the valley a lone black cloud was lacing the terrain with lightning and sheets of rain. After the cloud passed the ground steamed as the mud dried into hardpan only to be churned back into dust. We learned these quick violent storms were typical of the plateau. It sounds as if we were never satisfied but the choice between dust or mud gave us something to gripe about. Actually, when we were away from the heavily traveled roads we enjoyed the sheer beauty and remoteness of the mountain land and its leaf carpeted ground.

I usually rode in one of our armored scout cars which are open topped. Many of the narrow roads and trails we traveled were overhung with vegetation that we plowed thru. We painfully learned to watch ahead and duck our heads to keep from being whacked by tree limbs. One was particularly alert to avoid a particularly mean looking thorn tree with sturdy three pointed thorns shaped like a cross. I've never seen these trees anyplace else. To get entangled in one of those while on a moving vehicle would be most painful.

We did a lot of digging that summer. To make maneuvers realistic, whenever we stopped for any length of time, foxholes, slit trenches and defensive positions had to be dug in usually stony ground. To make things worse we had to fill them when we moved on. Double work and something we wouldn't do in combat.

As in Carolina, a particular maneuver would last maybe a week to a week and a half. In between we might have up to a week to rest, clean up and get ready for the next one. Critiques were held to show us why we had won or lost that particular exercise while plans and orders were received and prepared for the maneuver coming up. During these periods we set up a camp in the maneuver area rather than return to Camp Forrest. Given a couple of days in any one spot, soldiers would fix things as comfortable as possible. Some fellow were quite innovative in the living quarters they could rig up from shelter halfs, jerry cans, tree limbs and whatever else was at hand. These breaks also gave us a chance to visit nearby towns like Murfreesboro, Lebanon, Cookeville and many others. There were two day passes to Nashville for the lucky applicants. It was usually a forty to fifty mile trip so a company truck was used to haul the twenty or so men from each company that got to go.

I managed to make a couple of those safaris during the course of the summer. Nashville was a nice town, but crowded with G.I.s and the main thing we looked for were the taverns of course. I did take time to visit some of the sights it had to offer; the State Capital standing on a hill and the replica of the Parthenon in Centennial Park. I was surprised when I looked down on the Cumberland River from a high bridge and saw a group of destroyers moored to each other. I thought, "what in the world are they hiding up here for; fifteen hundred miles from the ocean." Later I learned they were corvettes that were built in Nashville and would be floated down the Cumberland, Ohio and Mississippi to the Gulf of Mexico. Our war production was amazing.

During the course of hauling G.I.s into Nashville during rest breaks, a truck swerved off an overpass and landed upside down on the railroad tracks below. We were told about eighteen soldiers died but of course the way rumors spread in the army its hard to separate truth from fact.

Having opened the subject of accidents I may as well mention several I was aware of. I'm sure a lot more occurred that we never heard of. One night several M-10 gun carriages from one of our battalions floundered over a steep embankment. At least one of the vehicles turned over, shearing its turret off and killing several of the crew and injuring the rest. I nearly had an accident with our scout car one day. The scout car is a wheeled vehicle with a quarter inch armor plate body which makes it pretty heavy. I hit a curve on Hwy 70 too fast and before I realized it the centrifugal force of the heavy vehicle had it bouncing toward a drop-off on the outside of the curve. I finally brought it under control when the wheels dug into the dirt of the berm. I was lucky as these heavy military vehicles aren't too forgiving when one makes a mistake. A lot of fellows learned the hard way that the jeep with its short wheelbase was prone to spin at the slightest excuse. Of course this same characteristic to spin around in its tracks was handy in combat. Seeing a bad situation ahead, the driver could spin around be well on his way to safety before the enemy reacted.

We were encamped on top of a mountain near Cookeville. I was in the command post truck and the major was on the phone when a bolt of lighting hit so close that it made a sharp crack right in the truck. It nearly knocked the major out as he had the phone to his ear. A moment later we heard calls for help outside. Running alongside an old barbed wire fence in the rain, we cam to several men standing by a pup tent. On the other side of the fence a smoking body lay on a pile of rocks. Inside the tent somebody was starting to moan. The man on the rock pile was dead. A witness said the lighting bold hurled him over the fence onto the rocks. Turning our attention to the tent we noted it was a mountain variety, fully enclosed with a long zipper. The zipper was welded solid so we slit the side of the tent and a bluish cloud of smoke with the smell of ozone came out and hung in the damp air. By that time medics arrived with a stretcher and the victim was soon on his way to a hospital. Last that we knew, he survived. Years later I read in Ripley's Believe It or Not, this incident about the lightning bolt that welded the zipper shut on a tent during maneuvers in Tennessee. I know one thing, and that is to stay away from mountain tops during thunderstorms.

One of our more interesting maneuvers was crossing the Cumberland using assault boats and constructing a pontoon bridge. Several drowned when an assault boat capsized in the turbulent water. Even a soldier that can swim has to divest himself quickly of his equipment to avoid being dragged under. Its pretty hard to stay afloat with the weight of combat pack, ammunition belt, bayonet, gas mask and heavy boots; not to mention rifle and helmet. Enough about accidents.

I suppose among the events of that summer I should mention the night the Sgt fell into the garbage pit. However this was not an accident. Cecil was among a group that had gone to Nashville on a weekend pass. Our base camp was on a wooded hillside and probably several hundred yards from the road. At night our vehicles parked down by the road to avoid accidentally running over someone in the sleeping area. A rope had been strung down to the parking area to serve as a guide. By following the rope one knew it would lead safely thru the dark to the vicinity of the mess tent.

It was known the group returning from Nashville would arrive late at night and follow the rope up from the parking lot. Some pranksters decided it would be good sport to relocate the rope a few feet so that it passed over the center of the garbage pit. Now the garbage pit was about five feet square and about the same depth. We had used this camp a number of times during the summer so there were several layers of ripe garbage fermenting in it.

About midnight we were awakened by the most dreadful curses and howling. Rushing over to the pit, our flashlights revealed Cecil trying to climb up the crumbling dirt walls. I was sorry he was the one who fell in but sure glad it wasn't me. What a mess! We poured several buckets of water on him and scraped off what we could with sticks. None of which I think he appreciated. The culprits wisely kept silent because he was hopping up and down and livid with fury. It sure is frustrating not to know who to vent your anger on, so I think he held all of us who had been in camp to blame. It doesn't pay to get the Sgt mad at you.

My father was an ardent, active Roosevelt supporter and I felt he would be hurt if I failed to visit nearby Carthage, Tenn., the hometown of dignified, white haired Corell Hull, Roosevelt's Secretary of State. So on one of our breaks I made a special effort to get up there. Carthage was located on the north bank of the Cumberland river and was a quiet county seat town. The courthouse on its square was the dominate feature. Occupying its benches or standing in small groups was the typical crowd one usually finds around a rural courthouse, many in bib overalls and chewing tobacco as they solved local and national problems, seemingly without another thing in the world to do. It certainly was not the town a G.I. looking for action would pick, but I felt it would please my dad when I wrote him of my pilgrimage. I wondered how anyone from such a small, quiet out-of- the-way place could rise to Secretary of State and yet one of our most fiery and controversial presidents came from this same area (Andrew Jackson).

Maneuvers finished up late in August and Brigade returned to Camp Forrest. I managed to get a two weeks furlough and took the L & N up thru Tennessee and Kentucky to Cincinnati. It seemed there was a tunnel every few miles on that run. As I recall, I had to change trains at Cincinnati and again at Lima, Ohio. It was quite a walk between the B & O and Erie Railroad stations at Lima. Someone asked my why I didn't drive the model A home at that time and save it. I guess if I could have gotten tires and gas ration coupons I would have considered it. On the other hand by the time it had sat there all summer while we were on maneuvers, all four tiers were flat, it had sunk in the mud and really didn't look like it would ever move again. After returning from furlough, I proceeded to lose the car in a crap game. We had traveled a lot of miles together and it had given me my fifty dollars worth so no tears were shed. At this particular day and time it was just another old car, useless because of war shortages and rationing.

It had been an interesting summer as we rambled over the Cumberland Plateau and we had seen Tennessee from some of its best to its worse. Beautiful farms spread out on the lush flatlands while back in the remoteness of mountain coves many lived a primitive marginal existence. Weather-beaten unpainted shacks surrounded by a random collection of decrepit outbuildings. Even old log houses and barns little changed from the days of Davie Crockett. Yet many were picturesque in their setting of hillside, corn patch and crowding dark primordial forest. Most of the mountain people were clannish and reluctant to talk. The kids, though bashful, were curious with this influx of strange men and vehicles that invaded their land, probably the most exciting thing to happen in their secluded existence. Some of the old country stores hadn't changed much since the turn of the century, even the clothing especially that of the women seemed forty years behind the times. Moonshine was more readily available than an ice cold coca cola. These were good, independent people for whom life even in the best of times was rough. They and their kinfolk had occupied these same mountain plots for generations and they were as much a part of the land as the trees. We were richer for the experience.

We had expected to be shipped overseas following Tennessee maneuvers. Instead we were shocked to receive a communication in September stating that Brigade HQ may be disbanded. Military thinking had now shifted to assault instead of defensive containment of panzer forces. Experiences in North Africa indicated the mass use of tank destroyers was not feasible and therefore our brigade organization was superfluous. The tank destroyer was a defensive weapon rather than assault. The existing battalions would probably be assigned to Infantry and armored divisions as needed. Even there the battalion would be broken up with individual companies assigned to two regiments within the division to bolster its anti-tank defenses. Some of the TD battalions were re-equipped with alligator amphibious vehicles for use in island assaults in the Pacific Theater.

Now I regretted my decision to stick with the brigade rather than take the college or officer candidate school opportunities offered me at Camp Hood. Too late to cry over spilled milk. General Gordor, Lt. Col. King, Lt. Col. Ayers and I were detached for temporary assignment at 2nd Army headquarters in Memphis. We would set up a TD Section to oversee the final training (combat certification) of TD battalions remaining in 2nd Army. It was sort of a dead-end assignment as no new units were to be formed. 2nd Brigade HQ under Col. Mattox would move to Camp Breckenridge, KY and eventually be disbanded, its personnel distributed among the various TD units. It was tough to see our team broken up. After a full summer of maneuvers we probably were at the height of our proficiency. In any event it was another round of farewells as our company was split up. At least I had a pretty nice assignment for the present as 2nd Army HQ was right in the heart of Memphis.

I should have woven the following data into my story much earlier. Having failed to do that, I will treat it as a separate appendage of general information regarding tank destroyers (TD).

In the chain of command, Brigade HQ was in tactical control over several Group HQ. In turn, each group contained a varying number of TD battalions as for example, an infantry regiment contains four battalions. Camp Hood, the hatchery for TDs had been very prolific. We already know that a number of battalions had been sent into the North African campaign. We can assume a number of others were already deployed in England or at Ports of Embarkation. In addition to those there were seven TD Group HQ and twenty eight TD battalions still on this side in 2nd Army. During the past maneuvers most of these units came under 2nd Brigade command at one time or another.

There were two types of TD battalions. The SP (self propelled) units equipped with (36) M-3 half track mounted 57mm or 75mm gun, or with (36) M-10 gun carriage with a 3-inch M-7 gun. Later, a T-70 gun carriage with a 76mm gun became popular for its mobility. Each battalion had (6) M-8 armored cars which carried a turret mounted 37mm gun. The SP type battalion had 671 officers and enlisted men organized in four companies.

The Towed TD Battalion was equipped with (36) M-5 3-in gun. This weapon looked like a conventional field piece with two wheels, split trail and was towed by a half track. In use it was detached from the vehicle and emplaced in a fixed position. Obviously it lacked the mobility of an M-10 but was easier to conceal. The only difference between the M-10 mounted 3-inch gun (M-7) and the towed gun (M-5) was that the first had a vertical slide (breech) block while the other had a horizontal slide block. Both fired up to a 27 pound projectile at a muzzle velocity of 2800 feet per second. Each towed battalion had four M-8 armored cars. It too was organized in four companies having a total of 797 officers and enlisted men.

I am aware that when I give vehicle designations and descriptions I leave myself open to correction. Weapon systems were constantly modified and these changes were noted by adding letters and numerals to the basic designation. Thus the basic half track was the M-3, but as a carriage for an anti-tank gun it might become a M-3AI. the half track carried everything from a 57mm to a 105 howitzer. I'm afraid I don't remember the different sub-designations so I just refer to the half track anti-tank vehicle as an M-3 which with its 57mm or 75mm gun looked pretty good when the Germans were still using the PZKpfw Mark III and Mark IV tanks with two inches of armor plate. When they met the PZKpfw Tiger tank with four inches of armor and an 88mm gun, the M-3 was totally inadequate. The M-10 gun carriage proved to be a practical weapon but it too went thru a series of improvements and adaptations. Thus there was the M-10A1, M-10GMC, M-15, some equipped with a 3-inch gun while others had a 90mm or 105mm gun. It was a moderately heavy armored vehicle and weighed up to 32 tons. The T-70 with its 76mm gun was an excellent weapon but it sacrificed armor for high mobility. It had a road speed of 55mph compared to about 30mph for most tanks. Its welded hull was only one inch thick. As anti-tank weapons and projectiles improved, so too did the tanks. Our 3-inch AP shell penetrated about four inches of armor at 1000 yards, but the King Tiger German tank had seven inches of frontal armor. On the other hand the German 88 could penetrate nine inches of armor which was rough on our Shermans which only had three inch thick armor. So it was a constant race; when a more powerful gun was built, a stronger tank followed.

37 MM GUN & CREW

REPLACING A TANK TREAD

CHANGING OUT A TANK ENGINE

BUILDING A PONTOON BRIDGE ACROSS THE CUMBERLAND
UMPIRES RULE THE BRIDGE TO CARTHAGE DESTROYEN

DITCH AROUND THOSE TENTS

FIELD KITCHEN

A HAZARD IN THE DARK

SCOUT CAR

A BLESSING * HOT CHOW INSTEAD OF K RATIONS

SIX DAY FURLOUGH
Two days going & Two days coming back

THE TRAIN WAS ALWAYS LATE AND NEVER ENOUGH SEATS

TANK WITH SIDE ARMOR ADDED

TANK DESTROYER TURRET

M-10 TANK DESTROYER

SERVING 3" GUN ON M-10 TD

40mm ANTI-AIRCRAFT GUN

GEN. LEE TANK – WELDED HULL

MEMPHIS

2nd ARMY HQ

MEMPHIS

Arrived in Memphis on a nice September day. 2nd Army headquarters was on the spacious fairgrounds in the heart of town and the main buildings were brick with red tile roofs. The main business area was maybe a mile west overlooking the Mississippi and wooded Overton Park within walking distance to the north. The street car line came right by the fairgrounds which was convenient. Of course, I felt pretty lost in the unfamiliarity of a big headquarters for the first week or so. Plenty of brass around. Fortunately M/Sgt Tomberlain helped us get established and acquainted with proper official procedures. Our section was responsible to oversee the twenty plus TD battalions and six or seven TD Group HQs still under 2nd Army jurisdiction. Many of these units had served under our 2nd Brigade during the summers maneuvers. We were to provide administrative control and oversee final training to bring these units up to combat readiness. As soon as they passed inspection and were judged qualified, they would ship out to some overseas theater.

General Gordor, Col King and Col Ayers were often out on inspection trips of our scattered units. My work consisted mostly of struggling with the paper work; inspection reports, performance ratings, movement orders, personnel transfers, filing, etc. Not very glamorous but the fringe benefits were great. Free to go into town most evenings unless on barracks duty (charge of quarters) Memphis was a big town and there was plenty to do. I soon had a circle of new friends. Tomberlain and Ayraud from the artillery section, Kiesling and Miller from the signal section, all M/Sgts. I was in high class company. Then there was Provost Sgt McAulif (MPs), always a good friend to have around in case of trouble. Of course they knew their way around town and where to go for an interesting evening. There were a lot of sailors in Memphis from the big naval station at Millingen. Sailors, soldiers and liquor don't mix well and on weekends when the dives were crowded, brawls frequently erupted. My buddies and I were usually in agreement that it was better to retreat and live to drink another day, than fight and end up with a bandaged head in local stockade. Several times we managed to get out of a place just before the MPs or the Shore Patrol arrived and waded in, swinging Billy clubs indiscriminately.

The Peabody Hotel was pretty much officers territory but I found the big U.S.O. club downtown and its advantages. They had a dance every Saturday night and it was a good place to meet girls. I dated several girls I met there unlike the bars; the U.S.O. was a pretty safe place to go. Only soft drinks served there. If anyone started making trouble, the MPs soon hustled them off to the stockade where they could sober up and cool off. The U.S.O. was also a sanctuary where one could kill a quiet Sunday afternoon.

I enjoyed the streetcars of Memphis though they swayed and bounced like a bucking bronco at times as they rushed between stops. If you had a seat, that wasn't so bad, but usually the car was crowded and standing room only. Hanging onto a leather strap sometimes required a little balancing act. Some nights on the way back to the barracks, I would have given anything to have been able to sit, but even if there were any seats in the back of the car, that was taboo. This was the south and the back of the cars were for blacks only. Being a northern boy, this Jim Crow law bothered my conscience at times. Especially when the situation was reversed with unoccupied seats in the white only part of the car while black women and children stood uncomfortably in the crowded rear part.

One Sunday afternoon I was standing downtown wondering what I could do when a slick chick walked by and my heart did a flip. I caught up with her but she ignored my advances. Normally I would have dropped it at that, but this one I really wanted to meet so I persisted in my efforts. When she walked into a drugstore, I followed her in and then back out. Finally as we were crossing a small park my tenacity paid off and she stopped and allowed me to

61

plea my case. We went over to the nearby Peabody Hotel bar where we had a drink and talked a while. When she had to leave for work, I had the promise of a date and I floated on air the rest of the evening.

In the months that followed, the time I spent with Lois was the only ones that counted. We enjoyed each others company and found plenty to do. Dances, bar hopping, hiking in Overton Park, or visiting the zoo. It really didn't matter as long as we were together. Our favorite meeting place was a bar called The Stables, for its décor and privacy. It was great to be in love. We went over to Forrest City, Arkansas (about 40 miles west of Memphis) several times and visited her family. It was a typical small Arkansas town in the cotton and rice belt. Really two towns; the white part and the black part. Even the businesses kept to their own side of the street, so to speak. I imagine the police kept law and order with an iron hand (and a club). Yet everyone was on a first name basis and life seemed to move in a relaxed, serene way. Always enjoyed the bus ride across the thirty miles or so of flat Mississippi flood plain between Memphis and F.C. The flat rich fields stretching our endlessly on each side. Occasionally we passed rows of one room sharecroppers shacks built on stilts alongside the road. Hot in the summer, wet in the rainy season and cold in the winter. They looked old enough to have been slave cabins. The absentee landlords of the rich land probably lived somewhere else.

Meanwhile, as more and more units were shipped overseas, the role of 2nd Army diminished. Late in February it was rumored drastic changes were to take place and the headquarters would be reduced to a skeleton force. Out of its personnel a cadre would form the 8th Army HQ for service in the Pacific and the eventual invasion of the Philippines and Japan. Other personnel would be distributed to outfits scheduled to be shipped overseas. My days in Memphis were numbered. On March 5, 1944 Lois Miller and I were married in the Methodist church at Forrest City.

Shortly thereafter I learned I would not be part of the 8th Army cadre as there would be no Tank Destroyer Section in its organization. Nor was there any place for me with my rank in the remaining TD units. Again I was a black sheep. I was told to pick any division sized organization in 2nd Army jurisdiction and I would be transferred to it. I picked the 104th (Timberwolf) Division at Camp Carson, Colorado. It would be nice to see Colorado and just maybe Lois could join me there for a while. Its commanding general was the well known "Bloody" Terry Allen, former CG of Big Red One in North Africa. The 104th was rated tops and would soon be moving overseas. I certainly hoped I get overseas before the war was over. It would have been nice to go with 8th Army HQ and fellows I knew, but such was not to be the case. We had a going away shindig at an open air beer garden near the fairgrounds. The next day I kissed my bride goodbye and headed west.

PROGRESS OF WAR – APRIL 1943 THRU MARCH 1944

American war production and our rapidly expanded armed forces start taking effect. The remaining axis troops in Africa surrender in May. In July the American 5th Army and British 8th Army invade and take Sicily. Italy was next with landings at Taranto and Salerno. Political chaos erupted and Italy tried to surrender, but German troops free Mussolini and set him up as a puppet backed by German bayonets. The advance up the mountainous spine of the peninsula proves slow and costly, finally bogging down at the Gustov line south of Rome. Monte Cassino becomes a symbol as the struggle for it drags thru February and March. Meanwhile a new beach head at Anzio is threatened by heavy German counterattacks.

In Russia the big German offensive at Kursh, involving over six thousand tanks becomes instead a big Russian victory. Russian armies advance generally on all fronts during this period, the winter was particularly rough on the Nazi war machine.

On the sea, new defensive weapons like radar, escort carriers and blimps bring submarine warfare under control. Wolf packs of 40 to 50 submarines attacking convoys becomes a thing of the past. Sinkings continue, but the hunters (subs) have now become the hunted and they pay a price for each success.

Allied bomber fleets increase the scope and weight of their attacks and now, thousand plane raids are not uncommon. Heavy losses at times become critical concern, but German fighter losses were heavy too. Fire storms in Hamburg were estimated to have killed over fifty thousand.

In the pacific, new aircraft carriers are taking their place with the fleet and no longer are we on the defensive. The Gilbert Island were the first to be wrested from the Japanese. However the losses inflicted on our marines at Tarawa was appalling. The myth that air attack and naval bombardment alone could take an island was put to rest. Many of us wondered if the nation was willing to pay that price to take the thousands of little specks of coral and sand that dotted the Pacific. Our assault forces forged on into the vast expanses of that ocean world, taking key strongholds in the Marshall Islands (Kwajalein) and the Admiralty Islands, bypassing other Japanese strongholds which hopefully would wither on the vine. In the South Pacific the enemy was gradually being pushed back on New Guinea and the Solomons. Even the Japanese threat to India was stalled in Burma. While the pendulum was swinging in our favor, we saw many years of warfare ahead before both Germany and Japan could be brought to their knees.

SOLDIERS & SAILORS CROWDED THE BARS

A QUIET SUNDAY AFTERNOON AT THE U.S.O.

UNIT	CO	STATION	R. C. D.
602nd Bn	Lt.Col Kopcsak	Cp Forrest, Tenn	(15 Mar 44 AF RO 19th AM) ~~lost~~
808th Bn	Lt Col Mc Donald	Cp McCoy, Wis	
772nd Bn	Maj McClellan	Ft L. Wood, Mo	
2nd Brig	Col Mattox	Cp Breckinridge	
820th Bn	Maj Eldridge	Cp Breckinridge	
821st Bn	Lt.Col Arbury	Cp Breckinridge	lost mar 44
822nd Bn	Lt Col Mains	Cp Breckinridge	
8th Gp	Col Larter	Cp Rucker, Ala	lost
653 Bn(SP)	Lt Col Krueger	Ft Benning, Ga	

UNIT	CO	STATION	R. C. D.
8th Gp	Col Larter	Cp Rucker, Ala.	1 mar 44 fm
609th Bn	Lt.Col Browne	Cp Shelby, Miss	} atchd 21st Gp
690th Bn	Lt.Col Burcham	Cp Rucker, Ala	
631st Bn	Lt.Col Nathan	Cp Shelby, Miss	
653rd Bn	Lt.Col Krueger	Ft Benning, Ga	
806th Bn	Lt.Col Greer	Cp Rucker, Ala	} atchd 21st Gp
?			
9th Gp	Col McVicker	Cp Atterbury, Ind	✓ 15 mar 44 AF
610th Bn	Lt.Col Herold	Cp Atterbury, Ind	✓ 15 mar 44 AF
13th Gp	Lt.Col Darling	Cp Gordon, Ga	/ Col MATTOX
774th Bn	Lt.Col Sturges	Cp Gordon, Ga	15 mar 44 AF
812th Bn	Lt.Col Etherton	Cp Gordon, Ga.	will face in Feb.
816		Ft Jackson	(16 Gp in TMA)

UNIT	CO	STATION	R. C. D.
14th Gp	Col Hedden	Cp Campbell, Ky	→ 1 May AL XVI Corps
692nd Bn	Lt Col Shelton	Cp Campbell, Ky	
808th Bn	Lt.Col McDonald	Cp McCoy, Wis	← Asgd
817th Bn	Maj Bardes	Cp Campbell, Ky	
825th Bn	Lt Col Mieding	Cp Campbell, Ky	
16th Gp	Col Wheaton	Ft Jackson, S.C.	
605th Bn	Lt.Col Buchwald	Ft Jackson, S.C.	
647th Bn	Lt.Col Mayo	Ft Jackson, S.C.	
648th Bn	Lt.Col Farr	Ft Jackson, S.C.	
19th Gp	Col Tucker	Cp Gruber, Okla	LMA
643rd Bn	Lt.Col Stevens	Cp Gruber, Okla	15 mar AL
811th Bn	Lt.Col Brownfield	Cp Gruber, Okla	lost to LMA
638th Bn		Cp Gruber Okla	
21st Gp		Cp Shelby, Miss	
670th Bn		Cp Shelby, Miss	
609 ✓		" "	
631 ✓		" "	

NOTE: I was to meet again with the
811 & 820 TD battalions during the
desperate fighting in the Ardennes.

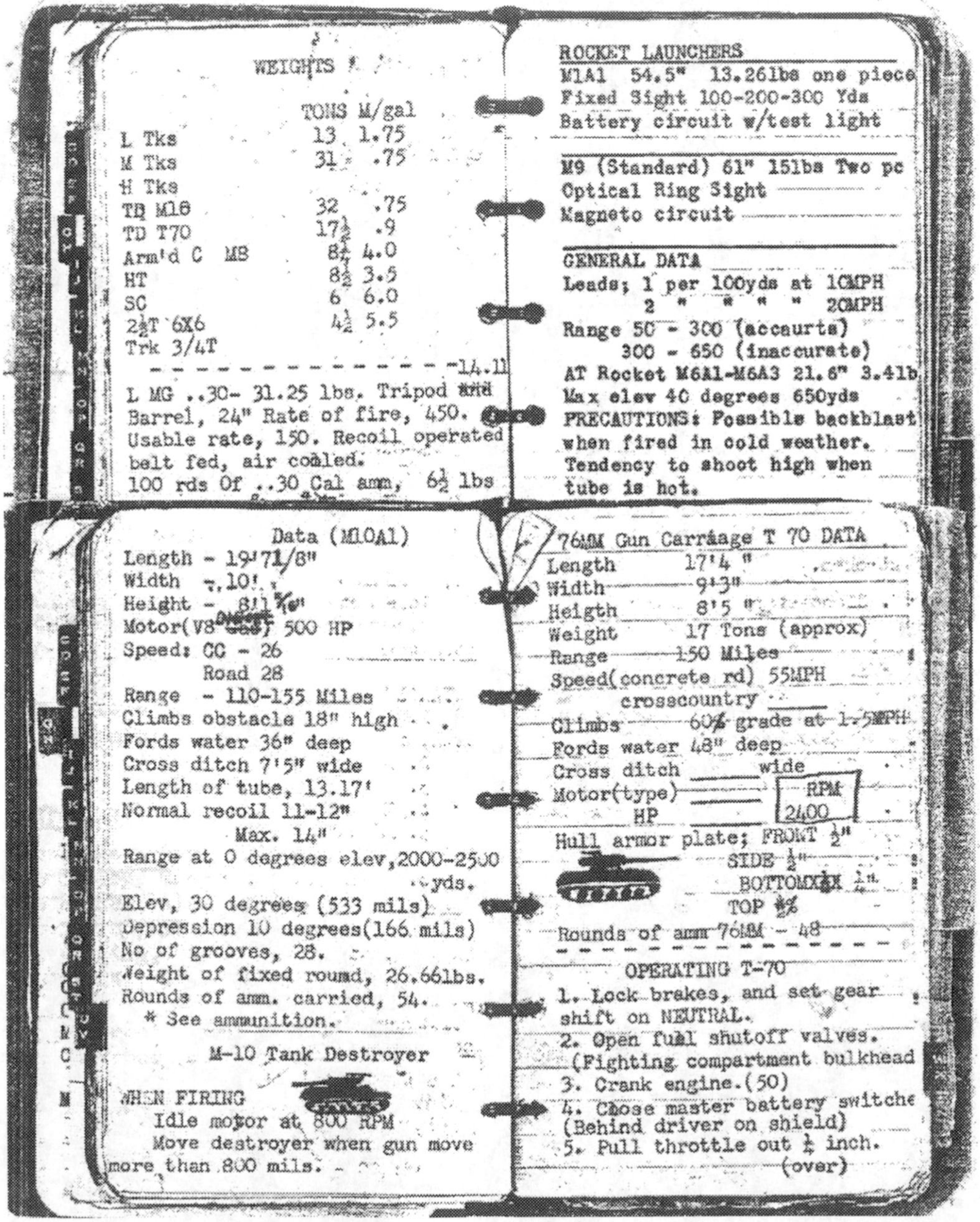

WEIGHTS

	TONS	M/gal
L Tks	13	1.75
M Tks	31	.75
H Tks		
TD M18	32	.75
TD T70	17½	.9
Arm'd C MB	8¼	4.0
HT	8½	3.5
SC	6	6.0
2½T 6X6	4½	5.5
Trk 3/4T		

- - - - - - - - - - - - - - - - - -14.11

L MG ..30- 31.25 lbs. Tripod and
Barrel, 24" Rate of fire, 450.
Usable rate, 150. Recoil operated
belt fed, air cooled.
100 rds Of ..30 Cal amm, 6½ lbs

Data (M10A1)

Length - 19'71/8"
Width - 10'
Height - 8'1 ⅝"
Motor(V8 Gas) 500 HP
Speed: CC - 26
        Road 28
Range - 110-155 Miles
Climbs obstacle 18" high
Fords water 36" deep
Cross ditch 7'5" wide
Length of tube, 13.17'
Normal recoil 11-12"
        Max. 14"
Range at 0 degrees elev,2000-2500
                     yds.
Elev, 30 degrees (533 mils)
Depression 10 degrees(166 mils)
No of grooves, 28.
Weight of fixed round, 26.66lbs.
Rounds of amm. carried, 54.
    * See ammunition.

M-10 Tank Destroyer

WHEN FIRING
    Idle motor at 800 RPM
    Move destroyer when gun move
more than 800 mils.

ROCKET LAUNCHERS

M1A1 54.5" 13.26lbs one piece
Fixed Sight 100-200-300 Yds
Battery circuit w/test light

M9 (Standard) 61" 15lbs Two pc
Optical Ring Sight
Magneto circuit

GENERAL DATA

Leads; 1 per 100yds at 10MPH
       2 " " "   20MPH
Range 50 - 300 (accaurte)
      300 - 650 (inaccurate)
AT Rocket M6A1-M6A3 21.6" 3.41b
Max elev 40 degrees 650yds
PRECAUTIONS: Possible backblast
when fired in cold weather.
Tendency to shoot high when
tube is hot.

76MM Gun Carriage T 70 DATA

Length	17'4 "
Width	9'3"
Height	8'5"
Weight	17 Tons (approx)
Range	150 Miles
Speed(concrete rd)	55MPH
crosscountry	
Climbs	60% grade at 1.5MPH
Fords water	48" deep
Cross ditch	wide
Motor(type)	RPM 2400
HP	

Hull armor plate; FRONT ½"
                  SIDE ½"
                  BOTTOM 1"
                  TOP ⅜"
Rounds of amm 76MM - 48

OPERATING T-70

1. Lock brakes, and set gear
shift on NEUTRAL.
2. Open fuel shutoff valves.
(Fighting compartment bulkhead
3. Crank engine.(50)
4. Chose master battery switche
(Behind driver on shield)
5. Pull throttle out ½ inch.
            (over)

THE GIRL THAT FOLLOWED ME TO COLORADO
AND SHE IS STILL WITH ME

104th Div.

106th Div.

TIMBER WOLF   GOLDEN LION

BACK TO THE INFANTRY

COLORADO

APRIL THRU OCTOBER 1944

CAMP CARSON

I arrived at Colorado Springs, Colorado about the first of April. The snow covered, crisp cold winter day that greeted me as a I emerged from the station was a change from the warm spring weather I had left in Memphis. The first thing I looked for was Pikes Peak, which I easily spotted in the distant haze. Reporting to the local Transportation Officer, I was soon on my way to Cam Carson along with several other new arrivals. At division headquarters, I was not exactly greeted with enthusiasm. If I had been a private or corporal, fine but a M/Sgt created a problem since those positions were already filled. In any event I was assigned to the 414th Inf. Regiment for lack of a better place. Lets just say neither I nor the 414th were happy with the situation but orders are orders, especially when my orders originated from 2nd Army HQs.

The 104th Division (Timberwolf) had completed its training and expected to head for a port of embarkation soon. However, training continued on the barren, snow covered terrain of the reservation and I worked with the S-3 (Operations) section. Typical work such as training schedules, tactical exercises, field orders, etc. After a taste of spring, it was demoralizing going out into snow and slush again. On the other hand I found the cold dry western air easier to take than our moist eastern winters.

There was another division completing its training in the area, the 10th Mountain Division. I can't think of its camp, which was located higher in the mountains. They were trained for mountain combat and used skis and mules. Even their artillery used special light cannon which could be disassembled and carried on mules. Having had some experience with skis, I inquired to see if they might have an opening for a homeless M/Sgt. No luck as they had a full complement. Regardless, I enjoyed the opportunity to visit this unusual outfit. I think they ended up in the Italian campaign. Unhappy with my surplus status with the division, I even considered re-activating my O.C.S. (Officers Candidate School) papers. Even that didn't look good as many of the schools were curtailing their classes. Quartermaster school was the only one that seemed certain and I didn't particularly want to become a quartermaster officer. At any rate, Lois was working on a transfer to the Colorado Springs telephone office so it would have been a bad time for me to move again. Decided I'd have to stick it out and see what happened when the division moved out.

Lois got her transfer, effective the 1st of June, and I took a week's furlough to go back to Arkansas and accompany her back to Colorado. I was lucky and had a ride with a Colonel's wife going east. We shared the expenses and the driving. Lois and I took a bus back thru Kansas. The bus was crowded and went out of its way to stop at every town in Kansas I think. It was a long tiring trip across that monotonous landscape. We were lucky to find a small furnished apartment in Colorado Springs and I was able to secure permission to live off base. Of course I had to report out to camp every morning which wasn't too convenient, but some how I managed. Lois' shift at work wasn't the best either (2 pm till 10 pm) but she managed to trade occasionally. The summer weather was great; the air so dry clear and invigorating, so different from the humidity of Louisiana or Tennessee. Every afternoon at about the same time, a cloud would drift over and give us a brisk shower for fifteen or twenty minutes. Often the sun kept shining right through the shower. Even if one got a little wet, clothing dried quickly in the dry air.

We didn't have much money to spend on transportation so we walked everyplace we went. We hiked around Manitou Springs and beyond thru the Garden of the Gods. This was an extensive area of grotesquely shaped red rock formations. After climbing among these for a day we wondered if we had enough energy left for the long walk home. Another place we liked was Broadmoor, a big hotel at the edge of town with park like grounds including a lake, ice skating rink and rodeo ring.

We even hiked out to the base of Pikes Peak and then decided the cog railroad to the top was too expensive for us. Army pay wasn't what it is today. Strange as it may seem, it didn't bother us to miss going up the main tourist attraction in the area. There were too many other interesting things to do. One day we walked clear out to Seven Falls on the far side of Cheyenne Mountain. Most of the way was uphill. We climbed to the top of the falls where the grave of Helen Jackson lay (Author of Ramona). It was marked by a large cairn of stones carried up from the foot of the falls by visitors. We added our two stones. After climbing along the top of the cliff, enjoying the spectacular view of the gorge far below, we realized we had lingered too long. Darkness would catch us long before we could retrace our steps home.

The shortest route seemed to be right up over the top of Cheyenne Mountain and down the other side to the zoo on its lower slope. From there we could follow the road back to Colorado Springs. Already tired, it was no way to start climbing a 11,000 foot mountain but we were young and never gave it a thought. Well, that was some experience. In the higher elevations breathing was so difficult we could only go a short distance and then rest an equal length of time. In addition there was no stream or water on this rocky vertical surface and thirst became a motivating factor as we thought of that fountain down at the zoo. When we finally topped the mountain and spotted the zoo far below and the city spread out beyond, it was an exhilarating feeling of achievement. However it was another hour of scrambling down over boulders and crevasses before we could slake our thirst and parched throats. Those were good days. Since that time, that mountain has been hollowed out for HQs of our North American Defense System. I doubt anyone climbs over it now except maybe the guards.

When I think of all the hiking we did, I sure have to give Lois credit for her spunk. After all I had been in the infantry for years and conditioned for this yet she kept up and even outdid me at times. Those months in Colorado will always have a special place in our hearts.

Occasionally we were extravagant and splurged. Once, shortly after she came out there, we went to the Copper Grove one of the nicer places in town. General Allen and some of his staff came in and took a table not far from ours. As we returned to our table after a dance, the general noted my Timberwolf shoulder patch and talked with us for a while. In the process he learned we were newly weds. A little later the waiter brought a bottle of wine over to our table and said, "Compliments of the General". We thought that was pretty nice of him.

It was at Camp Carson that I ran the Infantry Combat course and earned the Expert Infantryman badge. It was a pretty rugged set of tests and much more realistic that obstacle courses of earlier times. We had to qualify with the bayonet, the offhand firing as we traversed the course at bob-up targets. Barbed wire entanglements to negotiate, mud to crawl through, walls and nets to climb over and grenades to throw. All this while MGs fired overhead and dynamite charges in the ground simulated shell bursts. Speed was the key.

One incidence sticks in my mind at Camp Carson. We had an Irishman from New York in the outfit. He was a likable fellow and sharp as a tack, but always alert for a job that would excuse him from training. One of these was assignment to clean and do odd jobs at the bachelors' officers' quarters. This suited him fine, but one day he was found flat on his back and kicking in front of the officers' quarters. Rushed to the base hospital, he admitted drinking out of a bottle in one of the officers rooms. His stomach was pumped and he did recover. Investigating, it was found the whiskey bottle contained wood alcohol. I guess an Irishman will drink anything. We figure he had been nipping out of the bottles he found in the officers quarters and he finally picked the wrong one. Of course the officer never admitted he had deliberately set a trap. In any event this ended his happy job at the bachelors' officers' quarters and he faced a "dry" future.

In August the 104th Division was packing for its move overseas and I was ordered to the 106th Division at Camp Atterbury, Indiana. The 106th had been stripped of half its men, who were sent overseas as combat replacements, so it was in need of men. Lois planned to follow me as soon as she could. We were thankful for the summer we had in beautiful Colorado.

ROUGH RIDE

CAMP CARSON RESERVATION

BROADMOOR (OFFICERS COUNTRY)

THE RODEO FIELD

72

GARDEN OF THE GODS

LONELY JUNCTION

MULES USED BY 10th MOUNTAIN DIV.

MY ROOM IN THE BARRACKS

COG RAILROAD TO PIKES PEAK

RIFLE GRENADES

COMBAT OBSTACLE COURSE

CANNON Co's 75mm HOWIZTERS

NEW SHERMAN WITH CAST HULL

<u>106th Division Organization</u>   APPROX. 15,000 MEN

Div. Commander: Maj Gen. Alan Jones
Ass't. Div. Comm. : Brig. Gen. Herbert Perrin
Div. Artillery Comm. : Brig. Gen. Leo McMahon

Special Troops:

106th Division HQ Co.
106th Signal Co.
106th Quartermaster Co.
106th Reconnaisance Co.
806th Ordnance Co.

81st Engineer Battalion   (Lt Col. Riggs)   800 MEN

331st Medical Battalion   (Lt Col. Belzer)

592nd FA Battalion- 155 Howitzers   (Lt Col. Webber) ⎫
                                                        ⎪
589th "   "   105   "   (Lt Col. Kelly)   ⎪
                                                        ⎬ 800 MEN EACH
590th "   "   "   "   .   (Lt Col. Lackey)   ⎪
                                                        ⎪
591st "   "   "   "   (Lt Col Hoover)   ⎭

422nd Infantry Regiment   (Col. Descheneaux) ⎫
                                                ⎪
423rd Infantry Regiment   (Col. Cavender)   ⎬ 3000 MEN EACH
                                                ⎪
424th Infantry Regiment   (Col. Reed)   ⎭

Note: Each regiment consisted of 3 Infantry battalions and
      1 special unit battalion that included Cannon & Anti-Tank Co's.

CAMP ATTERBURY INDIANA

Arriving in Indiana, I reported in at Division HQ at Camp Atterbury. I was first sent to the 422nd Inf regiment but in a few days reassigned as S-3 Sgt in the 424th Inf. A lucky break for me in view of what happened later in combat. My advent into the S-3 position ruffled some feelings as the Tech/Sgt already there had expected to advance to M/Sgt. That is the disadvantage when an outsider arrives and takes a top position. It blocks a whole string of fellows from moving up a rank. Obviously there is going to be disappointments and anger.

The division was alerted to move overseas shortly but it was in a bad way. Seven thousand trained men pulled out of its combat units for overseas replacements since April. Many of the new men sent to the division came from various army special training schools which were being curtailed as expansion of the armed forces slowed down. Naturally many were disgruntled in being reassigned to the infantry. At any rate training was on a crash basis to try to mold the division back into an effective team. Maneuvers would have been the best way to build up a strong Esprit de Corp in the division, unfortunately there was no time for that now.

Atterbury was our closest town and Indianapolis the biggest city in the area. Our bus service to Atterbury was rather unusual. They had taken big moving vans and converted them into two-decker transports by building a second floor inside with stairs. Pretty crude with wood benches, low headroom and no windows, but they could pack a load of G.I.s in them. We called them cattle trucks.

Lois left Colorado Springs the first of September, just as the first snowfall arrived out there. Arriving at Camp Atterbury, she stayed in one of the rooms for dependents at the camp recreation center, until she found a private room in town. Again I was able to get permission to live off base. The landlady was a spiritist and held séances occasionally in the house. An activity that disturbed Lois, but we considered ourselves lucky to find any place to live in the crowded town.

We didn't have much time anyway as the advance parties from the division left for England the first week in October and the rest of us entrained October 14 for the overseas staging area at Camp Miles Standish, Mass. I was glad to be on my way finally. After the breakout of Normandy and Patton's dash across France, I thought the war would be over before I got overseas. Having joined up before Pearl Harbor it would have been embarrassing to have spent all my time in the States. I didn't know it, but the Germans still had some fight left in them and our biggest battle of the war was still to be fought.

So, while I was on the first step of my way to England, Lois returned to Arkansas for the duration.

PROGRESS OF WAR – APRIL 1944 THRU OCTOBER 1944

May sees new landings at Hollandia in the long New Guinea campaign while carriers and battleships continue to raid Japanese island bases. Sevastopol (Crimea) is retaken by the Russians. Monte Cassino finally falls on May 18 after months of assault. After this, the bridehead at Anzio is relieved and Rome falls June 5. the big even was the long awaited cross channel landings. The ferocious fighting to hold and enlarge the bridgeheads around Caen and the hedgerows of Normandy drag on thru June and July.

During this same period, landings are made on Saipan and Guam and the Battle of Philippines Sea is fought. The Russians open their summer offensive with many successes. The first of German V weapons appear as buzz bombs begin to fall on England. With Patton's III Army sweep out of the beachheads, the German positions are untenable. Paris falls and with new landings in the south, the Nazis relinquish most of France and Belgium. The allied armies pause as they outrun their supplies. In mid-September, Montgomery's attempt to reach the Rhine at Arnhem is defeated an in October the Americans meet bitter resistance at Aachen and the Hurtgen Forest. The enemy is dug in and determined to defend the Fatherland. In the Pacific our carrier task forces roam at will while army and marines are locked in small bitter battles to wrest key island strongholds from the Japanese. In Italy, our advance continues slowly against tenacious German resistance.

ENGLAND
OCT 15 – DEC 16 - 1944

ENGLAND HERE WE COME!

(ENGLAND) – OCT 15 TO DEC 15, 1944

After nearly four years of training, maneuvers, serving as cadre for new units, etc. it appeared I was finally on my way overseas. The 106th Division arrived in Camp Myles Standish, Mass (overseas staging area) the second week of October, 1944. A few days later we boarded troop trains for a Port of Embarkation. We assumed this would be Boston, a few miles distant. With all our gear and duffle bags the accommodations were pretty crowded. It wasn't long before a few card games started and space was cleared in the aisle for a crap game too. We had time to kill.

About dark, our train pulled out for what would prove to be an all nights ride much of the time waiting on lonely sidetracks. It was blackout conditions so with the passage of time, talking died down and between catnaps, we sat looking out at the darkness engrossed in our own thoughts. One thought was that they were sure taking us the long way around to Boston. Maybe they just wanted us to think we were going to Europe and we were on our way to the Pacific instead. Sometime in the early morning our speed picked up and the rails clicked with a purposeful regularity, a welcome change to sitting on a sidetrack listening to the pulsing of the air compressors. We were paralleling a large valley and watching the lights below had a strange hallucinating effect. At times it seemed as if we were disembodied and motionless and it was the lights in the valley that were moving swiftly past upstream into the darkness.

Then we entered an large urban area. We passed thru miles of dismal darkened city, the shadows of buildings rushing past and quick glimpses of deserted streets below us. Finally the train slowed and threaded its way thru a maze of tracks, finally coming to a stop by a dimly lighted station platform. Again the usual wait before it was our turn to debark. Eventually we unloaded amid a clatter of equipment and lined up burdened with full field packs, duffle bags, rifles and accouterments (a good 90 to 100 pounds of it). I looked up and there was a sign reading "Hoboken, N.J.". I thought how ironic, my dad shipped out of here in 1917, and across the river was New York, where my dad married my mother in 1920. So, here I was starting my adventure from a place I had heard of often. My reminiscing was cut short as we shouldered our equipment and moved out.

It was just a short march at route step thru the station and down a ramp to crowd onto a ferry boat. I think it was an Erie RR ferry, but not sure. Well, I left Meadville on an Erie RR troop train with Company B nearly four years ago. A rookie then; now with Master Sgt stripes, I'll ride the Erie to the troopship. It was a dismal time of the morning; ahead we could see the black silhouette of the Manhattan skyline. As we approached the far shore, the vague shape of the piers emerged and then we made out the shape of a large ship against the shadowy background. The ferry docked at the end of the pier. We marched up thru the cavernous darkened building and over a gangplank into the dimly lighted interior of the large ship. We wound our way thru the narrow corridors and up steps, stopping frequently as men were assigned quarters. It seemed as if the ship was already full. From the noise and vibration, we felt the ship get underway before we reached the quarters assigned us. We ended up in a long narrow room toward the bow. The outside wall flared sharply outward. It was probably crew quarters in peacetime, meant for 6 or 8. Now there were 20 of us crowded into it. Eventually we learned this was an English ship, the Aquatania, with about 10,000 on board. It was a fast ship (23 knots) and she would cross unescorted.

Apparently we were the last troops to board the ship before it sailed in the darkness before dawn. We were given instructions to remain in our crowded quarters or immediate area for the trip. There would be only two meals a day since she was an English ship (breakfast & supper). Once a day, weather permitting, we would have one hour on deck. Later there would be lifeboat drills and lifebelt instructions, etc. Portholes were blacked out and secured against opening at night.

Soon after sailing we were told to take our mess kits and line up for breakfast, so we joined a long line in the passageway. Crowded, hot and amidst the odor of wool, the line moved at a snails pace thru the endless passageways, up and down ladders (stairs) into the bowels of the ship. Every door we passed revealed jammed quarters and humanity like our own. Soon added to the throbbing of the ship we became aware of a rolling and pitching motion as the ship approached Sandy Hook and the open Atlantic. What seemed like hours later we reached a narrow, confined set of stairs leading down to the galley (kitchen). A hot, steamy grease laden breeze swept up the stairs with a variety of unappetizing odors. With stomachs already getting queasy from motion, this odorous breeze was too much and a number of GIs lost all desire for food. However with the press of those behind, there was no escape but to be pressed into the mess area along with the rest.

We entered a large open space with a serving line across one end and dozens of long high tables arranged abeam the ship and finally a wash line of hot steamy water for utensils at the far end. We were served a dipper of soggy dehydrated eggs, sausage and a cup of lukewarm weak coffee. All looked and smelled greasy including the coffee. One ate standing up at the tables which had a low wooden curb around them. As the ship rolled, mess kits slid, cups spilled and a sloppy gruel flowed back and forth within the table curbs. My stomach heaved and all I wanted was to get out of there. I dumped my food into the garbage and forced myself to stand the ordeal of the steamy wash line. When I finished, my mess gear still felt greasy.

For the next three days I and a lot of others suffered the throes of seasickness; vomiting, dry heaves, nausea. Even water wouldn't stay down, everywhere the sour stench of vomit. Confinement below decks didn't help. The brief time on deck each day was a blessing in spite of the gray cold wind. The occasional salt water showers never left one feeling clean either.

Eventually recovering from the miseries of Mal de Mar, we were starved and the two meals a day just weren't enough. Anyone with a candy bar to sell could get top dollar. The boredom of the days was broken up with housekeeping chores, fire and lifeboat drills and occasional work parties. Even KP was a good deal if one got on it as it offered an opportunity to scrounge a little extra food. The rest of the time was occupied with reading, writing letters or participating in a card game or shooting craps, or maybe wondering about the future. Then too, the crowded conditions aggravated tempers, and fights and arguments would occur to break the routine. One night we were startled by gunfire. We were told the gun crews had fired at some floating debris from a sunken ship.

We, did'nt know what our route was, but rumor had it that we swung down toward the Azores, then northeast toward Ireland. The evening of the sixth day we were enjoying our hour on deck. It was gray and stormy with as trong cold wind whipping spray on us from the big white caps. Someone yelled, "There's a ship" and sure enough, approaching us was a gray warship wallowing with its decks half awash in the heavy seas. Looking down form the high deck of the Aquatania it looked small, but from its gun turrents. I judged it to be at least a light cruiser. It flashed a signal or message with its blinker light as passed us and then forged ahead. On the other side we saw several small vessels in the distance. Probably destroyers or corvettes. I remember my dad telling of the swarm of little sub-chasers that came out from the coast of France to meet their ship in 1917.

We awoke the next morning to a sunny sky and sparkling sea. The first sun we had seen in a week. Someone said we had passed along the southern coast of Ireland during the night and were entering the Irish Sea. I had mentioned we stayed hungry on two meals a day. The ships cooks operated the black market of sorts. Several of us had managed to buy one of the treasured slips of paper that had the time marked to report to the galley. So at the proper time I went down and with 6 or 7 others were allowed in the kitchen. We were soon standing by a couple of portholes, eating our stew and looking across the water at a big four stacker about a mile away. It was moving in the same direction as us but at a slower space. Suddenly the stew stuck in my throat as I spotted a black pole like thing sticking out of the water right between the two ships. We could see it was moving from the spray.

Of course our first thought was Periscope; and if so, then it probably was German because no allied sub would be submerged in these waters. I said a sub has torpedo tubes fore and aft so he can nail us both from where he is. No use running as we are at the water line with at least six decks crowded with troops above us. We waited with baited breath for the shock of an explosion or for the alarm bells to sound. Gradually we pulled ahead of that periscope and the other ship and nothing happened. Baffled, I looked ahead and noted a small tug like vessel that we were overtaking. I said if that wasn't a periscope, I think I know what it was. That is probably a Minesweeper where the end of their cable is. Apparently that was the situation, but it sure gave us a scare. We did finish our stew.

Later that day, the sunshine gave way to gray and mist again. Some time during the night we became aware that the throbbing and motion of the ship stopped and then heard the rumble of the anchor chain being lowered. Next morning we saw we were in a great roadstead (harbor) and all about us in the grayness we could see anchored ships. One of them was a big aircraft carrier. Debarking was by lighters. Small vessels that held 200 to 300 crowded on their decks. It takes a long time to unload 10,000 people that way, so it was late in the day before our turn came. During the waiting, we cleaned up our areas, mopped decks and packed our equipment. When we got on the lighter, it was standing room only for the hour- long trip to shore. Then it was another hour wait at the pier while somebody decided what to do with us. Same old army.

While waiting and looking to see what we could of the stark Scottish landscape I noted several big dirty white pelicans sitting on the mushroomed tops of the pier pilings. One of them leisurely tucked in his bill and took off, heading right over us and had the audacity to relive him-self. We saw the strung out mess arching down toward us, but we were shoulder-to-shoulder and no way to take evading action. All we could do was tilt our helmets and pull in our necks and hope it hit someplace else. It hit one of those bass horn like ships ventilators and splattered about a dozen of us, myself included. There were quite a few foul comments directed toward the big beaked fowl. My thoughts were, "We haven't even landed and here this German pelican has dive bombed us."

Eventually we learned we had landed at Greenock, Scotland after our seven day trip across the Atlantic. We boarded a train a short march from the pier. The cars were unique to us with their running boards and private compartments, if you can call ten men to a compartment private. Soon the engine gave its shrill European screech and amid huffing and puffing we were off for somewhere, anything better than waiting. We soon passed thru Glasgow, not very pretty under the gray evening sky. Reached Edinburgh just before dark and assumed the castle we saw silhouetted on a hill was historic sinister Edinburgh Castle.

Our train traveled all night down thru the Scottish highlands and into the Midlands of England. Noted a lot of military of all description at the dimly lit stations we passed. Ladies passed out crumpets at one station stop. Rather tasteless and heavy with a consistency of sawdust, but it was probably the best they could do with shortages of everything in a crowded land. In the early morning we pulled onto a sidetrack in a small station and unloaded. I noted the name of the station was Adderbury, England; a coincidence because we had started our journey from Atterbury, Indiana about a month before.

We were scattered by units to billets in picturesque little towns with storybook names like Banbury Cross, Chipping Norton, Stow on Wald, etc. This was Robin Hood country except the forests of old twisted English oak had long since vanished. Our regimental headquarters was at an old English manor in Adderbury. Enlisted men's quarters were a fine old two story carriage house on the estate. No central heating in either the Manor or the carriage house. Only little fireplaces and no wood for those, so we were constantly chilly in the cold damp weather typical for the time of year. It was a new experience exploring the quaint lanes with their thatched stone houses and the smoky pubs with their warm beer and dart boards. I guess the locals didn't appreciate the new influx of noisy, boisterous GIs to disrupt the tranquility of their way of life. Given the chance, we would have drunk up their week's quota of beer and stout in one night, but I guess a lot of soldiers had passed this way before and the villagers accepted the disruptive inconveniences of war. At least we were on the same side.

As Regimental Operations Sgt, my duties were at HQs taking care of training schedules, maps, road priorities, combat courses, etc. The regiment was busy cleaning up equipment after the overseas movement and getting equipment, new manpower and ammunition to bring it up to combat strength. Combat training and rifle range work continued, so it was long days. November was a busy month.

My friend, Sgt Switzer from Brooklyn, was a rough fellow. We were as different as black and white, but got along very well. He was Regimental Transportation Sgt until he got into an argument with his officer on some administrative matter. He was too bullheaded to back off, so they busted him and sent him to a line company. I never saw him again and don't know how he fared in the fighting that was ahead of us. Then there was Capt (x), the S-2 officer. As the time came closer for us to go into combat, he got morose and nervous and obviously unfit for combat, so one day he was gone to a rear echelon assignment and a Cpt Ferlman took his place, and so things went.

I managed to get a one day pass for a quick visit to London, and spent my time sightseeing on foot. Saw the parliamentary buildings and Big Ben, Piccadilly Circus, Trafalgar Square and block after empty block from the Blitz. Passed a big hospital by the Thames that was entirely fire gutted. London looked like an exciting, spirited place to be, but I had no time to partake in any of that.

After Deddington, A buddy and I decided to try Oxford. As I recall, we had to walk a couple of miles to Banburg to catch a train to Oxford about 25 miles away. Somehow or other we met a couple of Irish nurses in Oxford, but they had to go on duty so we made a date with them for that evening. They gave the name of the hospital and the road. Well, it was dark and it had been thundering and raining intermittently when we started looking for their place. You'd have to experience blackout conditions to appreciate our problems. There must have been a half dozen field hospitals along that road and we had to check each one of them, and then we were constantly stepping in puddles of water in the dark or trying to avoid being run over by vehicles with shuttered headlights. We finally found their hospital. It was an insane asylum. It was an old Victorian building setting spookily back in the darkness behind a stone wall with high iron grill fencing. The lightning effects were appropriate for the setting, and it was with some apprehension that we opened the iron gate and approached the dark forbidding structure.

We were greeted at the door by a voice coming out of the darkness asking who we wished to see. We were led through a darkened entrance hall into the lighted interior of a waiting room. It was about as dismal as the exterior, with high ceilings, Spartan furniture and bare light bulbs reflecting dully from green paint peeling from ceilings and walls. The woman said the girls we asked for were on duty, but she would send them down. As it turned out, their shift had been changed and they had to work. So we made plans to try and see them the following week if we could get down and then left and found our way back to Oxford. This wasn't to be the end of our bad luck. We missed the last train back to Banbury so we started walking and hoping we would catch a ride. We probably walked 7 or 8 miles and only saw two vehicles; both of which didn't even slow down. By this time, it was getting quite cold and we were wet and the beer we had consumed wasn't setting too well. We found a haystack not too far from the road and burrowed into it for warmth. We took turns watching for a vehicle. Seemed like a couple of hours before one came along and we desperately flagged it down. It was two officers returning from London and they gave us a ride to Adderbury. We got there about an hour before reveille. Believe me, the next day was a long one for us.

We didn't get back to Oxford, because the following week orders came to prepare for cross-channel movement to the combat zone. Just before leaving the states, our division had been stripped of several thousand combat troops for replacements in Europe. We were scheduled to have until Christmas to bring the new replacements up to combat efficiency. Again it was rush as we turned from a training program to preparation for a cross-channel movement, too bad as we were just starting to enjoy this little patch of England. We loaded on troop trains for a slow ride thru the English countryside and then marched thru a heavily bombed port area to embark on a troopship about the 2nd of December. I thought it was Plymouth and it wasn't until the end of the war that I learned we shipped out of Liverpool. The ship was the Monawai, said to have been an Australian cattle boat before the war. Apparently they hadn't changed it much in converting it for troops.

We left on the evening tide, moving slowly through a fantastic conglomeration of shipping in the port. I thought it would be a couple of hours across the channel, instead we steamed all nite and as time passed, the seas got rougher. In the morning the ship anchored within sight of a low shoreline to the south and in the midst of a large group of assorted types of landline craft, all of us weathering heavily in the white capped seas coming from the west. We were told they were carrying the division artillery and vehicles. We were supposed to land at LeHarve, but the passage thru the mine fields and sunken wrecks was too dangerous to attempt in a channel storm. We were to sit there riding out the storm for the next four days. We lived on K rations because the ship had no facilities for hot meals. The second day the big doors on an LST apparently were damaged by the pounding waves, and it slipped its anchors to turn its stern to the waves. A dangerous maneuver for a shallow riding flat bottom craft. For a time it looked bad as it lay broached to the waves, but finally got safely around. We were told another LST had sunk during the nite.

Time was heavy on our hands waiting out that storm. Eventually the storm subsided and we got underway again. The ship edged its way into the Seine estuary, changing course frequently to follow some unseen lane thru the minefields. On our port side we watched the fortified promontory slip by. It was steep and high, almost a cliff and there were so many shell craters they overlapped. One time there must have been many trees but now only blackened stumps and shattered trunks. Here and there we could make out a pillbox or tunnel opening that must have housed guns at one time. There were strong pockets of Germans a short way up the coast still holding out. We entered the ports breakwater with the blasted remnants of blockhouses. The harbor was strewn with sunken wrecks, showing their upper works or on their sides. The piers and buildings as far as we could see were shattered debris. I thought I recognized the French Line pier where my mother and I landed in 1928. The pier structure was blackened twisted framework and a large vessel lay on her side next to the pier.

Our ship anchored out in the harbor and the crew rigged rope nets over the side for us to clamber down to the Higgins landing craft that came along side. Now climbing down a limp rope net with sixty pounds of equipment hanging on you takes a little bit of courage. In addition, you have to time your jump from the net to the boat because the boat was bobbing up and down on the sizeable harbor swells. If you missed you got crushed between the ship and the boat or else you sunk like a rock to the bottom with all your equipment. They had dumped duffle bags into each landing craft too, so when it hit the beach and the ramp dropped, we each hefted a duffle bag along with our other equipment and staggered across the rocky shingle beach and up the seawall. We were exhausted, but grateful we didn't have to do it in the face of enemy fire.

After resting a moment, we moved on to our assigned waiting areas along the debris strewn street by the seawall. The stone seawall at this location was about twenty feet high and narrow steep stone steps went down to a small landing by the water. Moored to the landing and extending outward moored to each other were a half dozen American corvettes (sub chasers). On the street close to us was a large German pill box or really, blockhouse. It like everything else had been shelled and had several gaping holes. In the darkness we decided not to explore its interior.

We were told to make ourselves comfortable as trucks would pick us up and haul us to our bivouac areas. With the cold channel wind and misty rain it wasn't too easy to make ourselves comfortable. Some of the outfits down the street were gathering wood from gutted buildings and building fires to keep warm. As time dragged on, our discomfort obviously increased and we began contemplating the comforts of the vessels below us. Eventually some of the more adventurous went down the stone steps and we watched the sailors let them on board. So soon the rest of us were going down the steps. The first vessels had as many as they could handle so we clambered from one to another until we found room. The sailors gave us mugs of hot coffee; even if it was too hot to drink it warmed our hands and stopped our chattering teeth. Concerned about missing the trucks, as soon as we could finish the coffee. we headed back. About halfway up the steps, there was a flash and loud explosion up on the street. Reaching the street I could see a lot of activity around one of the fires I mentioned earlier. Apparently a dud shell had been in the debris where they built the fire and heat set it off, wounding 3 or 4 men. How badly we didn't learn because the quartermaster trucks arrived, the tailgates clanged down and we loaded up. There was a mad scramble up the seawall as our men abandoned the comforts of the sub chasers below.

The Dodge 6x6s slowly ground their way out of LeHavre and were fairly snug under the canvas protected from the rain. I would have been happy to ride all night, but all good things come to an end. In an hour or so the trucks stopped and a voice outside yelled, "Everybody out." Lifting the canvas flap, it wasn't a very pretty scene that greeted our eyes. The rain was coming down in sheets the road was potted with mud holes and empty fields of mud faded into the darkness. No shelters, no barns, nothing. The same voice, now emitting from a bulky shadow by the bank, said, "Service Co and HQs is about a half mile back down the road. You'll see your kitchen set up." So shouldering our equipment we staggered off blinded by the headlights of the endless line of trucks. Funny, in England everything was blackout; here close to the front, the trucks are lit up as if they were in the states. So, working our way around trucks and GIs going the opposite direction, stumbling in potholes, slipping into ditches we fumbled our way past a half dozen company kitchens under dripping canvas flies before we heard the welcome call, "Service Co over here."

The space under the fly already was crowded with shivering forms. Hot coffee was all that was available as the cooks struggled to set up their equipment in the mud and get it operating. Kruse, Justis and I looked at the muddy field around us, cursed and decided we try to spend the night in one of the parked trucks we had passed along the road. Going back to the road, we crawled into the first one we came to. Feeling around in the dark revealed it had a loose load of potatoes, maybe a lumpy bed, but certainly dry. So stripping off most of our wet clothes we wiggled into our sleeping bags. Later, a couple other fellows slipped over the tailgate to join us, we awakened to the jolting of the truck and realized the driver was headed someplace we didn't want to go. We got his attention and he pulled over and gave us a few minutes to crawl into our wet stiff clothes. During the night it had quit raining the feel of snow was in the air. Half dressed and carrying our equipment haphazardly we started looking for our outfit, not knowing how far the truck had carried us.

We were lucky to find the company in about an hour. After getting some breakfast, I noted the small headquarters field tent had miraculously been erected during the night. The officers had spent about as miserable a night as us. At least the comforting hiss of the Coleman lanterns kept the tent warm as well as light. We learned we were in the vicinity of Yerville. We kept busy the next few days bringing some kind of order and operational capability out of the confusion of the cross-channel movement. We learned we were to relieve the 2nd Division of the VIII Corp and would become part of the 1st Army. Maps, plans and orders had to be prepared for the movement to the front. We were to move via Amiens, St. Quentin, and St. Vith and after spending several days in these muddy half frozen fields, the regiment along with the other units of the division began its move. We were glad to be on the move again; surely things could only get better.

I rode in a jeep with Capt Edwards as we had to check to see the battalions maintained proper positions and time schedules. It was bitter cold in the open jeep and we passed thru occasional snow flurries. The roads were rough from heavy traffic and former shellfire. Wrecked or burned vehicles alongside the road were not an uncommon sight. We made slow headway, as supply convoys had the priority to the front. At one point I noted a German flak tower. This one had a large concrete column supporting a reinforced concrete platform with shield walls. It could hold several of the multi-barrel 40mm flak guns to discourage our planes from low level strafing and bombing. From the scars, it had been shot up by our planes.

We passed thru Amiens, St. Quentin and stopped that night at a place called LaCapelle. Earlier, I had abandoned the jeep for a truck, which was much warmer with the canvas buttoned up, though we couldn't see anything. At one point when we were stopped, there was a lot of commotion outside our vehicle. I lifted the flap and peered out to see the shadowy bulk of a railroad locomotive being slowly towed by on rollers. No wonder the road was full of potholes. Next day we passed thru a place called Phillipville. I thought of my close friend, Phil Carrier, who had joined the marines. Last I had heard he was in the South Pacific and I envied him in the sun and sand instead of this dreary, morbidly cold country. (I later learned that Phil was killed on Iwo Jima). After this we got into very hilly terrain and I remember coming down into Dinant, an old fortress city that has seen the passage of many armies. Somewhere on the trip during a rest stop, several of us were invited into a Belgium home to get warm. While sitting there, I became aware of a throbbing vibration that seemed to come from the floor and then awareness of a noise like a heavily loaded truck struggling up a steep grade.

The Belgiums showed apprehension and one of them took the burner lids off the iron cooking stove. They managed to explain to us that what we were hearing was a V-1 (buzz bomb) and even a near hit often collapsed a building from the vacuum, removing the stove lids helped equalize the pressure thru the chimney. At any rate, the buzz bomb made a peculiar noise that you never forget and you always wanted to hold your breath until it passed over and the noise started fading away. You never mistook it for an airplane. I thought of Exodus where the angel of death passed over Egypt.

That evening we stopped in the village of Poteau, Belgium, and established the regimental CP at a crossroad. The battalion convoys were stopped as they passed this point and were given directions to assigned bivouac areas in the surrounding fir forests. By the time the last convoys straggled in, several hours had lapsed and we were colder than ever. There was a stone house on the corner and the family was friendly. Gillem and I gave the kids candy. There were four children, the oldest a friendly girl of about 11. We could only communicate by sign language a few simple words. The family invited us in and we got warm for the first time since England, I washed and shaved too (also the first time since England).

It was a plain little home; stone floor, a fireplace for heat, basically one big room downstairs and steep stairs going up to sleeping quarters on the second floor. They invited us to sleep there, which we gladly accepted, assuring them that the floor by the fireplace was fine for our sleeping bags. The Colonel and Exec Officers moved in with us. Capt. Edward spent a good part of the night riding in a jeep with the Exec, locating the various battalion HQs. It was quite a job to locate them in the snow and dark woods. The only shelter most of them had, was what they could improvise. The next morning was busy as plans were finalized to relieve the 23rd Infantry Regiment. They sent guides to lead our troops to the correct areas. So, about noon we began the final movement to the front. We thanked the friendly Belgium family and left them some chocolate and coffee from our K rations, neither of us aware of the holocaust that would overwhelm us all in a few days.

Now we passed thru magnificent dark fir forests, their limbs heavy with snow. We noticed many of them festooned with long strips of metal foil as if decorated for Christmas. Later we learned this was dropped by our bombers to confuse the enemy radar. We stopped in St Vith which was our Division HQs. It was a sizeable town. Here the guides took advance parties from each company forward so they would lead their units in under cover of darkness and the 23rd would withdraw. Relieving a unit on the line is always a tough operation, because if the enemy gets wind of it they will shell the devil out of the positions hoping to catch a lot of troops in the open. Regimental HQs was more sheltered from enemy observation, so we moved in and began our exchange.

HQ was located in a large two story stone farmhouse on the edge of the village of Heckhalenfeld, southeast of St Vith and on the Belgium-German border. It was a typical type farmhouse, with living quarters on one end, a hayloft and storage area in the middle portion and livestock area on the far end; all under one roof. It sat on the side of a hill overlooking the narrow cobble street that wound down into the main village. As the 23rd packed, we unpacked. Map boards had to be set up and information transferred on unit locations, then there were fire and patrol schedules to be noted, enemy dispositions recorded, our communication facilities established, problems to be rectified; like some of their machine guns and mortars were frozen in the mud and couldn't be moved so we exchanged our guns for theirs. Even some of their trailers were embedded in frozen mud, that we had to give them ours, but they were on their way to attack the Roer River. We didn't know the enemy had other plans for our quiet sector. Eventually they were gone and we were sole possessors of the land and we looked around to see what we had inherited.

The regiment occupied a line about five miles long with the dragon teeth of the Siegfried Line marching across our front about a helf mile away. The 112th Infantry Regiment of the 28th Division was on our right flank, the other two regiments of our division occupied a large volcanic mass on our left flank. Our dispositions placed the 2nd Battalion on our right, the 3rd battalion in the center. However, our left was wide open because Division at the last minute took our 1st battalion away from us for Division reserve. This was the key sector in our area because it contained the town of Winterspelt and a straight road from the German position in Prum to St Vith, our Division HQs. To fill this gap, Cannon Company left it's guns with Service Company and moved into Winterspelt as infantry, but they didn't have the machine guns or mortars that a normal infantry company has and they were not trained to fight as infantry. Colonel Reid convinced Division to let him have the 106th Recon Company which he used to extend the line north of Cannon Company. So here we were with two full battalions holding unimportant positions and two improvised rifle companies holding the one area the Germans might attack and no regimental reserves left.

FINALLY ON OUR WAY OVERSEAS

My father passed thru here in 1917

QUAINT ENGLISH LANE

MRS. M. M. KUNSELMAN
600 FIFTH STREET
HOT SPRINGS, ARK.

SHIPBOARD SCENE

WAITING TO UNLOAD AT GREEOCK
(PORT OF GLASGOW)

THE VILLAGE

GIRL AT THE VILLAGE PUMP

ADDERBURY, ENGLAND

V···— MAIL

Regimental HQ.

90

REST STOP

NOTHING BUT A WET AND MUDDY FIELD

Cold Ride To Belgium

Smashed Vehicles Litter the Roads

We Discover The Address They Gave Us Was An Insane Asylem

WAITING TO LAND AT LE HARVE

OVERSEAS TO ENGLAND THEN ON TO BELGIUM

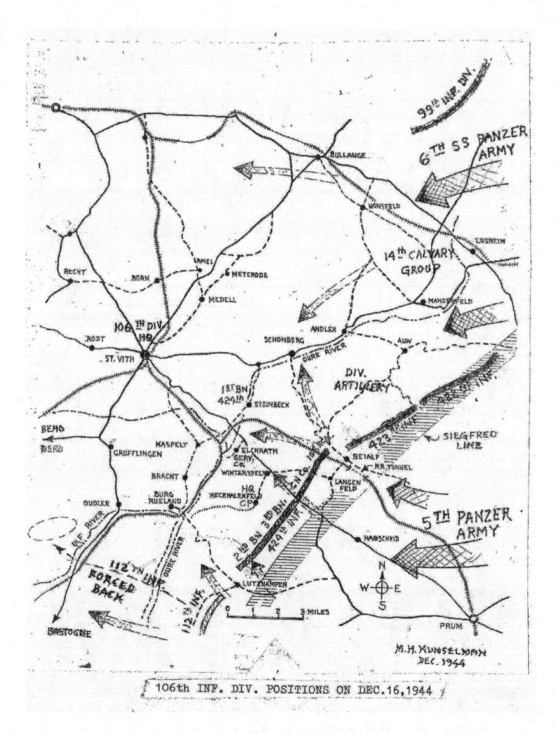

106th INF. DIV. POSITIONS ON DEC. 16, 1944

M.H. KUNSELMAN
DEC. 1944

COMMENTS FOR THE FOLLOWING CHAPTER

The Battle of the Bulge was costly to both sides; After 6 bitter weeks the Germans were back where they had started. Over 100,000 casualties on each side, What had the Germans hoped to gain?

Pondering that question I concluded it had no significance for us. Maybe it delayed the defeat of Germany a month or so, but it was a battle we could well have done without. I think we have to look at the German side of the picture to understand why this terrible battle ever occurred. The allied armies had swept thru France and Belgium and stood on the border of Germany. They were preparing to sweep into Germanys industrial heartland, the Ruhr valley. On the eastern front the Russians were advancing with alarming speed. The situation was desperate. Moreover, Hitler had boasted that the only enemy soldiers on the soil of the Fatherland would be either dead or captive.

The germans knew the American lines in the rugged Ardennes region were thinly held and few available reserves. The Ardennes and it's Losheim Gap was a well known invasion route for his armies. It was used in 1870, 1914, and 1940. they decided to gamble everything there. With great secrecy they assembled a powerful armored force and launched a surprise attack on the 3 American divisions in their path. They planned to knife quickly through this thin line of defense and wheel north into the rear areas of the allied armies wreaking havoc on communications and supply depots, I guess like Sherman's march to the sea. To create confusion, paratroopers and saboteurs were dropped behind the lines and a brigade (150th) composed of soldiers wearing American uniforms and using captured American tanks was slipped in among our troops.

The purpose of the battle was fourfold: First, to seize the initiative from the allies and protect the industrial Ruhr from attack; Second, to split the American armies and cause dissention among the allies; Third, to fulfill Hitler's boast to drive the invader from German soil; Fourth, and this is the most significant, if the panzer armies could take their prime objective (Port of Antwerp) the American, Canadian, and British armies would be cut off from their chief supply point and their position made untenable. Hitler hoped this would enable him to negotiate a separate peace on the western front, enabling him to mass his forces against the Russians. So the implications of the Ardennes Campaign were political, economic, military, and diplomatic. It was a bold gamble.

BELGIUM
DEC. 16, 1944 – FEB. 4, 1945

GERMAN PANTHER TANK

How close did it come to success? The tenacious defense on the northern shoulder and the seven day defense of St Vith doomed his gamble. Unable to advance his jammed columns on the north, the attack shifted south only to be forced into time consuming detours around Bastogne. The panzer columns finally got within four miles of the bridges across the Meuse, sixty miles behind our lines, but by then it was too late. A new American defense line had been established and the door to Liège and Antwerp was closed.

Our regimental combat team consisted of the 424th Infantry Regiment, 591st Field Artillery, C Co. 81st Engineers, 106th Recon Company, and a platoon from the 820th Tank Destroyer battalion. To the northeast (left) of us lay a volcanic mountain mass called the Schee Eifel. Our sister regiments, 423rd and 422nd with the 589th, 590th and 592 FA battalions occupied its length. A road called Skyline Drive and the Siegried Line ran along its crest and thru their positions. To the north of that was notorious Losheim Gap, a favorite invasion route for the Germans into France. Attached to our Division (106th) were the 14th Calvary Group consisting of the 18th and 32nd Squadrons (armored cars and light tanks), Company A 820 TD and the 275th Armored Artillery battalion. They held a seven mile front of the most valuable or rather vulnerable territory in the division area. I'll never understand how anyone could make that mistake. Cavalry is for reconnaissance, not holding ground against a panzer attack, but both VIII Corp and 2nd Division assured us the Germans would never launch an attach thru this forbidding terrain. I guess they never read their history.

I suppose I should describe the basic makeup of a WWII American Infantry Division. It consisted of 3 Infantry Regiments, 3 FA (Field Artillery) battalions 105 howitzers, 1 FA battalion 155 howitzers, 1 Engineer battalion plus Quartermaster, Ordnance and Medical units, totaling about 15,000 men. Each regiment consisted of 3 Infantry battalions plus a Service-HQ Company, Cannon Company (75mm) and the Anti-tank Company (57mm), totaling about 3000 men. Each battalion consisted of 3 Infantry Companies and a Heavy Weapons Company (MGs and mortars). Each Infantry Company consisted of 3 Infantry Platoons and a Heavy Weapons platoon (MGs and mortars). In normal tactical use, whether in attack or defense, the division places 2 regiments on the line and holds one back for reserve. Likewise, the regiment uses 2 battalions on the line and one in reserve. The battalion follows the same principal of two companies in contact and one in reserve and even the company utilizes 2 infantry platoon on the line and one in reserve. This principal serves two purposes as it allows each unit from company sizes to division to have 1/3 of its force for rest and recuperation. In our overextended line, everything was needed on the line, leaving no reserve and at that, held only strong points depending on patrols to cover the area between. If the enemy should attack and break thru in strength anyplace, there was nothing to stop him.

Now to get back to my story, our first crisis was the fire on December 13th. One of the fellows was heating water on a homemade gasoline heater in the hay loft part of the building. He tipped it over and in seconds the whole area was in flames, with fire and smoke shooting thru the door into the main quarters. There was no stopping it and in a mad scramble field desks, maps, and personal equipment was thrown out of the heat and smoke filled rooms. The dozens of telephone lines were cut from the regimental switchboard and that heavy piece of equipment was lowered out a window to the ground. The last of us vacated the building with flames hot on our tail. Many of the townspeople came up to watch sullenly as the flames consumed the big building. Hostile, but I felt sorry that our carelessness had destroyed somebody's home. Our adjutant walked across the road and commandeered a similar house, moving the equipment and reestablishing our headquarters. The fire was bad, because the loss of telephone communications and the confusion of moving delayed the Colonels plan to realign our forces and strengthen the weak left flank.

That night, there were several fires in our regimental area. One man died in the fire at Service Company, apparently when he could not escape in time from his zippered sleeping bag. Two more fires occurred in our neighboring regiment and at first sabotage were suspected, but more than likely carelessness was responsible. Strange though after this rash of fires in one day, we never again were bothered. Our original building burned all night affording an excellent target to draw enemy artillery fire, but none fell on us. Later we figured the Germans were moving troops up for the surprise attack and didn't want to risk drawing counter battery artillery fire from us. The next two days were busy ones as communications were improved (telephone and radio), fire lanes cleared for MGs mortar crews fire ranging shots, mine fields were plotted and additional ones laid, logistics planned (ammunition and food), counterattack plans prepared, patrols established, and in any spare time fixing shelters to survive the cold and mud.

Our positions were just across the Belgium border in Germany and in addition to Winterspelt and Heckhalenfeld, there were a half dozen other villages in our area. The civilians for the most part stayed out of sight and were considered passively hostile. At night there always were several of us on duty at the Command post, hereafter referred to as CP. Messages would come in from the battalions or from division, mostly requiring routine action. Of course in a combat area, one doesn't just plug into a wall socket for lights. There isn't any electricity. We had a small gasoline generator for electricity. It was located in a shed about a hundred feet from our building. Periodically one of us would have to go out to put gasoline in it. We didn't like the duty, because it was pitch black outside, not even starlight thru the thick cloud cover. The generator is a noisy thing and sometimes a German patrol attracted by its noise will lay in wait, knowing sooner or later some GI will wander out there to service it. So it was with this thought in mind one night that I fumbled my way out to the shed. It was so dark I had to find the shed by tracing the wire with my hands. About the time I located the darker shadow of the doorway, the generator gave a couple of gasps and quit and the silence was unnerving. I straightened and stepped toward the opening and something crashed into my helmet and I saw stars. My first thought was, "They got me!", and I fell to the ground. However everything was silent except for my heart pounding and the helmet rolling around on the ground. Finally, feeling around in the dark, I discovered I had run into the half open door. I guess that was when my hair started turning gray.

VII Corp had requested prisoners and we had sent combat patrols out for that purpose. Several prisoners were taken and they were passed up to us, where our S-2 officer questioned them and learned new units were being moved in with an indication of an enemy buildup. The prisoners were passed on to division. Other than that, things remained pretty quiet the next two days. Occasional artillery or mortar fire would search out a position. At night flares would cast their eerie glow for a minute and die out, and from time-to-time the noise of small arms fire. More than likely some soldier with a nervous trigger finger. Most of our men had been without shelter for over a week and many were becoming casualties of trench foot. We only had combat boots which stayed soggy. Many would lose toes, feet, and even legs before rubber boots would be available. The weather can be just as deadly as the enemy. Early on the night of the 15th, our patrols reported the sound of motors and tanks, but the word came back from Corp not to worry as the Germans often played these sounds on PA systems to confuse and worry new troops. So we relaxed and figured in time we would learn all these disturbing but harmless tricks of the enemy. Oh yes; with snow on the ground we were badly in need of winter camouflage suits. We finally receive a few, enough to give about a dozen to each battalion when they really needed hundreds.

Dec. 16, 1944 – I remained on duty by the field phone in the CP until about 3 am. The battalions made their routine reports. The several patrols that were out, reported some sounds of enemy activity, but nothing unusual. A rocket barrage hit K Co. in the 3rd battalion area. Turning the duty over to Jim Gillum, I went up to the attic and crawled into my sleeping bag. I had hardly gone to sleep when Gillum was shaking me awake and I was aware of a bedlam of noise around me. Half awake, my first thought was that the building was on fire. Jim said heavy artillery fire was falling on all our positions and they wanted everybody downstairs. Suddenly I realized that wasn't hail rattling on the stone roof above, but shrapnel and we got out of there. I flashed the light on my watch and noted it was about 5:50 am.

It's quite an experience to come under heavy shellfire the first time and I will admit my stomach felt like jello for a while. I suppose some others felt the same way, but none of us would admit it. It is one thing to experience it under training exercises but when the real thing hits, you think "Hey this is for keeps." Communications from the forward positions was busy but those to division HQs were cut, probably by the shellfire. Cannon Company reported big searchlights were shining up and reflecting from the low clouds to the north of them and that flares revealed enemy swarming in the minefields in front of their positions. Things picked up fast then as our 591st artillery started responding to calls for help. All along the line there were reports of activity in the darkness in front of our positions, and the twinkling of dim red and green lights, apparently signaling devices to control the movement of the assaulting forces. 3rd Battalion, last to be hit, was being attacked by infantry and tanks. With communications to division out, we didn't know if this was just a local attack on our positions, or if the whole division was involved.

Stepping outside, I saw the eerie effects of the searchlights to the northeast and the reddish glow of artillery fire flaring up and dying all along the dark hill masses. To the southeast a swarm of screaming mimis trailing fire rose over a ridge and fell, to explode with a muttering roar somewhere in our battalion positions. A fearsome sight and I compared it to Dante's Hell. Meanwhile shells ripped and howled overhead (both incoming and outgoing). I thought, if this was a quiet sector it sure is going to get rough when we meet the real thing. About that time a couple of shells exploded in the lower village, throwing out a shower of sparks and I ducked back into the shelter of the building.

By eight o'clock, the 3rd Battalion had counterattacked and retaken their positions and 2nd Battalion had repulsed their attack, claiming two tanks destroyed and the others withdrawing. They reported many enemy dead and wounded in front of and in their positions, and 200 prisoners taken. However, Cannon Company was slowly giving ground along the Prum-St Vith highway in face of persistent heavy attacks. In heavy weapons, they only had a couple of 50-caliber and 30-caliber machine guns (MGs). They reported the enemy up Hwy 265 in big halftrack personnel carriers, unloading and marching up the road four abreast. They were being mowed down, but more took their place. Colonel Reid ordered Company C 81st Engr. who were in the east end of our village to move northeast and cover Cannon Company's right flank. Meanwhile the 106th Recon Company on Cannon Company's left flank just vanished. The radio was jammed and telephone lines to 106 recon and Cannon Company were soon cut, either by enemy patrols or shellfire. It was imperative to know what was going on in those areas.

Later an officer from Cannon Company reported they had been overrun by masses of infantry supported by armored vehicles advancing up the road from Prum. Cannon Company was falling back toward Winterspelt and needed ammunition as well as reinforcements. Unfortunately our 1st Battalion was still division reserve and unavailable to us. Company C 81st Engr were ordered to move up and support Cannon while the I & R Platoon under Sgt McKenna established a defense between the regimental C.P. and the Winterspelt Road. Meanwhile the messenger sent to contact 106 Recon Company on our far left flank returned reporting he could not contact them because of Germans swarming in that area. He did see an officer from the 423rd Regiment who said a strong force of Germans were advancing around the southern tip of Schnee Eifel and threatening the town of Blielf. Also, the messenger said he had been fired on. It certainly looked as if our left flank was in real trouble.

Communications were reestablished with division around 8am and we learned the whole VIII Corps area was heavily attacked by panzers (tanks) and infantry, but thought to be just a spoiling attack to force First Army to halt its attack on the Roer River dams. Later in the morning, General Perrin (Div Exec) visited our area to access the situation. Recognizing the danger on our left, he secured the release of our 1st Battalion (Lt Col Welsh) from division reserve to stabilize the situation. They move down quickly from Steinbruck, sending C Company ahead to support Cannon Company at Eigelscheid while the rest of the battalion dug in around Winterspelt. We could plainly see the church steeple at Winterspelt, about a mile north of our command post (CP). The Germans continued to attack along the highway and the antitank platoon knocked out two tanks, but a third tank destroyed the gun with a direct hit. C Company and the remainder of Cannon Company fell back into the perimeter of Winterspelt. With the momentum of the German attack, one of their combat patrols penetrated the town and grenaded the battalion CP, located in a basement. Luckily the CP personnel spotted the danger and they vacated the basement just before the grenades demolished it. However, the 1st Battalion held fast to their positions and the southern route to St. Vith was blocked for the time being. Although the enemy attacks and shelling continued all along our regimental sector, our positions held the rest of the day and into the night.

To our south it appeared the 28th Division had been overrun and it's 112th Infantry Regiment separated from the rest of the division. In turn, B Company 112th had been forced out of Lutzhampen and into our rear area on the

Burg Rueland Road. They were separated from the rest of their regiment (112th) and asked for help. Colonel Reid ordered our 2nd Battalion to send a platoon and ammunition. Ironically I had gone into service back in 1941 with B Company from Meadville, Pa. Later in the afternoon, our Service Company at Elcherath (to our rear) was attacked by enemy soldiers wearing American uniforms and using an American halftrack towing a 3-inch antitank gun. At first, they thought it was Americans so they ere taken by surprise. We were to learn later that the 150th Panzer Brigade was composed of Germans wearing our uniforms and using captured American vehicles and tanks was slipped into our rear areas to confuse and demoralize our troops. For the duration of the campaign this deceit had to be dealt with using special passwords that were uniquely American and carefully screening any strange unit we might meet. German patrols in our rear areas would cut into our phone lines and using American speaking Germans would try to give false orders or information, and of course the same was true with radio. Sometimes they were successful.

To our immediate northeast (left flank), we had no contact with the 423 and 422 Infantry Regiments on Schnee Iffel and there was a gap between us in which then enemy was moving. Further north in the Losheim Gap, the real catastrophe was taking shape as the Sixth Panzer Army was rolling over the 18th Cavalry Squadron and its attached units, threatening to break thru and sweep down behind our regiments on the mountain mass surrounding them. Already their escape road to the north was blocked, and the artillery was defending itself from tanks with direct fire. If the enemy broke thru at the railroad tunnel and took Beialf, the southern escape route would be blocked and 2/3 of our division trapped. All of this and in less than a week we arrived.

There were a lot of heroes this day, but one would have to read the division history to learn their stories. I will only mention several incidences I observed. One was a young battalion messenger. Early in the fighting he was driving his jeep to our Command Post when a bullet passed thru the lower edge of his helmet and thru his neck. He had a bloody bandage tied around his neck and refused to be evacuated, continued running messages the rest of the day.

A lot of prisoners had accumulated in our stockade by afternoon and it was necessary to get them back to division and off our hands. My friend M/Sgt Gene Justis took three truckloads and after turning them over to the Division Provost, offered to guide 15 truckloads of badly needed ammunition back to regiment. Ten of them with artillery ammo were dropped off in the artillery rear area and he continued with the other five. As they entered one village in a rear area, they were surprised to see armed Germans in the street. Firing their 50 caliber MGs from the truck ring mounts, they barreled their way thru the surprised enemy. Three trucks with the badly needed ammo made it. Further along he reported seeing several houses with candles burning in the windows. They shot one out as they passed, figuring it was a signal for the advancing Germans. We know the enemy was in contact with the civilians in our area because we discovered the local people had gathered in sturdy basements prior to the opening barrages that morning. Several of our men remembered seeing a woman going from house-to-house the evening before, probably warning the people. I guess we would try to do the same if it were our people.

From identities of prisoners taken that day in our sector it appeared we were being attacked by the 116th Panzer Division, 62nd VG (Inf) Division and part of the 110 Luftwaffe Division. Papers and maps found on a captain from the 116th Panzer, captured by 2nd Battalion showed their first day's objective was Crombach, about nine miles to our rear and their major objective was Liège, Belgium, a major communication and supply center for the whole American front. This was no small local attack. Apparently we had managed to upset their timetable – for a little while anyway.

None of us slept much that night; maybe catching a catnap as the opportunity afforded itself. We stuck close to the field phones and message center while S-2 continued to question prisoners and glean a little more information. We had no real idea what was happening in the rest of the Corp area and not sure what was happening in our own. As we added new reports of enemy units to our map with a red grease pencil, our own position began to look like a peninsula jutting into a German sea. That night, division reported it was being shelled by 14-inch guns. That would be big railroad guns. Artillery grumbled and flares hung low in the sky over our forward positions as they watched for and reported seeing strong enemy patrols bypass them and move to our rear, at least no reports of tanks. Several buzz bombs droned over, probably headed for Liège. Several platoons from the 168th Engr were sent up to reinforce Company C 81st Engr. Communications improved as our wire crews repaired and replaced the lines that had been badly torn up by artillery fire. Messengers were kept busy as static jammed radios left a lot to be desired in performance.

We received news that CCB 9th Armored Division was assigned to our division and would attack in the morning to reestablish the line between Winterspelt and Beialf. That was good news to know there would be tanks to oppose tanks. More good news as we learned CCB 7th Armored was to move thru St. Vith and attack in the Losheim Gap and drive the enemy out of there. So as the day drew to a close, things were looking up.

Since our destiny henceforth will be tied to armored divisions, I will try to clarify their makeup. As an infantry division has three combat teams, each with its own artillery, engineers, antitank units, etc. the armored division has two combat teams made up of tank battalions, armored artillery, armored infantry, engineers, tank destroyers, etc. these are called Combat Command A and Combat Command B (referred to as CCA and CCB). There is also a CCR which is mainly supply and support units but it does have combat capabilities too. So what was being sent down for the attacks in the morning was not two armored divisions, but a combat command from each.

December 17, 1944 – Before dawn the sound of heavy fighting erupted from the vicinity of Winterspelt. We could distinctly hear burp guns and tank cannon. Of course, it was only a mile north of us. About an hour later Lt. Huddleson, the popular 1st Battalion S-2 officer, came into the CP and said the Germans had the town. Tanks and infantry broke thru the perimeter and moved into the center of town, the tanks firing directly into the buildings. He said the tanks looked like Tiger MkVs. These are monstrous 60-ton tanks with 88mm guns, about twice the weight of our Shermans, which didn't matter since so far we had not seen any of our tanks. As daylight broke, we watched the engineers withdrawing over the hill to our front with mortar or shellfire exploding among them as they fell back to the far edge of Heckhalenfeld. Meanwhile, anyone not absolutely needed at the CP were sent to prepare and occupy defensive positions on the Winterspelt side. A couple of others and myself went up to the attic and dug holes thru the thick gable thatch for firing ports, quite a job we found out as that thatch was so thick and densely packed, I think it almost would stop a bullet. Rifle fire was falling around the CP, making it risky to venture outside. It seemed to be coming from the south instead of from Winterspelt, so the Intelligence and Recon platoon (I&R) moved out to try and locate its source.

When 1st Battalion was forced out of their positions, C Company fell back toward us thus forming a screen between the CP and the enemy. There was a stream and depression between the two towns that offered some favorable defensive shelter. The rest of the battalion was pushed up the St. Vith road a couple of miles and eventually reestablished themselves at the Oure Berg with the river at their back. With the enemy streaming up the highway on our flank, C Company said the road was bumper-to-bumper with enemy armor and infantry; it was only a matter of time until they sent a force down to bag us. Already they had struck Elcherath and after a short fight, put our Service Company to flight. How quickly things change. Here we had been expecting CCB 9th Armored to be attacking this morning instead the Germans had successfully beat them to the punch and were now beginning to circle our rear. Colonel Reid made Lt. Huddleson task commander to organize such men as he could find into a defensive force along Winterspeler Creek and block the enemy from moving southward behind us. Artillery ammunition was becoming a critical concern as the guns fired continuously. Many prime targets had to be ignored as they gave close in fire to protect our precarious positions.

Where was CCB 9th Arm.? Their arrival had been delayed by masses of traffic and refugees on the roads west of St. Vith. About 11:30am, the 9th Arm. launched their attack from the vicinity of Steinbruck. We listened to the sharp bark of tank gun fire to our left rear, but as time passed it got no closer and eventually died out.

Meanwhile, with daylight the enemy continued to launch attacks against the 2nd and 3rd Battalion positions to the south but they and B Company 112th held their positions. Patrols reported no sign of the 28th Division to the south and large groups of Germans seemed to be moving freely in the area. A message from division arrived a day late, reporting German paratroopers dropped in the vicinity of Malmady before daylight the morning of the 16th. Malmady was north of St. Vith. With no communications to division, our broken left flank, and the apparent failure of the armored attack; the question came up of withdrawing. I remember Colonel Reid's decision, he said "since we don't know conditions to the rear are any better we will hold our positions." So the day passed as the roar of battle shifted in the north and we continued to receive shelling, rocketing, and small probing attacks; but our positions held.

We heard planes several times to the north, but whether ours or theirs we never knew. It certainly wasn't flying weather with the sullen low cloud ceiling and mist shrouding the higher hills. However occasionally we'd see our little artillery observation planes doing their risky job and at times could see German antiaircraft fire (tracers) reaching for them.

A message arrived in the afternoon from division instructing us to withdraw to a line along the west bank of the Oure River with regimental HQ to be at Burg Rueland. We learned too that CCB's attack had stalled after taking Elcherath. This was 9th Armored's first combat. In face of the heavy enemy forces, they withdrew to the northeast to try to blunt the panzer attacks toward St. Vith. The enemy had hit Beialf this morning at the same time they swept our forces out of Winterspelt. HQ Company, Service Company of the 423rd regiment, and B Company 81st Engr had borne the brunt of the fighting around the railroad tunnel, suffering heavy casualties, but were overwhelmed by tanks and infantry. These forces swept northwest toward Schonberg where they would join another enemy armored column moving southwest from Andler completing the encirclement of our forces in Schnee Iffel.

Commenting on the report of the roads west of St. Vith filled with panic stricken troops and refugees, it was never clear who these troops were. Certainly most of the 106th Division units were accounted for. Two of the regimental combat teams were trapped on the mountain mass and many of the rear echelon units were preparing to defend St. Vith including the division band which exchanged their instruments for rifles. I'm sure many individuals and small units given the chance headed west. The 32nd Cavalry sent up to support the 18th may have been part of this traffic. Add to these the many VIII Corp support units such as Ordinance, Quartermaster, heavy artillery, and it could quickly jam up the roads. Of course, there would be legitimate traffic too, such as supply convoys. Trying to buck this traffic, CCB 7th Armored was delayed 12 crucial hours preventing the planned attack into the Losheim Gap. Instead their units were committed piecemeal as they arrived to the defensive line desperately being formed to the east of St. Vith.

We prepared for our withdrawal to the Oure about three miles away. Only one road was available to us at the south end of our positions. It was planned to pass the 2nd and 3rd Battalion vehicles and the two batteries of the 591st FA down that road while the rifle companies would move cross-country to a bailey bridge at Weigel. The field artillery would have the most dangerous move as they were emplaced close to us and to reach the road in the south they would have to use a trail that came within 300 yards of enemy positions at one point. The only exit road for us on the north end was firmly in enemy hands. An old logging trail to our rear led to a point close to Burg Rueland and we would have to use that. The pioneer platoon was sent to clear and improve it best they could for the passage of vehicles in the time they had. The whole area was rugged woods, crisscrossed with ravines so it was going to be rough traversing it at night with only shielded lights to guide the vehicles. Guides were sent out to familiarize themselves with the ground they would have to know.

Withdrawing from a position in the face of continuing probing attacks is always a dangerous situation. If the enemy even suspects a withdrawal in progress, he drops heavy artillery barrages over the lines and rear areas, following this with strong attacks while the defenders are in the open and off balance. For this reason each company left a platoon in the defensive positions with orders to fire flares and weapons occasionally to give the impression the lines are still fully manned. Most important was to get the withdrawal well under way before the hostile civilians learned of it as they probably would try to inform the enemy. It was well after dark by the time we had the equipment and our things loaded in trucks. A last check of the area to see if anything or anyone was missed and we crawled on top of a load of duffle bags and boxes in an open truck. Of course in spite of our check some things were still missed, one of them being Captain Perlman's duffle bag, for which he never forgave me; it was my mistake in assuming his sergeant had taken it.

It was a cold starless night again, only searchlights cast their eerie glow off the clouds to the northwest, probably the Schonberg area. To the east all was darkness. Occasional bursts of shellfire erupted along our positions, but the rumble of distant artillery was strongest to the northwest. As we lay there waiting to get underway, we heard the approaching throbbing drone of a buzz bomb. Suddenly a graceful stream of tracers arched up from a dark hill mass to the east. One of the 634th AA guns must have been on that hill and we never knew it. Who was going to warn them that when we pulled out they would be all alone? I hoped someone would get a message to them in time. As for us, our motor coughed into life and we slowly lurched out into the shadowy line of vehicles. The buzz bomb passed low directly over us and we watched its tail flame disappear impassively into the western darkness.

The passage thru the forest was painstakingly slow as the truck jolted into potholes and slipped, churned, and fought for traction as the snow covered passage turned into a quagmire. Shadowy figures with dim lights whispered instructions; "watch that next turn, keep close to this, or avoid that," etc. The truck was constantly scraping trees or we were getting whacked by unseen branches. Here and there we passed ghostlike forms trying to retrieve a vehicle that had slid off the trail. At times we had to hang on to keep from falling out the front of the truck as it skidded down into deep ravines and at least at one place we had to winch up the other side. Into this nightmare world filtered the sound of the continuous artillery and occasionally an opening in the canopy above the weak reflected Glow from the sleepless searchlights could be seen. Eventually we emerged from the woods, bounced over a deep ditch onto a road. Several times in the darkness we saw mysterious fires and wandered what they were; what had caused them. then without warning our truck started slipping to the left, went into a ditch and tipped over on its side dumping us and the baggage onto the ground. The snow cushioned our fall and after taking stock, decided other than bruises we were fine. Shouldering our gear, we walked the rest of the way not really seeing where we were but following the direction of traffic we crossed some kind of bridge into Burg Rueland. Getting directions we walked east thru the dark twisting narrow street till we came to the edge of town which ended abruptly as if cut off by a knife. A short way beyond we came to the new HQ location in a house with some walls and other structures just off the right side of the road. Some of the communications platoon was already at work. A Coleman lantern gave some light inside as we got busy and hung blankets over the windows and other openings so no light would show on the outside – standard procedure!

December 18, 1944 – The truck was up righted and reached us a couple hours later which gave us a chance to get a little sleep. We unloaded the truck and put the HQ in operational order. That just amounted to setting up the field desks and crank phones, the map boards, and message center. As soon as the phones were hooked up we started receiving reports from the battalions. 2nd and 3rd Battalions made the move without incident and the artillery reported themselves in new positions near Grufflingen. Burg Rueland was along the Ulf River at its confluence with the Oure. The rivers ran in rather deep narrow valleys. Steep wooded hills on each side except the one our building was on, was very steep and barren. It may have had vineyards on it and at the ridgeline above we could see some old ruins that looked like a castle. To the east of us a few hundred yards was the edge of Burg Rueland, which ended abruptly in a line of stone houses and connecting stone walls broken only where the road entered it.

2nd Battalion held the right flank extending southward from the Ulf along the bank of the Oure, which I think was the border between Belgium and German. The 3rd Battalion held the middle from the Ulf northward to Bracht while the 1st Battalion was on the left flank and scattered from Bracht te Lemmersweiler. CCB 9th Armor was somewhere to the north but a sizeable gap existed between it and the 1st Battalion. We found Company A 27th Arm. Inf. and a platoon of the 634th AA Battalion at Maspelt, north of Bracht.

The house was dirty and had the typical musky odor. We cleaned up enough trash to make it livable and have enough room to lay out our sleeping bags then we collected a supply of firewood for the rusty iron stove and set up the gasoline generator so we could have electric lights instead of Coleman lanterns. After that, I studied the photo maps of the area to familiarize myself with the lay of the land. With everything shipshape, decided I would head up toward Bracht which at most would be three miles.

Taking my carbine and map case, I walked down thru the town and noted the broken railroad trestle crossing the Ulf and a little further on the bridge we must have crossed in the dark. Normally we would have blown the bridge, but Colonel Reid still hoped the 9th Armored would try to relieve our regiments on the mountain. They would need the bridges for their attack. North of the town I came across with a wire crew laying line to the 1st Battalion area. They are always busy; laying wire, retrieving wire, or locating broken wire and repairing it. Right now things were quiet, but they have to go right on with their work even under shell fire, day or night. At least a rifleman has the solitude of his foxhole.

A combat area is festooned with hundreds of telephone wires hanging from trees, bushes and running every which way. Along roads, a weapons carrier with a winch can ease the burden of this work, but cross country, it's two men dragging a heavy reel with them. One of the normal dangers in a combat zone is wires knocked down by shell fire and hanging low across the roads. A man riding a vehicle never sees them until too late and then zip, off goes his head. Most vehicles, jeeps especially, carry a cutting bar welded to the front bumper. All this amounts to is a piece of angle iron projecting vertically above the head at least to the height of a man's head. It will snap the wire and save the driver. I rode with them in the weapons carrier as they were making pretty good progress. I wanted to hear their experiences during the last two days anyway. I always felt a kinship for the communication boys as that's what I did when I first went in. I knew what it felt like to wear climbing caulks and hanging on to a swaying tree.

The road and railroad follow the river north a half mile then the road swings away and starts climbing and soon was in dense fir forest. Venturing into them was like entering a cave; it was so dark under the snow laden limbs. These forests are all planted, as the trees are in rows marching off into infinity; though this effect is broken by the rise and fall of the land. Passing by these trees one, minute you can see a hundred yards into the shadowy depths between the trunks then another step and the trunks limit your view to fifty feet. Of course this effect is only when one is in the forest. Along the road, where the trees get light, the limbs grow low and are bent to the ground by the weight of snow so we really could not see into the woods at all. Every quarter mile a fire lane, 75 to 100 feet across, bisects the forest. You cross these clearings as quickly as possible, because you never knew when a machine gun or sniper would have it covered waiting for a target to cross.

Saw some 3rd Battalion people and here and there beaten trails disappearing into the woods to their positions. At a bend, one of our antitank squads was camouflaging their 57mm with fir limbs and snow. Riding the truck was ok, but the two men walking stringing the wire in the trees, were cold and soaked from the snow falling from the trees onto them. as we got higher, it started misting and we passed thru patches of fog adding to the discomfort. When we reached an intersecting road I saw it was going to take them tome time to get the wire across the opening. Anyway they weren't very good company, grumpy from their discomfort and they hadn't slept in 24 hours, so I left them and headed back to Regimental HQ. We had been hearing incoming artillery to the north probably in the 9th Armored area.

Luckily I caught a ride back on a jeep towing a trailer load of ammunition. They had come through Bracht which was being shelled intermittently. He told me that C Company 81st Engr. had driven into Bracht in Service Company's trucks a short time ago. After the fight at Winterspelt yesterday, they had been sent down Winterspelter Creek to bolster Lt. Huddleson's force. Apparently they got separated and ended up in Elcherath. This was interesting as the Germans must not have reoccupied that town after 9th Armored withdrew. At any rate they spent the night there. Hearing heavy firing just north of them in the morning, they hiked to the river where they found Service Company's trucks abandoned by a foot bridge. They were tired of walking and decided to save the trucks if possible. The first two bogged down in the middle of the river, but the third one snorted and clawed its way across. Using its winch, they towed the other two out and after some rough going along the river bank followed a trail up to the Bracht road. I can imagine Service Company's embarrassment when the engineers presented the trucks to them.

All too shortly my ride came to an end as they dropped me off before turning and slipping and sliding down a side trail into the woods with the trailer of ammunition. I walked a couple hundred feet and then a messenger from 3rd Battalion picked me up and I rode all the way back to HQ. Passing thru Burg Rueland I saw a C Company 331 Medic's ambulance turn up a side alley. I made a note to check and see if that was one of their collecting stations. Also observed a TD gun had been emplaced to cover the bridge which the engineers were working on to prepare for demolition. Lucky the Germans had not followed us up or we would have been fighting for that bridge by now.

Back at the CP I checked to see what was new. VIII Corp HQ had moved out of Bastogne and was to the southwest of us. That sounded bad. The engineers were preparing the four bridges over the river for demolition, which I had already observed and the enemy was shelling Grufflingen making it hazardous for our supply vehicles that had to come thru there. Also one of our men left in the old positions last night had reported in about noon. He had fallen asleep and when he woke up, it was daylight and everyone was gone so he high-tailed it back thru the woods to rejoin his outfit. He said they were still shelling the positions, so apparently they still thought we were there. That was good. I went to one of the back rooms and dropped off to sleep. We had learned to grab some sleep whenever the opportunity offered itself.

I got up around 6pm (1800 hrs) and relieved Jim Gillum at the S-3 desk. Saw there had been some action up around Bracht and several prisoners taken. Identified as being from the 182 and 190 Inf Regiments which would be part of the 62nd VG Div. Our patrols that had been sent out to locate the 112th Reg't to the south and the 9th Armored to the north and both returned without success. Were we alone? Later that night, one of our patrols stopped a jeep coming from Ondler toward Burg Rueland because he had his headlights on. The passenger got out and walked to the front of the jeep and our fellows saw he was wearing German boots. When they move to seize him, he turned to jump back in the vehicle and they shot him, but the driver backing wildly and turning in the road got away in a blaze of gunfire. They brought the wounded man to the CP and Captain Perlman tried to find out what they were doing behind our lines. He was groaning with pain and the Captain told his guards to take the prisoner to the aid station and then the stockade, pretty brazen to be driving in our rear area with headlights on. They must have thought they were in a German held area. A search was made for the jeep and driver but he was never found.

A short time later we received a call from 3rd Battalion that they thought a tank was prowling in Burg Rueland itself. Earlier in the evening two of the bridges over the river had been blown, but Colonel Reid still saved two of them still hoping a counter attack might be made. Regardless if a tank was in town, it must have entered by some other route as the bridges were guarded. It could easily have forded the river or perhaps it came from the west. After all what was the jeep with the two Germans doing in our rear area.

We had a normal guard around HQ, but nothing to stop a tank. Captain Edwards told me I had better see if I could find a bazooka team to cover the exit from the town. I went down to message center as there are always some strays hanging around and got two riflemen who shouldn't have been there any way. I gave them a bazooka and three rounds of ammo, which was one more than they would ever need, because if you haven't hit the tank with the second round you'd better drop everything and run like hell. Ordering them to follow me I got the usual hassle about not being their NCO, but in the end grumbling they followed me though reluctant to leave the warmth of the message center. We checked thru our guards making sure of the password and countersign and warning them to watch for me as I would be returning in about a half hour. I vaguely remembered the lay of the land, but in the dark and with a foot or more of snow on the ground, it would be hard to locate the place I had in mind. There was a small stream about 200 feet from where the road exited the village so we worked our way along it until we found a satisfactory spot. It didn't offer any protection but one could see the darker opening along the edge of the village marking the road and well

104

within the range of the rocket. It was bitter cold and quiet except for the distant rumbling of artillery, we listened for any sound of a tank. Several times we heard, or thought we heard, a muted clatter and once a definite squeal as un-lubricated metal might make. After that the quiet was unbroken for 15 or 20 minutes so I told them I'd check back in an hour. They grumbled about being there and I mollified them with sympathy and the promise to bring them a canteen of hot coffee.

I didn't feel safe going back to HQ as nervous guards sometimes shoot first and challenge afterwards. Checking back with Burg Rueland revealed no new developments and patrols were still searching for any signs of the tank. So an hour later I filled a canteen with hot coffee, bundled up, and headed for the post; crawling the last hundred feet whispering the password, but no answer; again and again no answer. Moving in cautiously I verified this was where I had left them by the packed snow. What had happened? Surely they had not deserted the post! In a combat zone soldiers are shot for that. Were they taken prisoner? Hardly likely as the guards would surely have heard some commotion. I didn't relish the idea of crawling around in the dark whispering the password in hopes of locating them; especially if Germans really had captured them. However, I could think of no other options so I crawled downstream quietly calling the password and shortly heard them respond. Relieved, I still gave them hell for changing positions. They claimed they had found a more sheltered position. It was pretty miserable sitting still and exposed in this weather and they were ready to be relieved, but I told them they would have to stand one more tour and then I would have them relieve. Leaving the coffee, which was only lukewarm now, I returned to CP. During the next hour patrols reported the town clear. If there was a tank, it either was well hidden or was gone. So I just relieved them without replacements. Never did hear any more about the tank. So assume it was a false alarm.

December 19, 1944 – What little information that trickled down from division indicated a continuing deterioration of the situation in the north and another big enemy armored spearhead south of us thru the 28th Division. If division HQ was fighting at St. Vith, that was bad because who ever heard of a division HQ actually engaged in combat. That was supposed to be as safe a billet as being at home. At any rate it began to look as if we might become enveloped like the other two regiments, so the Colonel had us prepare another withdrawal plan just in case. Our chief concern was the plight of our sister regiments now encircled on the mountain. I had heard of the lost battalion in World War I, but surely we weren't going to lose two whole regiments. With the failure of the 9th Arm. and now the 7th Arm. Getting embroiled at St. Vith, the prospects of breaking the encirclement was nil. Best hope was to supply them by air so they could hold out until the Germans were driven back. We still didn't realize three German armies had been thrown into the attack.

While others were fighting for their lives, we had another relatively quiet day. The usual artillery fire interdicting Grufflingen and Bracht and the 1st Battalion again was hit by some small probing attacks from the northwest. A motor patrol sent south along the Oure River went 1 or 2 miles without locating the elusive 112th Regiment. Their Company B was still with our 2nd Battalion. I would liked to go down and see if any of the hometown fellows were still with the outfit, but they were on the extreme south end of our line and I couldn't justify the time.

Late in the afternoon, the 112th was located about five miles to our southwest and occupying a east-west line (facing south). They had beaten off several strong attacks the last two days. B Company prepared to rejoin their regiment and following an exchange of messages, Colonel Nelson (112th) came to our HQ after dark to coordinate plans between our two regiments. The discussions were to be secret, so the room was cleared. I went into the entry hall to the outside to wait until they were finished. It was pitch black in this small room about 6 foot by 8 foot in size. I had been there but a few minutes when the outside door opened partially and a shadowy bulk slipped in and melted in the darkness. I started to speak then thought better of it, because he had not made a move once inside. I could hear him breathing. How peculiar; who the devil was he and how did he get by the guard outside the door. I had heard no challenge. I couldn't think of any good reasons, so I started thinking of some bad ones.

What if he was one of these German saboteurs they slipped behind our lines, maybe just to spy or maybe he's going to toss a grenade into the CP. I did not have a weapon except that sheath knife tucked in my boot, but it had a strap with a snap. I'd have to unsnap the button and the noise would give me away. The way my heart was beating it seemed he should hear it. He shuffled his feet once, but otherwise remained quiet. When was he going to make his move; we couldn't stand here all night and anyway I felt like I wanted to sneeze. I bent over quietly and pulled the knife out of my boot, sheath and all. I remembered what a GI from 3rd Battalion told us. He tried to kill a German with a knife while his buddy held him, but he couldn't get the knife thru the soldier's heavy overcoat. They finally dispatched the German with a rifle butt. On top of that he badly cut his buddy's hands and wrist with the knife in the struggle. Great! I wondered if this fellow had on an overcoat.

When he made his move, it was to open the door and slip out as quietly as he had slipped in. now I drew my knife and stepped outside. All I saw in the darkness was the guard; collar turned up against the cold. Baffled, I said, "Who just came out that door?" he said "Nobody!"

Look I said, I stood inside with him for at least 15 minutes. You were in there all the time he asked? When I assured him I had been, he sheepishly confessed he had stepped inside to get out of the cold for a while. Good Lord, that was another case of deserting a post and I told him he was lucky I discovered it instead of the officer of the guard. I warned him of the penalty and court marshal he could face and left it go at that. Frankly I was relieved at the simplicity of the solution as to the mystery of, "Who Slipped in the Door?"

The meeting finished, Colonel Nelson returned to his regiment. They were now part of our division and would attack east in the morning to drive the enemy out of Beiler and occupy the high ground overlooking the Oure south of us. That would eliminate the big gap on our right flank. Meanwhile combat patrols would keep in contact with them the rest of the night. Later this night we received the sad and unbelievable news that apparently the two regiments and artillery on Schnee Iffel had surrendered after attacking Schonberg in a breakout attempt. Things looked blacker, 8000 men – unbelievable!

December 20, 1944 – the early hours of the 20th started with some rockets sailing in over the house and exploding with a roar on the steep slope above us. Most of us were sleeping when they howled over, and it brought us scrambling to our feet. They make a fierce noise. They kept coming over about every half hour and luckily kept hitting behind us on the slope. They stopped about daylight, but we did not get much sleep. I don't know if they were trying to hit Burg Rueland or us, but apparently to clear the ridges along the river they were hitting high.

About noon a message from the 112th informed us they had successfully made their attack and were occupying a line anchored near the river and extending west toward the Bastogne-St. Vith highway. At request of VIII Corp, one of their companies was moving south on the highway toward Batogne to help relieve that garrison. Meanwhile some enemy activity was observed in the vicinity of Maspelt in our 1st Battalion area. Late in the afternoon the Germans mounted a strong attack from northwest of Maspelt with infantry and tanks. At the same time they shelled Bracht and our artillery near Grufflingen. The 591st gunners stuck to their guns and with accurate fire directed by a small observation plane, forced the tanks to withdraw. During this attack some of our troops left their positions and marched thru Burg Rueland to our command post. Their officer said they were being overrun by tanks. Colonel Reid confronted them, told the officer firmly to turn his men around and get back to their positions; which they did. Strange because this battalion had faced the enemy well before and would do so again. Apparently rumor became a fact in their minds and they pulled out, but they certainly didn't panic, attested to by the orderly ranks on the road below regimental HQ.

These attacks coming from the northwest and west of the river indicated the enemy was still flanking us and threatening our rear. We now knew there was a 15-mile wide gap in the lines south of the 112th Infantry and the enemy was attacking or had surrounded Bastogne. The company that had been sent south to help the 101st Airborne Division at Bastogne had met strong enemy forces in the area and was withdrawing back to rejoin the 112th. In our effective strength report to division, Colonel Reid estimated we were down to 50%. Enemy action and bitter weather (trench foot) continued to whittle us down. The 112th was in about the same condition. With the disorganized situation in the rear, ammunition and supplies continued to be a problem. Trucks that did reach us reported enemy forces well to our rear. Hot meals were few and far between.

Still no sign of our air force, but luckily the enemy's was grounded too by bad weather. His buzz bombs continued to drone overhead, concealed in the heavy low clouds. During the night the 591st displaced to a new location to escape the severe counter-battery fire falling on them. The survivors of Cannon Company had formed a three gun battery and were serving with the 591st FA. We again received several volleys of rockets on the slope behind us to finish December 20th.

Information and specific details of events on other parts of our front was slow to reach us. Thru normal communications messengers: liaison officers, and supply truck drivers, we did our best to keep up. I will bring certain events up to date. As 7th Armored built up it's strength east of St. Vith called the Prumenburg position, 106t Division HQ withdrew to a new location at Veilsalm. On December 18 as division artillery and other units were withdrawing to new positions, they must have been spotted by the 1st SS Panzer which exploded southeastward and took Recht and then caught the convoys at Poteau, the place where we had stayed the night before moving into the line. As vehicles started exploding and burning from tank fire, panic issued and soon there was one huge traffic jam as individual vehicles tried to escape. A screening troop of the 32nd Cavalry put up a good but hopeless fight at Poteau. However, 18 ton tanks with 37mm cannon were no match for the 60 ton German monsters with 88mm gun and they were soon swept aside. 7th Armored had to enter the melee and finally forced the Germans out of the town and established a shaky holding line to the north. Out losses in men, vehicles, and tanks was heavy. Meanwhile CCB, 9th Armored was holding southeast of St. Vith, repelling numerous attacks from the direction of Schonberg & Winterspelt. I couldn't help but wonder what had happened to the family we had stayed with in Poteau.

December 21, 1944 – Things remained pretty quiet for us all morning, but pressure had been building up at St. Vith and a decisive battle for the town was expected today. The red marks on our operations map showed the enemy slowly but surely enveloping both us and St. Vith. In the afternoon our 3rd and 1st Battalions repulsed several attacks from the northeast and suffered casualties from heavy rocket and artillery barrages on Bracht. Of course we could plainly hear that action and received a few rounds of artillery ourselves. Later we received a report that 1st Battalion had discovered an enemy radio station in Bracht and killed the operator. He probably had been directing fire. At times we could hear distant rumbling of battle from the 9th Armored area and this continued all day.

We reexamined the ruins on the ridge as we had seen what we thought were wires on the dilapidated tower, wondered if maybe there was an enemy operator up there. Considered going up to investigate but somehow never got around to it. We heated water in our helmets to shave and maybe take a sponge bath, but none of us had bathed since England. I imagine we were pretty ripe, however since we were all in the same boat I guess we didn't notice ourselves or each other. The places we existed in had their own odors of damp and dirt plus the smell of wet wool and smoke.

Late that evening we learned that the 106th Infantry Division and the 7th Armored division were now part of the XVIII Airborne Corp which was establishing a new defensive line somewhere north of us.

December 22, 1944 – Received a message from 9th Armored about 3am to expect withdrawal orders as the enemy had penetrated the defenses along the Schonberg road and also 7th Armored positions east of St. Vith. Shortly official word came thru that our division was now attached to 7th Armored. Our 3rd Battalion was to move north and join elements of 9th Armored on a hill mass called the Braunlauf between Graufflingen and St. Vith. There to establish holding positions for the withdrawal of VIII Corp units from the pocket now threatened with encirclement. The remainder of our regiment was to move to the vicinity of Commenster with our two battalions establishing positions south of the Grufflingen-Beho road. The 112th would extend our line toward Bovigny and contact Task Force Jones. Units were to withdraw one at a time, providing covering fire for each other. 112th had the furthest to move so they had priority. We needed the time though as maps had to be studied, march orders and time schedules prepared, and vehicles and guns extricated from the snowy woods. It was daylight by the time we started moving out.

God was good as the leading edge of the blizzard that had paralyzed France and England the previous week reached us. A beautiful heavy snow started to fall to conceal our movement from any prying German eyes. Leaving a skeleton crew to keep the CP open until we opened at Commenster, we loaded into our truck. We slowly passed our slogging lines of infantry; heads down, collars up against the storm. At Oudler we stopped to check the guides who had been sent out earlier to make sure they knew their orders. Here too we met the traffic coming from the south. Its amazing the diversity and number of vehicles that move an army; we wondered who all these people were. Supply and support units that we didn't even know existed. Traffic moved slowly and I guess we could have walked to Grufflingen as quickly as we rode.

We were delayed quite a while in Grufflingen, which was one big traffic jam. Our spirits were already low with the uncertainty of the future and the cold wintry day. The snow was churned to brown ooze by the steady passage of trucks, half tracks and artillery caissons. I noticed a truck parked in the square with a load of dead GIs, their bodies frozen stiff in the position in which they died. The thought struck me that things must be bad; even the dead are getting out. The town had been shelled that last four days which was obvious from the debris and smashed vehicles. I wondered why they weren't shelling now, with the place packed with our troops. Someone said they had been shelling the crossroads to Beho intermittently all morning.

An officer from the north told us the Germans had broken the Prumenberg position last nite and probably St. Vith, 6 or 7 miles north was in their hands. They fired flares behind our tanks to silhouette them, and then blasted them with 88s. As tanks started to burn and explode, the defense crumbled. We finally got in the line of traffic and started for Commenster via Beho. Arriving at the turnoff, we merged again with traffic coming south from St. Vith and our movement became slower than ever. There were MPs, several light tanks, and armored cars at the intersection. I noted the MPs had dug slit trenches too, but we cleared the junction without any artillery fire falling and the endless column moved sluggishly southwest. Just to the north, was the Braunlauf and our 3rd Battalion; artillery was falling somewhere in that direction.

Reaching Beho, we turned north and finally arrived at Commenster late in the afternoon. Locating the advance party, we just unloaded the necessities to operate the command post, as it appeared we might no be here long. Our 591st FA was in position west of us along the Beho-Salm chateau road. We soon had telephone lines to them and Division HQ, but the rest of our communications was messengers or radio.

It was a hectic confusing night, as our units straggled in and established themselves. Their positions had to be closely established by map coordinates so that covering artillery fire could be provided if needed. Then there were new orders and orders countermanding orders and finally an order to move again. The 112th too had been moved and they were occupying a line Beho – then east of Commenster and extending northwest to Veilsalm. This was a final holding line and thru them, the delaying forces to the east (including our 3rd battalion would disengage and fall back to the bridges). Then the 112th would hope it could make it with Task Force Jones. Their chances wouldn't be good. Our two battalions were to move out after the rest of VIII Corp units got under way and pass thru Beho northwest to the bridge of Salm chateau. We lucked out again in not getting the final rearguard assignment for the troops in the pocket.

All night, we heard the rumble of trucks as Corp and division units pulled out. I think there was a road to Vielsalm and probably some of the traffic went that direction. It was going to take a lot of time to pass 30,000 men and all kinds of military vehicles across two bridges. We estimated 30 hours and that was if the Germans didn't throw a monkey wrench into the movement. Our regiment was to clear Beho by 6 am. Meanwhile enemy tanks were hitting Poteau and threatening the bridge at Veilsalm.

DECEMBER 23, 1944 – It was long before daylight when we headed west. Supposedly we were the last Americans out of Commenster and a heavy barrage hit the town shortly after we left. We fell in behind our battalions at Beho. This time they were riding, clustered like flies on 7th and 9th armored tanks and vehicles. The pace again was just a crawl. Along the dark road we passed a number of vehicles abandoned for one reason or another. I was riding in the jeep which had a 30 caliber MG on a pipe mount which I hoped we wouldn't have to use. We were all bundled up to our eyes against the biting cold. We finally dragged in to the outskirts of Salm Chateau sometime in the morning and there we finally came to a complete stop with a fantastic jam of vehicles and men ahead of us.

Groups of civilians stood shivering outside their houses, talking and watching us and glancing to the east. Some gathered around the vehicles and tried to converse, but the language barrier was too difficult to understand much. Their main concern was the Germans of course. These were Belgians and I along with others felt ashamed that we were pulling out leaving them under the yoke of the enemy again. When they were liberated a few months ago, I'm sure many of them took revenge on collaborators. Soon German sympathizers would crawl out of the woodwork to point them out to the Germans. Many probably would die before this was over. As the frosty ground haze started to dissipate we could see it was going to be a clear morning. The first sun we had seen since England. Unbelievable! A cold one though, as the breath froze on our faces. To the northeast, east, and southeast the sound of gunfire held the attention of both soldiers and civilians. I wondered what was holding us up and if the German panzers would cut us off yet. At what point did we abandon the vehicles and head for the river? Somewhere behind us men were buying time with their lives.

Unknown to us of course, our 3rd Battalion and 9th Armored tanks were fighting a desperate battle around Grufflingen, attacking the enemy to the north and southeast in order gain elbow room to extricate themselves and fall back toward the bridges. German tanks stopped the attack and then raked them with 88s and MGs as they fell back. Earlier a force of tanks and infantry came after our column as it cleared Beho, but ran into the 1st Battalion 112th and four 90 mm guns of the 811th TD (part of Task Force Jones). The 90mm guns stopped the tanks, but the desperate fight continued along the road behind us.

Sometime around 10 am we heard a strange drone of engines in the west and we saw hundreds of black specks approaching, soon revealing themselves to be our liberators (B-24s). They passed just a little to the south of us, streaking the frosty blue sky with their vapor trails. The column was endless, still coming as far as we could see. The Air Corp had finally entered the battle with this first break in the weather. A mighty cheer arose from our stalled columns of vehicles. We could see them wheeling and dropping their bombs over some target 10 or 15 miles to the east – assumed it was St. Vith; then the returning formations passed just to the north of us. We saw several planes drop out of formation and explode. Other planes, obviously damaged by German flak, struggled homeward at a slower pace, some trailing smoke. Except for short intervals, the show continued for over an hour and we could see a great pall of smoke over the target area. Above the sound of their engines though, the noise of artillery and tank fire continued. Some of it coming from due north and we wondered what was happening and why we were still sitting here.

It was afternoon before we finally crossed the high bridge over the Salm. German armor had penetrated to the river between Vielsalm and Salmchateau and self-propelled 76 mm guns were firing down the road toward the bridge. Several vehicles were burning on the road north of the bridge. The mass of vehicles crawling along the escape road was unbelievable; half tracks, tanks, ambulances, artillery, big engineering trucks hauling bulldozers, bridge equipment, tank retrieval vehicles, and of course jeeps and QM trucks. As we passed into the countryside northwest of the bridge we had a false sense of security. Unknown to us while north of us the 9th and 1st SS Panzer divisions were still advancing westward. If these two columns met, then our escape route would be slapped shut on us.

The nice clear day had given way to another storm bringing wind and show. We were thankful for the brief break in the weather that allowed our air force to launch that splendid raid. Along the road we passed many disabled vehicles abandoned in the ditches, even one of the Long Toms (155 mm long range gun). Also saw groups of refuges who had fled their homes with what they could carry. Forced off the road by military traffic, they huddled in open fields and woods without shelter to survive the terrible bitter cold blizzard that would develop as the day wore on.

Fortunately once we crossed the bridge the convoys maintained a slow but steady pace northward. The day had darkened with the winter storm and the wind was piling the snow in drifts. I thought Napoleons retreat from Moscow must have been like this, except they were horse-drawn or on foot. Numb with cold, we stoically watched the bleak landscape pass slowly by. Finally we passed thru part of the 82nd Airborne Division which was part of the new American Line being formed on the north flank of the breakthrough. We had escaped the German pincers. Our convoy stopped at a windswept intersection near Webomont until a officer from IVIII Corp assigned us a bivouac area. No shelter for the infantry; our area was an open field and the snow was now about two foot deep on the level. The whole regiment started building bonfire from fence posts, trees, old lumber. Soon an officer from Corp HQ drove up and ordered the fires extinguished as they would draw enemy artillery fire. Colonel Reed said, "my men are cold, hungry and without shelter. They need the fires to survive the night so go back to your warm headquarters and we will take a chance on any artillery."

Well it was a miserable night huddled around the fires. All night long we had to forage for fuel to keep the fires going until eventually there was no more wood to be found within walking distance. At least we had the comfort of knowing we had escaped the German trap. It had been a hectic eight days of fighting and falling back.

Now I will go back and cover the final collapse of the Salmchateau-Vielsalm bridgehead. I left the 112th, 1st Battalion desperately engaged with panzer units at Beho. They were slowly pushed back and joined other units of Task Force Jones withdrawing from the south. Together they continued to impede the Germans. Meanwhile 2nd Battalion of the 112th managed to disengage and withdraw across the river at Vielsalm about 4:30 pm. Enemy panzers however had forced their way into Salmchateau shortly after we crossed the bridge, blocking that escape route and trapping a mass of vehicles on the road from Beho. The 1st Battalion 112th found itself caught between the traffic jam on the north and the advancing enemy from the south. Enemy 88s were firing into the stalled columns and vehicles were starting to burn and explode. Panic was in the air. Colonel Nelson walked up the stalled column and found a light tank company which he extricated and with the 1st Battalion they found a side road toward the river. The road ended at a marsh or swamp. With the tanks helping the trucks and jeeps, they managed to cross both the frozen swamp and the river.

Having reached the west bank of the Salm, they still had to move north past the Germans at the bridge. The 229th FA laid a protective barrage of fire between them and the enemy as they raced north to join the tail of our column. Out of more than a hundred vehicles they only lost eighteen. Quite a feat – Western Pennsylvania can be proud of their National Guard Regiment. It didn't give up when things looked blackest.

Other units in that trapped column managed to escape. Many on foot managed to reach our lines the next day. The 440th Armored FA Battalion (part of Task Force Jones) found itself cut off at Salmchateau, charged up the road to Vielsalm in a running gunfight and crossed the bridge to safety. It lost one self propelled howitzer n the melee.

On Hwy 16 north of Houffalize at a crossroad named Baraque de Fraiture, the 3 gun battery of our 589 FA that had run the gauntlet of enemy tanks at Schonburg (where the rest of the battalion had been destroyed) had dropped its trails and formed a roadblock. They were joined by survivors of 589th Service Company. As time passed other groups joined them: 203rd AAA with 3 multiple 50 caliber MGs, a couple of light tanks from 87th Rec, a Tank Destroyer platoon and miscellaneous infantry and paratroopers. Virtually surrounded, this motley bunch held their position, blocking this key highway against enemy attacks starting on December 19th until they were overwhelmed on December 23 by the 2nd SS Panzer Division. Their action (unplanned) was one of the decisive delaying actions of the battle. Holding the Germans for four days certainly was decisive in the escape of our forces from the Vielsalm-

Salmchateau bridgehead and it gave time for the 82nd Airborne and 3rd Armored to establish themselves on the open north flank.

We learned the extent of the breakthrough this night. The 2nd Panzer Division (not to be confused the 2nd SS Panzer facing us) had penetrated nearly 60 miles west into our rear area and was near the Noselle River in France. The 9th SS Paner was a few miles east of us at a place called Trois Pnt and the 1st SS Panzer was stalled at Stavelot to the northeast. The 2nd SS Panzer was coming up from the south on Hwy 16 right at us. Meanwhile the 116th Panzer (that had hit us the first day) was moving in from the southwest. On top of all this, the 18th and 62nd Infantry Divisions and the Fuhrer Panzer Escort Brigade would be following up from Vielsalm-Salmchateau. We apparently jumped from the frying pan into the fire. The prize was National Hwy 16 that ran from Basel, Switzerland right north thru Werbomont, Liège and Antwerp. If these converging panzers could break through here they could romp right up to the North Sea in the rear areas of the US 9th Army, the British 2nd Army, and the Canadian 1st Army.

To oppose them on Hwy 16 we had the remnants of the 7th Armored Division and our 424th Infantry Regiment. To the west was the 3rd Armored Division and to the east was the 82nd Division. Elements of the 7th Armored were sent south the evening of the 23rd to occupy the villages of Grandmenel and Manhay thus closing the gap between 3rd Armored and 82nd Airborne Division. Again it seems strange that a battered outfit down to 40% effective strength should be sent to hold crucial Hwy 16 while two fresh divisions held the flanks.

DECEMBER 24 – We spent the day licking our wounds so to speak and preparing what shelter we could for comfort; no hot meals but a supply of unit size rations were a welcome change from K-rations. I learned that 7th Armored had been hit by 2nd Panzer before dawn and driven out of Grandmenel and Manhay, falling back toward Werbomont. Later that day we were ordered to provide one battalion to help 7th Armored retake the villages on Christmas day. Our 2nd Battalion was pegged for this, being in the best shape. Meanwhile we received several hundred replacements, mostly GIs who had escaped the surrender on Schnee Iffel. It still left us about 50% effective strength. That afternoon regimental headquarters moved south and established its CP in a building overlooking the broad valley wherein lay Grandmenel, Manhay, and the 2nd SS Panzers. All during the night heavy concentrations of our artillery fire screamed overhead on their way to targets in the valley.

DECEMBER 25 – The 7th Armored plan to retake the villages consisted of two battalions of infantry supported by two tank companies, our 2nd Battalion attacking down the west side of Hwy 16, and the 48th Arm. Infantry Battalion on the east side. After a preparatory shelling, the attack got under way and progressed slowly most of the day. The attack was over fairly open ground, exposing our troops to a wicked crossfire from MGs firing from basements in the two villages. The attack got within 50 yards of Manhay and then stalled. The supporting tanks never really got into the fight as they were held at bay by several well emplaced 88 mm tank guns.

Withdrawing at dusk the 2nd Battalion tried to regroup on Hill 522, a barren hump on the valley floor. German 88s and artillery caught them there in the open causing heavy casualties. What had been the strongest battalion in the regiment was now the weakest; suffering 35% casualties in the day's fighting. The rest of Christmas night the wounded and dead were dragged back thru the deep snow on improvised sleds and canvas shelter halves.

Meanwhile an officer, remaining on the outskirts of Manhay while our artillery was shelling to cover the withdrawal of the battalion, noticed the Germans were withdrawing (a tactic sometimes used during heavy shelling to reduce casualties – then reoccupying when the shelling stopped). With this information, elements of our attacking force including tanks returned and occupied Manhay ahead of the Germans and there things stood as Christmas day came to an end.

The rest of the regiment received the Christmas dinner Corp had promised us: turkey and most of the trimmings to go with it. It kind of stuck in our throats as we ate that nite thinking of the misery and suffering out on that bleak snow covered hill. Some Christmas! We didn't sing any carols.

DECEMBER 26 – The enemy returned before dawn. Charging with infantry and tanks, drove our forces out of Manhay again. Preparations were made for another attack. In yesterday's attack 2nd Battalion was attached to the 7th Arm. And our regiment was not otherwise involved. In today's fight we would have a major role with 2nd Battalion reinforced with L Co 3rd Battalion attacking Manhay astride Hwy 16 while 1st Battalion would attack Grandmenel. Also participating in the attack would be the 28th Arm Inf. Battalion, a battalion from the 82nd Airborne would attack from the east and a battalion from the newly arrived 75th Division would attack Grandmenel from the northwest. Tanks from 7th Arm. would add muscle to the effort.

110

Our artillery put two TOTs on Manhay just before the attack started around 9 am. TOT means Time on Target, in which each of the dispersed artillery battalions time their fire so that all the shells arrive and explode over the target at the same instant. This has a devastating effect as the enemy has no warning or time to seek shelter. Later inspection revealed about 350 Germans were killed and 80 vehicles destroyed by artillery fire in Manhay. Grandmenel was given the same treatment, but forewarned, the troops there sought shelter and the casualties were much less. Of course the artillery continued to shell the two villages as the infantry worked their way close enough for the final assault.

E Company 2nd Battalion attacking down Hwy 16 finally sought shelter in the roadside ditches from the punishing mortar, artillery, and MG fire sweeping the road. Their attack stopped, mortar fire was still exacting a toll in the ditches. Then one of those unexplainable things happened, the battalion chaplain drove down that fire swept road and stopped to give first aid to some of the wounded in the ditch. Then he carried a seriously wounded GI to his jeep and drove back up the road to the first aid station. Inspired by the chaplains actions, E Company got up from the ditches and charged into the outskirts of Manhay, closely followed by the rest of the battalion. About the same time the battalion from 82nd Airborne entered the east end of the village. After several hours of house-to-house fighting and mop up, Manhay was again in our hands. Tanks were quickly moved in to solidify the position.

The 1st Battalion attacked and entered Granmenel and fought house-to-house until they met the battalion from the 75th Division moving in from the northeast. Now both objectives were taken, not to be relinquished this time. The 2nd Panzer was stopped and now the buildup of our forces on the north flank would doom any further hopes of the Germans to break out. We were proud to have had a major role in the Battle of Manhay that stopped the momentum of a panzer attack dead in its tracks.

Yesterday, far to the west of us, our 2nd Armored Division and British units fought a desperate battle with the 2nd Panzer Division in France and stopped their westward drive. From now on we would do the attacking as the Germans would be slowly pushed back to where they started. Hitler's big gamble had lost. The delaying actions by the units overrun the first days caused the enemy to miss his time schedule and block his northern thrusts. He had made a penetration in our lines approximately 40 miles wide by 60 miles deep and all for nothing. Now, short on gasoline, many of his valuable tanks would have to be abandoned in the Ardennes.

DECEMBER 27-30, 1944 – During the attacks on Manhay and Grandmenel, our infantry complained that our tanks gave them little close support until the objectives were taken. They referred to the 7th Armored as the mechanized road blocks. To be fair one has to recognize that the 7th Armored had fought a desperate series of battles for over a week and in the process had lost heavily in tanks and tank crews. By the time of our action at Manhay and Grandmenel they had to conserve what tanks they had left. At that point infantry was expendable and could be replaced far quicker than tanks. Of course this reasoning was of no consolation infantry huddled in the snow and being raked by 88s, mortar, and machine gun fire.

After the retaking of the two villages, they were eventually abandoned as we built up defensive positions on the north slope of the valley. Behind us a massive array of artillery was concentrated on a three mile front straddling the highway. The Germans tried to concentrate a number of times in the succeeding days to resume their advance but the massed fire of 300 artillery pieces smothered them each time. The carnage inflicted must have been terrible. I was told the new proximity fuses were used here (first time in Europe). Shrapnel shells have to detonate in the air spraying their lethal splinter downward on the troops to be effective. This required calculating the time of flight for the shell to reach the target area and then setting the time fuse on it. Obviously error would result in some shells exploding too high in the air or hitting the ground before detonating. The proximity fuse detonated at a predetermined distance above the ground thus vastly reducing error and resulting in a much faster rate of fire; as calculations and setting of the old time fuses was eliminated.

In any event the days following our taking the two villages were constantly shaken by artillery drumfire. An almost continuous ripping and tearing in the air above us, hundreds of shells passed over us to fall on one target after another in the valley. It was quite an experience and we were grateful they were our shells.

Finally on the night of December 30, we were relieved by the 75th Div. It was a windless cold night , the snow lay heavy on the ground. As our men moved toward the rear, another shadowy line moved in the opposite direction. Any noise we made was drowned out by our artillery overhead. Looking back thru the darkness we could see the twinkling of little lights, flashing on the dark hills across the valley Like fire flies on a summer night. Except, they were our shells exploding along the German lines to make the enemy keep their heads down.

It hardly seemed possible only two weeks had passed since that first terrible barrage had hit us and the Germans came out of the eastern darkness. In that time our division had lost over half of its men. We were headed for a rear area; that meant baths, clean clothes, hot meals and replacements to bring us back to combat strength. Now we were veterans turning our positions over to a green outfit fresh from England. Their time of testing was coming up but their fortune too as they would be the first to meet the advancing Russian troops at the Elbe.

[To contain the German drive, 3rd Army under Patton cancelled its drive to the Rhine. Pivoting north it rammed into the southern flank of the bulge. The 1st Army under Hodges delayed its attack on the Roer river dams and plugged the northern exits from the bulge. By the end of December the momentum of the panzers had been stopped and their plans to wheel north defeated. Unable to capture large fuel supplies, the tanks ground to a stop and many were dug in to serve as steel pill boxes. With clearer weather our air force returned to the fray. Now we were ready to push him back from where he started.]

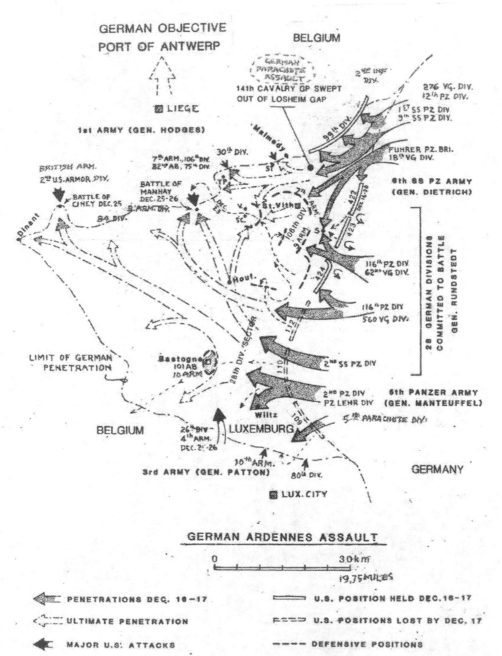

GERMAN OBJECTIVE
PORT OF ANTWERP

BELGIUM

GERMAN ARDENNES ASSAULT

0   30km

19.75 MILES

⇐   PENETRATIONS DEC. 16-17   ⎯   U.S. POSITION HELD DEC.16-17

⇐   ULTIMATE PENETRATION   ⊏⊐   U.S. POSITIONS LOST BY DEC. 17

◄   MAJOR U.S. ATTACKS   ⎯ ⎯   DEFENSIVE POSITIONS

SC (SALMCHATEAU)) TP (TROIS POINT) S (SCHONBERG)

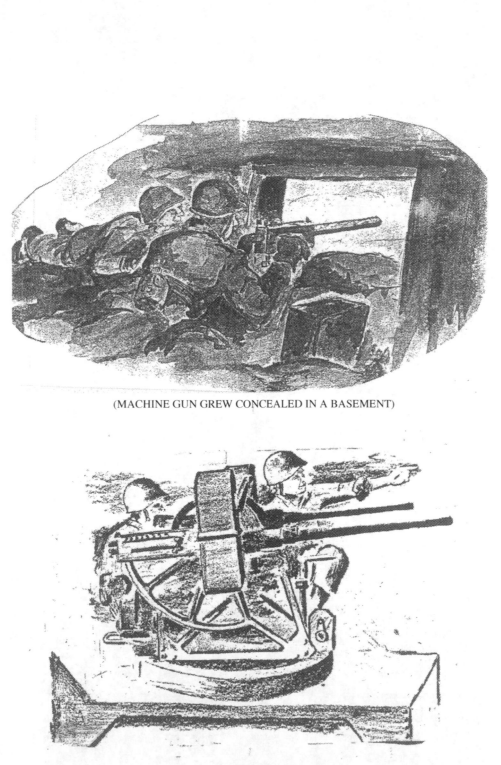

(MACHINE GUN GREW CONCEALED IN A BASEMENT)

DUAL FIFTIES, GUN MOUNT

57mm AT GUNCREW IN ACTION

WITHDRAWAL TOWARD THE BRIDGES AT VEILSALM & SALMCHATEAU

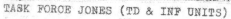

TASK FORCE JONES (TD & INF UNITS)

STRINGING TELEPHONE LINES

GERMANS ATTACK OUR ARTILLERY CONVOY AT POTEAU.
AMERICAN LIGHT TANKS NO MATCH AGAINST HEAVIER
ENEMY TANKS.

AMERICAN SPEAKING GERMANS WEARING OUR UNIFORMS
AND USING CAPTURED EQUIPMENT AMBUSHED OUR TROOPS

JANUARY 1 1945

New Years Eve found the regiment billeted in villages around the vicinity of Anthienes, Belgium (south of Liège). Here we were to recuperate from the trauma of the Ardennes for a few days. Four of us lucked out to get a vacant room on the 2nd floor of a building near the center of the village. No heat, no beds, but it beat the accommodations of the previous month. After attending to such duties as were required at headquarters we had the rest of the evening free. Washed up the best we could, shaved in lukewarm water, knocked the dirt and mud off our shoes and uniforms and prepared to see what the village had to offer. Fortunately we had the remnants of a bottle of Calvados and one of cognac to start on. Obviously the few cafes were jammed shoulder-to-shoulder with GIs, however it was relaxing to do what drunks do well together; sing, swap stories, swap drinks and bedevil the waitresses which were the only females around. Prudent parents kept their daughters locked in. we managed to avoid the fights that erupted without reason in that mob.

Calvados, cognac, and red wine are not to be recommended as a good mixture and by New Years hour our condition was deteriorating. It was a struggle to get through the crowd and reach the door, but the cold crisp air was a relief from the smoke and noise. One of our number was already past the point of locomotion so we took turns supporting Sgt. X between us as we staggered along the snow covered streets looking for our billet. None of us were too steady. Considering our condition we were lucky to find the right building but there it was; the three stone steps up to the narrow double door. Beyond the door a narrow flight of stairs culminating at the door to our room which opened out over the stairs. No landing at bottom or top; a difficult situation for a sober person, but a real challenge for 3 drunks and one completely limp body.

Well we managed the first obstacle: up the three steps and thru those confounded spring operated double doors. Each door was only 16 inches wide and seemed to have minds of their own, slamming shut on us as we struggled to drag the limp body of Sgt X up thru them. They pinched our hands and grabbed our feet. Finally thru the doors, we rested in the darkness on the stairs getting our breath for the final assault. Grasping Sgt X by the collar we reached the head of the stairs only to wait while we fumbled for the door. Suddenly Sgt X, who had been docile but complaining, started to flail his arms and stiffening out his legs; he shot out of our grasp. He bumped down the stairs and hit the doors with a thump. There was a brief glimmer of light as the doors slammed open and then shut with a vengeance. We stood aghast a moment in the darkness and ominous silence, then scrabbled down fearful that he probably broke his neck.

After passing thru the door he slid across the curb and to the gutter in the middle of the snow covered cobbled street. There he lay stiff as a board, but breathing peacefully. The Lord does watch over drunks. He had slid head first all the way; figured the helmet liner must have saved him. He gave us no trouble this time as we dragged him up and deposited him in his sleeping bag, clothes and all. Next morning we were a sad bunch with splitting hangovers. I guess we never learn. The Sgt remembered nothing of the nite before and in addition to his hangover, became obsessed with the bruises all over his body. As he pondered these he became convinced he had beaten him with clubs and got quite angry. So we finally told him what had happened which didn't help much and it was several days before our relationship normalized.

The next few days were busy but pleasant as we drew supplies. The company kitchens were set up and a steady diet of hot food instilled new life. Then company by company we were trucked to a big bath center where we shed our dirty uniforms and underwear, proceeded thru hot steamy showers, and ended up in clean clothes on the other side. They might not fit, but they were clean. Meanwhile weapons were cleaned and brought up to par; vehicles repaired and ammunitions built up to unit strength. Replacements fleshed out the line companies. I always felt sorry for the replacements because the combat platoon or squad is sort of a closed society of survivors forged in the rigors of shared hardships. It takes time before the newcomer is accepted (time and shared hardship), and sometimes he becomes a casualty and gone before anyone really knows his name.

During this period more of the men who had escaped the encirclement on Schnee Eifel joined our regiment. I will degress form my story to tell what happened to the lost reqiments during those four days (December 15-19, 1944). I had to refer to division history' ST. Vith-Lion int the Way " by Col. Dupuy (Infantry Journal) to fill gaps in my knowledge of events.

120

SCHNEE EIFEL Dec 16-21 1944

See map on page 126

The Schnee Eifel is described as an old volcanic mass of forested hills, valleys, and ravines dominating the surrounding landscape. One main road called Skyline Drive dissected the area with difficult twisting approaches at the north and south ends. Otherwise it was back roads and trails with small villages huddled in the depressions. The German Zeigfreid line of fortifications marched across its eastern face. North was the Losheim valley (German invasion route in 3 wars). East was Schonberg, the Oure River and Belgium. To the south was the Bliealf Gap. In winter the area was covered by low clouds above and fog mist and snow below; a perpetual gloom in the forests that sapped the spirit.

The defense line faced southeast along and amongst the Zeigreid fortifications; the 422 Regiment (Colonel Duscheneaux) on the left with the 1st and 3rd battalions on the line, the 2nd Battalion was regimental reserve. the 423 Regiment (Colonel Cavander) extending to the right or southwest with its 3rd and 1st Battalions, the 2nd Battalion was Division reserve near St. Vith, and the 589 and 592 FA Battalions were southwest of Auw. Further south near Radscheid was the 590 FA Battalion. Other units (804 TD Company, 81E A&B Company, 634AA) were scattered as supporting units.

16 DEC 1944 – About 5:30 am artillery, rockets and mortar fire pounded the front lines and rear areas disrupting the telephone system; mainstay of military communications. This was followed by German infantry advancing out of the predawn darkness. These attacks were all repulsed. Tree bursts flashed and cast lethal swarms of shrapnel and torn tree limbs downward. To the north enemy armor and infantry brushed the 18 Cavalry outpost at Roth aside and pushed west toward Auw. This forced the 422nd to commit its 2nd Battalion to extend its line westward thus the defense line was shaped like a V with the apex pointing northeast. By 9 am the attack from Roth was pushing up into Auw where the surprised engineers fought a desperate holding action house-to-house.

By early afternoon tanks were moving south on Skyline Drive and threatening the 589 FA which lowering its howitzers engaging the armored vehicles with direct fire. After several armored vehicles were damaged or destroyed, they withdrew to protected locations but continued their probing attacks. About 2 pm Colonel Descheneaux ordered Cannon and L Companies to attack Auw. While failing to retake the town it stabilized the situation for the time. German probing attacks continued the rest of the day.

The 106 Division HQ at St. Vith (6 miles to the west) became concerned about enemy armor approaching Schonberg from Andler. This was one of the keys to the defense of St. Vith and had to be held. At 12:30 pm if ordered Colonel Pruit to take the 2/423 Battalion with a platoon of 804 TD to Schonberg. However, seeing that the artillery south of Auw had to be moved immediately to safety, it changed Pruits orders and for him to continue on to provide a covering force while artillery was extracted, then to return to defend Schonberg.

During the night of December 16-17 the 592 FA successfully displaced to a new location west of St. Vith. The 589 FA was far more difficult because of its proximity to the enemy but most of it managed to displace to a new location on west side of the Bliealf-Schonberg Road. However, C Battery proved too difficult and its guns were destroyed and abandoned.

To the south the 423 Regiment weathered any direct attacks on its main line of defense but a strong enemy force coming around the southern tip of Schnee Eifel threatened his right rear. Already the 106 Rcn Company holding the road at Grosslangenfeld was under attack. Colonel Cavander created a provisional battalion of HQ and Ser Co personnel plus whoever else could be scraped up to help B Company 81 E hold Bliealf. So as December 16 ended the 422nd was threatened from the rear. The artillery had to displace and the 423rd was threatened on its right flank.

17 DEC 1944 – The planned U.S. armored counterattack to drive the Germans back never occurred. I've told what happened to it earlier in my journal. The Germans launched their attack on Bliealf at 6:30 am via railroad tunnel and the road, quickly driving the defenders out of the town. Soon the enemy was probing up the road to Schonberg and up Skyline Drive and now threatened the 590 FA positions. The 589 FA, just getting reestablished, found it had jumped from the frying pan into the fire. Germans moving up from Bliealf now forced it to make a run for the supposed safety of Schonberg only to arrive there about the same time as the tanks from Andler. Only 3 guns of Battery A managed to escape. As the trapped column disintegrated, many men managed to escape at least for a time. Later B Troop 18 Calvary and part of 106 Rcn Company tried the same escape route which ended in disaster.

Pruit and his 2nd Battalion prepared to return to Schonberg following the successful withdrawal of the artillery. A new enemy attack from Auw forced him to meet this new threat. Knocking out four armored vehicles they broke up the attack. Learning that Schonberg was now in German hands out of touch with Division at St. Vith and the 422 Regt he joined forces with the 590 FA and they moved east to the 423 Regt defense perimeters around Oberlascheid and Buchet.

The main division switchboard was destroyed when Schonberg was captured and communications depending solely on radio quickly deteriorated. Messages were delayed for hours. News that the 7th and 9th armored attack was scheduled for morning wasn't received until 3 pm. It raised false hopes not knowing the attack had already failed. 422nd reported rations getting low and the 423rd low on ammunition. Unknown to division the promised airdrops never occurred. The weather was cold, foggy, and misty with occasional snow flurries. The trails and roads were a muddy, frozen slush. Trench foot continued to take its toll and now battle casualties started to pile up at the collecting stations which no longer could send them back to the receiving hospital. December 17 ended with false expectations the relieving forces would reach them the coming day.

18 DEC 1944 – At 2:30 am a delayed message was received ordering a joint attack on Schonberg then to continue across the Oure River and establish a defensive line toward St. Vith. It failed to designate one of the regimental commanders to be in charge; a serious command mistake. Nor did it explain how it expected an infantry force without artillery or tanks and low on ammunition to break through a strong established panzer force. It would require abandonment of the defenses on the east so as they assembled for the attack they would be fighting a rear guard action as well. Further delay before Colonel Cavander could forward the order to the 422 Regt. They agreed to start moving to their assembly areas soon after dawn. The 422nd had the furthest to go, maybe 3 miles or so. Not far under normal conditions but in rugged terrain and slippery trails it was evening before the last, including prisoners, struggled into the assembly area. This was a ravine to the east of Skyline Drive. F Company missed the assembly area and contact with the regiment. It seems in view of the events of the following day it would have been better if the regiment had pushed on to the high ground overlooking Schonberg like the 423rd did. Now probably hungry as well as tired they tightened their belts and prepared for another cold night. Many had discarded their overcoats during the hard hike.

The 423 Regiment, its 2nd Battalion leading, started northwestward and on reaching Skyline Drive at Radscheid was attacked by the enemy moving up from Bliealf. The aggressive Pruit counterattacked driving them back toward the Schonberg Road, capturing a German 88 mm gun in the process. He then withdrew and dug in along the high ground. The third battalion bypassed the fight and continued toward the assembly area on hill 504 about a half mile south of Schonberg. The 1st Battalion was diverted and swung south to protect Pruits left flank. The 590 FA apparently remained in the vicinity of Oberlasheid while A Battery supported the 1st and 2nd Battalion action.

Later the 3rd Battalion lost contact with the rest of the regiment and as it was approaching hill 504 its left flank was fired on including flak. Attacking the battalion reached a position astride the road about a half mile south of the Schonberg and held the position in spite of heavy shelling. After nightfall companies F/422 and F/423 drifted into the assembly area. Later Company F/422 headed south (? Confusion) looking for its 422 regiment. Colonel Cavander ordered his 1st and 2nd Battalions to break contact with the enemy in the south and move to the assembly area leaving Company A as rear guard. The 422nd had relatively easy day compared to the 423rd which had to fight all the way. The medics and the wounded had to be left behind to whatever fate awaited them. What had happened to the air drops and where was that promised relief? The men settled down with mixed emotions to await the coming day as December 18 ended.

19 DECEMBER 1944 – The 423 Regiment was about at half strength as it prepared to attack Schonberg a half mile down the slope, 3rd Battalion on the left with 1st and 2nd Battalions ensconced to its right. At 9 am the air seemed to explode as artillery salvos fell on the troops followed by 20 and 40 mm flak sweeping the area. Shaken, the 3rd Battalion regrouped and started their attack about 10 am. For a moment they thought help had arrived as a Sherman tank lumbered into view. Instead it raked their flank with cannon and M.G. fire. What more could happen? Plenty!

The 590 FA was overrun by the Bliealf forces advancing from the south. Now there was no friendly artillery barrage to smother the resistance. The 3rd Battalion reached the outskirts of the town but could do no more. By 3 pm they had fallen back to the slopes of Hill 504. The 1st Battalion Company B, supported by HQ Company, reached the Schonberg road only to be pinned down. Having received no orders by 2 pm, Pruit decided to take his 2nd Battalion (regiment reserve) around to the right and attack from the east. Moving into the ravine of Linne Creek they met a blaze of gunfire from their right flank.

Shaken, they regrouped and resisted this surprise attack until the mistake was discovered – it was the 3/422 Battalion that had blundered into them and fired. Now, badly disorganized it ended their attack. So by 3pm Colonel Cavander found himself about back where had had started with remains of 3rd Battalion, the 1st Battalion destroyed and out of touch with the 2nd Battalion. I fail to understand this lack of communication. If radios failed, runners could have maintained contact.

The 422 Regiment began its attack at 9 am with its 1st Battalion on the right, 2nd Battalion to the left, and 3rd Battalion to follow as regimental reserve. Now we see the mistake of not pushing on the previous evening. C Company was hit by 20 mm and M.G. fire as it crossed Skyline Drive and disintegrated. One platoon managing to reach the high ground beyond. Tanks moving south from Auw overran A and B Companies and that finished the 1st Battalion.

The 2nd Battalion (less the lost Company F) managed to cross Skyline and reach the high ground overlooking Schonberg 1000 yards away. They could see the Andler-Schonberg Road jammed bumper to bumper with military vehicles. Somehow thinking these the long awaited relieving forces, they advanced out on the open slope; bad decision, for those were German transport and many carried 20 and 40 mm flak guns. A devastating fire swept the exposed battalion. H Company managed to get its mortars and heavy M.G.s in action until destroyed. Badly hit, the 2nd Battalion sought the shelter of the woods; OR reached the regimental motor pool perimeter on Hill 575.

The 3/422 Battalion, moving more westerly, avoided the fate of the 2/422 Battalion, but stumbled into the fire fight with 2/423 Battalion. Unable to organize to continue the attack and still unable to contact his 423 HQ, Pruit joined the 3/422 Battalion and formed a defensive perimeter. Both tanks and infantry were closing in on them. with the wounded piling up and no medicine, food or water it was the end and Colonel Duscheneaux sent out a white flag bout 3 pm. Colonel Pruit requested permission that he and his men be allowed to try and escape. That request was refused. Colonel Cavander in a similar situation reached the same conclusion about 4 pm and surrendered those of the 423 Regiment that were with him.

Isolated groups still wondered in the wooded hills, most eventually hunted down. The largest group of 500 or so formed a defensive perimeter on Hill 575 including some guns of the 634 AA and 804 TD. They held out until 8 am December 21. Others successfully made their escape back to our lines to fight again.

As I put this account together it made me thankful my original assignment to the 422 Regiment was changed to the 424 Regiment, thus sparing me the ordeal they suffered and the captivity (if one made it) that followed. Based on limited information, I did the best I could to explain what happened on Schel Eifel. Perfect or not I thought the story should be told.

In retrospect, was all this necessary or was it the result of bad command decisions? It was said some officers objected to the order to attack, arguing it would be better to remain in their defenses among the bunkers of the Zeigfreid line. Supplied by air they could hold out for weeks forcing the Germans to come to them. Good point!

Lets look at a similar situation to the south. The 101 AB and CCB10 Arm Divisions blocked the Germans from taking Bastonge but were quickly surrounded as 4 Panzer division bypassed on the north and south continuing deep into our rear areas. Supplied by air, 101 AB had enough to hang on but insufficient to attack the enemy supply columns flowing around them. In essence we not only lost the use of one of the best assault divisions but also the 3rd Army sent to their relief. How much better (maybe) if Patton had launched his planned attack into German instead; it would have brought the Germans to a screeching halt in the Ardennes as they deployed to meet Patton's threat. This would relieve the pressure all across the front.

(DEADLY SKERMISHES IN FOG

SHROUDED RAVINES AND FOREST)

124

Without tanks, airforce or artillery support
the infantry break-out attempt failed and the
survivors became prisoners of war.

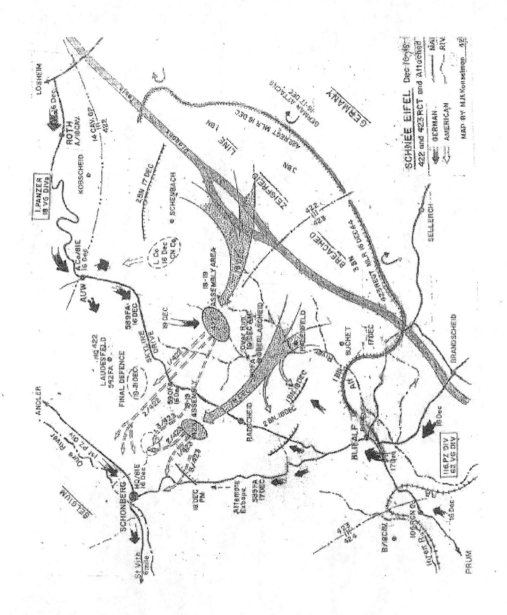

Now to pick up my story, we received orders to move to the vicinity of Trois Pont, Belgium and relieve the 112th Infantry. This was the area where the 1st and 9th SS Panzer divisions had been stopped in a free for all. It was elements of the 9th that had hit us at Vielsalm – Salmchateau.

It was a gray and misty day as we moved up. Not very cold, but the dampness chilled one to the bones. The busy traffic had churned many of the roads into a mixture of mud and snow. I was riding a jeep with the advance party. Though safely in a rear area, at one place we received some sniper fire. Later we found a fresh gouge on the jeep where a bullet had ricocheted. At an intersection outside of town, we threaded our way thru a junkyard of German vehicles, anti-tank guns, and equipment destroyed and abandoned – signs of a bitter struggle. As we went thru a railroad underpass, we noted a large unexploded bomb lying by the stone abutment. The railroad yards were a mess. Trois Pont was at the confluence of several rivers that flowed in steep, rugged valleys. We were supposed to set up our Regimental HQ at Aisemont on the high ground a few miles further south. However that village was so badly shot up there wasn't a suitable building available so we spent some time in Trois Pont while the adjutant scouted for another location for the CP. With time to kill we explored the town which appeared to be in the condition that the battle had left it. Apparently the surviving civilians had fled and not yet returned.

Some of the buildings had the entire front blown off, exposing the rooms like a dollhouse. In one of these rooms an old man lay dead in bed. No wound was apparent. He may have died of shock or exposure. In another house we found a boy of maybe 12 dead on the kitchen floor. The congealed blood from his head wound had frozen him to the rough wood flooring. The basement of a barn or out building was a macabre scene. In it were the frozen stacked bodies of 25 to 30 civilians; that they didn't all die of natural deaths was evident from the horrible discolored bruises or smashed features of the faces. Here and there outside, mounds in the snow indicated where other dead probably lay.

In a deep railroad cut leading to a tunnel, we found the remnants of a train that had been blown up. The debris from the cars littered the steep banks on both sides, but the trucks wheels and twisted floor frames remained on the tracks. All that remained of the engine were the big drive wheels and twisted pile of boiler tubes. It must have been a fancy engine with a big German imperial eagle on the front as we found the crumpled remains of the eagle about fifty yards up the track. I guess our fighter bombers must have been waiting and nailed the train as it came out of the tunnel. We also came across several dozen graves with German crosses. Unlike our practice of retrieving our dead, they often bury their dead where they died. As to whether the civilian dead here represented a German atrocity or were just the unfortunate victims of battle I don't know; however, a few miles east at Malmady 125 American prisoners were machine gunned by their SS captors and left dead in a field by the road. The SS troops had been ordered to not burden themselves with prisoners.

This was the furthest west that Peipers marauding panzer assault force reached. They needed the bridges at Trois Point so they could turn north toward Liège and Antwerp. A small force of engineers managed to blow the bridges in the face of the enemy and with elements of the 30th Infantry Division held the town despite desperate attacks by the Germans. Frustrated, the enemy withdrew a little to the east then struck north to La Gliese still trying to break out of this tangled rough terrain onto the flat land. Again they were blocked by hastily assembled elements of the 82nd Airborne Division. From that point the enemy would start retracing his steps abandoning many vehicles with empty fuel tanks along the way.

We set up the regimental HQ in the wreckage of a farmhouse clinging to the side of a steep hill on the road to Aisemont. It was a nasty place littered with debris and signs of recent German occupancy. They had relieved themselves all over the place and it stank. They also had left a number of potato masher grenades scattered about. These we didn't touch as some of them were probably booby trapped.

We learned that the 517th Parachute Regiment was moving into positions east of us at Stavelot, and together we were to drive the Germans out of their positions south of us. The engineers were busy with bulldozers clearing the roadways of snow for the coming attack. It was rough work and cleared roads still had a layer of snow and ice on them with four foot banks of snow on each side. The attack would pretty well be limited to the road network as it was virtually impossible to flounder cross-country in that snow. White camouflage was a must, as plain uniforms were deadly on that landscape. By this time there probably wasn't a bed sheet left in all Belgium.

The attack would be over relatively open high ground divided by a deep valley. We would have the high ground on the right of the valley and the 517th would attack parallel to us but on the left side of the valley. Our attack plan was with the 3rd Battalion on the left, 1st Battalion on the right, and 2nd battalion in reserve near Aisemont. The

517 would launch their attack by crossing the Ambleve River on rubber pontoon bridges from the vicinity of Stavelot. The 740th Tank Battalion attached a company of shermans to each regiment as support. However, because of mechanical failures and snow, the tanks proved of no use. Many of the American tanks still had standard pads on their treads which provided no traction on snow. Once they started to slide there was no stopping until they toppled into a ditch or hit some immovable object. The German tanks we saw had steel cleats and they could claw their way thru snow or ice.

13 JANUARY 1945 – At 8 am in bitter cold, the regiment started its attack and by midday the 1st Battalion had taken the enemy forward positions around Lavaux and repulsed one enemy counterattack. Continuing up over the high ground and into the Ponceau ravine, that battalion was stopped by heavy artillery crossfire and gunfire from enemy tanks and self propelled 75s (SPs). A Company Commander was killed and B Company Commander wounded. The battalion staff was caught in raking tank fire, mortally wounding the popular S-2 Lt Huddleson and the Battalion Commander – the S-3 1st Battalion fell back to the ridge and dug in. Lt. Huddleson had both fee blown off, but it was the cold and terrible delay in getting the wounded back to the aid station that probably caused his death. He was a brave and capable leader and we mourned our loss.

The 3rd Battalion in its attack on Henumont encountered strong resistance from well emplaced machinegun nests and rocket fire. After destroying several machinegun positions it launched a flanking attack then a frontal attack which were both repulsed. A tank supported assault was cancelled because the tanks never arrived. So the battalion dug in for the nite a half mile short of its objective. An air strike would have been helpful, but in all our fighting we never received direct air support. Henumont sat on 517th's side of the valley, but gunfire from it enfiladed our line of advance. Our artillery shelled it all night and in the morning, the 1st Battalion of the 517th entered the town from the east only to find the Germans had pulled out during the nite.

14 JANUARY 1945 – With Henumont no longer a threat, the 3rd Battalion shifted its attack to the south. During the night 2nd Battalion had moved up from reserve and moved thru the 1st Battalion to resume the attack on Coquaimont Ridge. By evening all objectives had been taken and the line companies were digging in against the expected German counterattacks. We moved regimental headquarters up to Aisomont. As reported it had been pretty well battered and the building we settled in only had several rooms habitable. As I was looking at one shattered room, an emaciated frightened cow climbed thru a wall looking for food or water. This had been a dairy area, but most of the cows were dead and bloated under the snow; thousands of them we were told. One can imagine the stench when spring comes.

The 517th had taken all their objectives too. However the paratroopers operate different from infantry. Any strong pockets of resistance they encounter on the way to the objective they just bypass. These pockets of Germans can be a nuisance and we continued to get mortar and gunfire from the 517 area across the valley.

I went out to familiarize myself with the village, starting with the medical collecting station. It was busy with wounded trickling back from the combat area. About a dozen dead were outside under shelter halfs. A medic said two of the bodies were civilians whose faces had been eaten away by pigs. Ugh! No I didn't want to see them. Next I went over to the prisoner cage which is just a figure of speech. The prisoners (about 75) were packed in the dark interior of a wrecked building. The older ones looked like they were glad to be out of the war, but the young ones were very ugly and vocal; I suppose cursing in German. I noticed some of them had the lightning insignia of the SS and those I wouldn't want to turn my back on.

Later that evening we received orders from XVIII Corps to take the town of Ennal and fortified R'emestre Ridge, which were strongly held by the enemy and was a thorn in the side of the 75th Division.

15 JANUARY 1945 – Colonel Reid and General Perrin (Division Commander) went forward to observe the attack. At daylight F Company advanced on Ennal while E & G Companies attacked the ridge. F Company entered the town and after some rough house to house fighting, seemed to have taken it then a surprise counterattack forced them to withdraw. Outside the town, they were pinned down by machinegun and mortar fire. Gen. Perrin & Col. Reed walked up this road urging the men to getup. COL. Reed Fell severly wounded, General Perrin waving his 45 led the remnants of F Company back into Ennal; after a rough and tumble fight the Germans withdrew. Later it was discovered the Germans had prepared a number of spider holes with camouflaged covers in which they hid when the fighting got too rough. When the fighting died down they emerged and took our men by surprise. Meanwhile E & G companies had taken the ridge and its bunkers, but the mopping up continued into the next day. The last few days had been tough on upper echelon officers; a Colonel, Lt. Colonel, and a Major plus several company commanders. With Ennal and the ridge neutralized, the 75th Division launched their attack across our front. The enemy tried to get their

tanks and motorized equipment out of the salient and our artillery had a field day picking off the vehicles as they streamed rearward.

While this was going on, I had an interesting experience. I was exploring a little outside Aisemont and came across a cleared side road which I followed. Soon ahead of me and straddling the road, I saw a large stone farmhouse and outbuildings all enclosed or connected by stone walls. It looked like a fort. Closer I noted the road seemed to terminate in the courtyard formed by the buildings. My map showed the dead-end road and I wondered why we hadn't used this substantial building for headquarters instead of the ramshackle one we were in. My curiosity led me on, but I was acutely conscious of my exposed approach with banks of snow on each side. I didn't know who might be watching me so using some guile I turned to the rear and raising my arms as if signaling a patrol to deploy to each side of the road I then gave the signal to advance and then continued into the courtyard.

I walked up to what appeared to be the farmhouse entrance and was appalled to see that the well trampled snow on the stoop was stained bright red from a very large amount of blood. As I stared at the blood trying to find a clue for its presence and also regretting I was even here. The door opened and I swung to face it with my sten gun. In the doorway stood a tall young blond headed man in the frock of a priest. Behind him in the darkness I could see the form of several others. He greeted me in French of which I only understand a few words. I pointed inquiringly to the blood and somehow or other including sign language he conveyed the idea that they had killed a chicken. This was not too convincing as I saw no signs of feathers. They invited me inside and it didn't seem I had much choice but before entering I turned and whistled and signaled my imaginary patrol to hold their position.

I think this may have saved my life because going with them into a small parlor I found there were eight of them. All young, all dressed as priests, and ominously several were blond. Only two of them spoke in French while the rest kept silent. They brought out a bottle of brandy and glasses. I kept my gun casually pointed in their direction and my back to the wall. From what I could understand they were sent into the area to take care of the dairy cattle. It didn't sound right – the only cattle were dead and under mounds of snow.

Meanwhile I noticed several of them wore black hobnailed boots under their frocks – hardly priestly. After a reasonable but strained period of time I indicated I had to move on. It was a relief to get safely to the door, but I realized it would be bad business to go back the way I cam as I would be exposed for a good quarter of a mile. Looking to the left I noted a small stone shed about 80 feet away and an opening in the wall, beyond the ground fell sharply into the valley. If I could get the stone shed between myself and the house I'd feel a lot safer. So again putting on my act I signaled my patrol to move east and I headed for the shed. With a sigh of relief I walked thru the opening and got the shed between myself and the house.

As I went down the slope the snow was nearly hip deep and the going was rough. As soon as I was below sight of the house I headed toward a thin stand of trees. Though tired from floundering thru the deep snow I found renewed energy to jump and scrabble and dodge until I got over the top of the hill. Eventually my path intersected the road and looking toward the farmhouse saw it was barely visible in the gathering darkness. Feeling reasonably safe I hightailed for regimental HQ.

Nobody knew about a group of priests being in our area so we assumed they could be a squad of Germans cut off by our attack and biding their time until they could escape back to their lines. The only combat unit at HQ was the I&R platoon, but part of them had taken a load of prisoners back to division. The rest had their hands full guarding prisoners or manning the several guard posts. It was decided because of darkness plus the fact they might be what they claimed to be it would be best to wait until morning to check them out. Never did get back, but I'll bet they were gone.

During my absence the ambulance transporting Colonel Reid to the field hospital had stopped so he could give instructions regarding change of command. They said though sedated he was conscious and his wounds though serious were not thought life threatening. For him the war was probably over.

We remained in the Trois Pont-Stavelot area for about a week as reserve. Weather got milder and a lot of the snow was replaced with mud. A Colonel Jeter arrived from the 99th Division to take command of the regiment. We never saw Colonel Reid again after he was wounded. Finally got orders assigning us to the 7th Armored again and we would relieve the 508th Parachute regiment somewhere north of St. Vith.

It was during this time that some of us visited an area where German armor had been destroyed by our air force. All that remained was fire blackened twisted wreckage; turrets blown off the hulls, large chunks of armor plate torn from the hulls and cast aside. Looking inside one I could see what appeared to be charred boots and bones in the debris. On the few days the weather cleared permitting our planes to fly they exacted a fearsome toll on the enemy.

23 JANUARY 1945 – QM trucks arrived and we started our move back to the front. Not a very pleasant trip because the Germans had mined the roads as they withdrew; there was the constant thought that the floorboards of the truck might erupt any time in a hail of flame and steel. The demolished and burned vehicles alongside of the road were a constant reminder the threat was real. Pity the engineers who have to dig up and deactivate the mines. There was an interesting sight in Stavelot (or maybe it was Malmedy). The center span of a bridge over the Ambleve had fallen with a huge 60 ton Tiger tank in the middle of it. The river was shallow and it was about a 50 foot drop so one can imagine what it did to the tank crew. Finally arrived in Diedenberg and it was dark by the time we effected the changeover with the 508th. The town was crowded with our HQ as well as the 2nd and 3rd Battalion CPs.

24 JANUARY 1945 – Received orders that we were to attack and secure Bullingen-St. Vith highway tomorrow. The 517th Parachute Regiment, our partner again, would be on our right this time. The 1st Division on our left would launch their attack a day after ours. The 2nd Battalion objective was the town of Mendel and a large hill mass beyond. The 3rd Battalion would take Meyerode and the Adesburg Ridge. On our left flank just over in 1st Division area was a German stronghold in Ambleve which we would by-pass. When the 1st Division attacks they also plan to by-pass it and later take it from the rear.

Our HQ was located in a stone farmhouse complex at the edge of town similar to the one described in Aisemont, though the outbuildings were closer grouped together around a small courtyard. The dominating feature was a huge manue pile steaming in the courtyard. After getting our operations map up to date with locations of all our units and helping prepare attack orders and map overlays for the next day, I retired to a potato cellar for some shut-eye. It smelled musty but at least was dry. I had been suffering with the GIs, a common ailment from dirty and greasy messkits and questionable water. Sometime during the night I woke up with stomach pains and an urge. Pulling on my boots I made a run for the apple orchard.

It was a cold clear night with a full moon and wispy patches of fog gathering in the low areas. I had just squatted down when I heard the crash of glass in the building nearest me and looked just in time to see a dull red flash and explosion. I fell forward on my face and lay there thinking; "a German patrol raiding the CP throwing hand grenades in the windows, and here I am in this field lit up by moonlight and without a gun." I expected to hear more explosions and the sound of burp guns. Instead there was some shouting and babble of voices followed by silence. Baffled and devoid of any rational explanation of the disturbance, I cautiously returned to the buildings.

The cause of events proved simple enough. One of our fellows had a hand grenade hooked by its handle in the buttonhole of his jacket which was a convenient way to carry them. As he pulled his jacket off, the grenade snagged on something and the pin pulled out. Grabbing the live grenade, he or someone else, tried to throw it out the window which unfortunately was covered by a blanket – standard blackout procedure. So the grenade hit the blanket breaking the glass on the opposite side, then bounced back and fell into a combat boot where it exploded wounding the two in the room. They were being loaded on an ambulance jeep when I got there.

The excitement had me fully awake so I went back to the CP. About an hour later we received a call reporting that the Germans had scored a direct hit on our artillery forward observation post killing or wounding everyone there. Someone must have been careless in approaching or leaving the position as they are very carefully concealed from the enemy. Losing this carefully selected observation post and the men was a serious blow.

25 Jan. 1945 Following a brief barrage, the infantry attack progressed favorably but it was not clear sailing. The 3rd Battalion cleared Adesburg ridge and reached Meyerode, where strong enemy resistance forced them to dig in for the night. The 2nd Battalion ran into German 88's and a company of tanks was committed to knock out the guns. In the process, one tank was lost to bazooka (panzerfust) fire. Resuming the attack, they found Medell strongly held by infantry and tanks. An airstrike was called for and after the planes plastered the town, five tanks were observed scampering east out of the town. Advancing again, they came under 88 gunfire. Finally behind an artillery barrage, they neutralized the gun positions and entered the town. By late afternoon it was cleared of Germans and in our hands. From there, the 2nd Battalion moved on to Deperts Berg but heavy resistance and darkness stalled the attack.

26 Jan. 1945 The 3rd Battalion with a company of tanks pushed into Meyerode and spent the rest of the day mopping up and advancing onto the Adesberg ridge. Meanwhile the 2nd Battalion took the Deperts position, repulsed the German counterattack. With the 1st Div to our north, launching their attack today, the St. Vith-Bullingen highway was now secure in our hands. During the day, we had an interesting experience at regimental HQ. General Hoge of 7th

Arm. CCA was in our crowded HQ conferring with Colonel Jeter on the progress of the attack, when we heard the rapidly approaching roar of aircraft. Before we could think, there was the crash of 20mm shellfire and ricocheting 50cal mg bullets everywhere. General Hoge held his dignity, but the rest of us dove for shelter, wherever it could be found.

      I ran out the door and crawled under a jeep in the lull after the first attack. I had a fleeting glimpse of a pair of twin-boomed planes completing their turn for a second attack. Seconds later, their gunfire was rattling off the cobblestones and fragments were flying everywhere. I decided crawling under the jeep was a bad decision and made a run for the stone shed by the manure pile. Once on the move, I just kept running on through the shed and into the familiar apple orchard and flopped into the nearest depression. From there, I could watch the planes which turned their attention to a tank company bivouced on the far side of the road beyond some trees. The planes were five P-38s (Lightnings) with red noses and the white star of our airforce on the wings. By now, there was a lot of our 50 cal fire directed at them. Apparently they finally saw our ground recognition panels and realized they were shooting up friendly units for they zoomed away into the blue yonder.

      General Hoge was furious and the air liaison officer was franticly trying to contact somebody who could call them off. It was all academic because they were gone almost as soon as they got here, but it was bedlam for a few seconds. For all the noise, there were only a few minor injuries and a few shell holes or gashes in vehicles. We hoped they did better against the real enemy. I had a sizeable gash on my right thumb, but whether from shrapnel or in my mad scramble to get the hell out of there, I don't know. The scar is still one of my identifying marks, along with the tattoo I got in New Orleans.

      In the days that followed, evidence was found in the fir forests around Deperts ridge and Meyerode that some of our troops (perhaps 150) who had escaped from Schnee Iffle had made their last stand in this area. Bodies found, reports from civilians. Civilians reported stories of GIs coming to their houses seeking food and information. All through December many German patrols were seen in and around the forest and gunfire was heard daily. There were rumors of German convoys being ambushed on roads through the forest. Apparently the Germans eventually killed all the Americans, so we will never know the heroism that may have occurred here by a handful of men. But that was the story of the whole Ardennes Campaign: small groups of men fighting it out in the cold, gloomy, fog-enshrouded forests.

      During the days that followed, we observed several overflights of B-17s and B-24s heading into Germany on massive raids. The formations took several hours to pass. On one occasion they returned from a raid, over our positions. This time some of the formations were ragged and it was obvious that planes were missing. A number of the big bombers were obviously in distress, and we saw one pull out of formation and explode in a brilliant flash. Immediately afterward, we could see pieces of debris spiraling earthward. Several parachutes blossomed from another plane as it continued losing altitude and left a large trail of smoke smudging the sky. Our patrols recovered two of the airmen, but failed to find the others. The Germans probably got the others, as they all landed in no-mans land. Strangely enough, we had orders to keep all recovered airmen under guard until returned to division. We never learned why, unless the enemy would sometimes infiltrate spies and saboteurs by making it appear they were downed airmen.

      On the 27th, the 82nd Airborne Division arrived and spent the rest of the day taking over our positions. It was rough getting to our advanced battalions because of the ravines, forest, and narrow, clogged trails. They wasted no time and launched a new offensive against the demoralized krauts the next morning, as we started our move back to the Huy- Liège area. It was cold and the snow had returned, a real wintry day. We passed through some familiar territory, such as Poteau, where the panzers had smashed our cavalry screen and shot up our division artillery as it was withdrawing from St. Vith. There were smashed and burned vehicles, including a number of light tanks, lining the roads. The house where we had stayed with the friendly Belgian family in early December was a burned hulk. Were they there during the fighting, or had they fled into the blizzard and jammed roads? Either option could have been fatal. I'll never know what happened to them. From there, we passed through Recht and Veilsalm. The German attach had swept all along this area and much other the debris remained under a mantle of snow, very depressing.

      Jan. 29, 1945 When we were relieved by the 82nd, we also were released from 7th Armored Division and returned to control of the 106th Infantry Division located in the Huy- Liège area as XVIII Corp reserve. Our regimental HQ was located in a large, picturesque hunting lodge in the sinister setting of a gloomy forest. It even had a moat and drawbridge. The main hall was dark, with high, vaulted ceilings and a huge, ornate fireplace. In the days that followed, the fireplace would require a large share of our free time scouring the forest searching for firewood to feed it. Other features of the hunting lodge were mounted stag and boar heads festooning the walls. The Ardennes boar is a fearsome-looking creature with a double set of razor-sharp tusks, like something out of a nightmare.

Here, we received our delayed mail and first packages since England. Along with welcome letters from Lois and my parents was a box with a cake. Needless to say, the box and cake were well mashed, but not a crumb was wasted. Again we were mated with our errant duffle bags which we thought the Germans had pawed through a long time ago. We owed our thanks to engineers who had saved Service Companies trucks throughout the confusion of the long retreat. I retrieved a round loaf of French bread that I had cacheted in mine. It proved to be hard as a rock and nearly defied the attack of a bayonet. Being 90 percent crust, it was a definite threat to one's teeth. Although it was like chewing leather, it was a welcome change in our diet.

We soon found our paradise wasn't perfect. We had scarcely settled in when the first buzz bomb droned over. Thereafter, it was a steady stream, day and night. Liège was the target and we were between it and the German launching locations somwheres to the east. The buzz bomb wasn't the most accurate device, so a lot of them fell short of the target and those were the ones that bothered us. I don't know how they guided them; whether it was as simple as a timer that cut the engine after they flew a predetermined path for a certain amount of time or perhaps they followed a radio beam until they reached an intersecting beam at the target. I'm sure our side tried countermeasures to foul up their guidance system. Maybe that's why it seemed more of them were falling on us, than continuing on to Liège.

We couldn't seek cover every time one came along. Instead we'd listen carefully to the sound, which I would liken to the throbbing of helicopter blades. As mentioned before, the throbbing would seem to get slower as it got closer until one could picture it hovering directly overhead (above the low laying clouds) then, as the throbbing started to accelerate, one knew he was safe. If the sound stopped, we'd run for shelter in the unnerving silence because the bomb was on the way down. If one was lucky, he had maybe 45 seconds, but never over a minute before it hit. To keep things interesting, the Germans mixed in a few dive bombers. These, instead of gliding in, would now tip over and hit the ground with their ram-jet going full blast.

Typical of the weather in the Ardennes, low clouds obscured our view of the buzz bombs. Only once did I see one break out of the clouds as it dove earthwards. With a half ton of explosive, they created a huge crater, some large enough to hide a two story house in. The craters quickly filled with ground water. When one exploded, even a mile away, one could feel the pressure change on his eardrums. In spite of the number of bombs that hit in our area, I only know of a few men injured, including several from my company who had eye injuries from pulverized glass. I was told that Liège was block after block of rubble, much of which could be attributed to the buzz bombs. Some of the older damage probably was from our bombers, when it was in German hands. Liège was a main supply, hospital, and communications center for the 1st army.

SCENE AT COMMAND POST

ARTILLERY IN ACTION

DIG DEEP AND LIVE

PANZERS BREAK INTO WINTERSPELT

MUST BE BAD. EVEN THE DEAD ARE LEAVING

SNOW TWO FEET DEEP & COLD RATIONS TONITE

FALLING BACK TO BERG RUELAND

ABANDONED AMERICAN TRUCKS

MENDEL, BELGIUM

PATROL IN SNOW COVERED FOREST

GERMANY
FEB. 5 – MAR. 15, 1945

We were actually glad when we received orders moving us back to the front. This rear echelon stuff wasn't the safest place to be with these flying bombs around. At least at the front you had a chance to hit back instead of being sitting ducks.

5 Feb. 1945   Our regiment had received orders the day before, attaching it to the 99th Division in the vicinity of the Losheim-Neuhof. This was along the original line our division (106th) held at the beginning of the German offensive in December. The panzers had smashed the 18th cavalry group in the Losheim Gap and then enveloped our units on the Schnee Iffel. So it looked as if the enemy had finally been pushed back to where he started six long weeks before.

We began our movement, as some milder weather and some sunshine returned. On the way, we passed thru a sizable town that had been hit by our airforce the day before. Unfortunately, it had been occupied for some time by the 1st Army troops. One of those mistakes of war. There was still smoke rising from the debris and groups of people standing around or digging. One thing that sticks in my mind was a G.I. truck wrapped around a granite monument in the town square. Later, we were held up when a truck from another unit hit a mine. I guess they checked to see if they could locate any other mines in the vicinity. When we got moving again, we passed the truck. It looked bad; I don't see how anyone on it could have escaped alive. Of course, any casualties had been removed. Finally arrived in the vicinity of Honsfeld, where we located our CP in the basement of a substantial, but wrecked house. It had a concrete first floor which offered some comfort against artillery.

Our position was on the right flank of the 1st Army, which was about ready to begin its long delayed push into the Rhineland now that the Roer River dams had been neutralized. The Kyll River flowed in a deep valley across our front, then turned east toward the Rhine. The terrain to the east was very rugged with a t number of sizeable streams in deep ravines flowing into the Kyll. In the far distance, around the town of Berk, Germany, lay the Ziegfred line fortifications. We expected the Germans to follow Hitler's orders to hold them to the last man. Our front extended about 4 miles with 2nd Bn. on the northern half (left flank) and 1st Bn. on the south (right flank). We had the 591st FA (105mm) in support. The enemy had made massive use of mines and booby traps as he withdrew from our area, so we soon began having casualties from these.

We were only supposed to anchor 1st Army's right flank when they began their big offensive to the north, so our action was limited to patrols probing the enemy's defenses. These often ended up in sharp little firefights. A nightmare for the patrols was getting thru minefields when they couldn't avoid them. One case involved several men wounded when they stumbled into a minefield. A medic, trying to reach them, was killed by the Germans. Later, others reaching the wounded men had the nerve-racking job of untangling tripwires before the wounded men could be dragged to safety. We had seen rough terrain, but this was the worst; a jumble of ravines, fallen trees, and streams. Much effort was devoted to building trails and log bridges. While the rain melted snow in the open, it still lay heavy in these forests and depressions. No vehicles could get in to most of the units.

141

The rains continued, and our basement started flooding and we had to do some bailing and some improvisions to diver or block the worse leaks. We had built a stove from an oil drum by cutting some holes in it for a door and stovepipe. Ran the stovepipe to the nearest cellar window, but enough smoke escaped to irritate our throats and eyes. One night, I had the duty tour and I was having a rough time keeping my eyes open. Everyone else in the basement were asleep. Thought I'd heat some water on the stove and shave to wake up. So I went up the outside stairs and poured a basin of water from a jerry can and balanced the basin on the oildrum stove to heat. I was half asleep again, when Capt Pealman woke up, sniffed, then asked where the odor of the gasoline was coming from. Suddenly, I realized we also had a can of gasoline at the top of the stairs for the coleman lanterns and I probably had used it. I jumped up, fully awake, pulled on gloves, and grabbed the boiling basin of gasoline from the stove, went to the door, and threw it out. It's a wonder the fumes had not exploded and killed all of us. I was thoroughly cussed out, and deserved it.

About 12th of Feb. our regimental commander, Col Jeter was transferred back to the 99th Div and Lt. Col. Stump arrived to take over. The 99th which had been in continuous combat since early December was relieved by the 69th Inf. Div. We reverted back to control of the 106th Div. This was the first combat roll for the 69th. I went over and visited the 272 If. Regt. of the 69th. On the way over, passed some wrecked enemy SP's and examined them. They were a tracked armoured vehicle equipped with a high velocity 75. I mentioned before, that the Germans used them as a nuisance weapon. They would sneak them up to close range, fire several rounds, and then get out before we could locate and get artillery on them. These had not been so lucky and several dead crew members lay inside or alongside the vehicles.

We finally were issued some small tracked vehicles called Weasels, to facilitate moving ammunition and supplies up to the front line troops. About the size of the British bren gun carrier, it was not nearly so attractive. Looked like a bath tub on caterpillar treads, but it could negotiate that rough terrain. I rode one up to the 2nd Bn area with a load of mortar ammunition. It clawed its way thru terrain a man would have difficulty crawling thru. We passed a number of little signs warning of mines on each side of the trail. Not very reassuring when riding on a pile of mortar shells. The battalion CP was located in a large enemy bunker. The battalions positions were a salient bulging into the German line. Like infantrymen everywhere, our men had made themselves as safe and comfortable as the miserable conditions permitted by digging deep and roofing over these holes with logs. One danger I've not mentioned before are shell damaged trees that often topple without warning or reason when least expected. Also, an artillery shell hitting a tree and bursting is far more dangerous than one exploding in the ground. In all this forest fighting, tree bursts have cause a lot of casualties among our troops. While I was at 2nd Bn, a patrol brought in three prisoners. From their appearance, existence on the other side was just as rough as it was on this side.

One day when we were driving over to the 1st Bn, we heard the roar of low flyplanes coming on fast. Then we spotted a hedgehopping German with three of our airplanes hot on his tail. I think they were mustangs, but it was only a glimpse. Last we saw, all four were hightailing into Germany. On Feb. 17, some rockets and 150's shelled our HQ, causing some anxiety, but other than creating a little more rubble and causome work for the wire crews (telephone), it proved harmless. Div HQ's received a shelling about the same time. About this time, 1st Bn pulled off a successful raid on a large troublesome enemy bunker that commanded a sizeable part of the Kyll river valley. It had been carefully planned and a platoon from C Co. planted shaped charge, killing four Germans and taking 9 captive.

One night I was sleeping in the attic, sheltered by a portion of the roof that still had some tiles. All at once I awakened in the middle of a gun battle. In my sleep groggy condition, I thought the Germans had made another breakthru like last Dec. I fumbled my way across the exposed ceiling beams to an opening in the roof and saw the flashing of gunfire all along the woods. Below me a number of our fellows were firing back, so I joined in, though no one could see anything in the blackness. Fortunately some steadier heads realized the situation and got the firing stopped. Seems a quartermaster truck company had pulled into a field for the night. Neither group knew the other was there because of the strip of woods and sometime during the night a guard spooked at something he heard and fired. Everybody else then just joined in. We heard some of the quartermaster boys jumped into their trucks and took off when the shooting started. If true, they probably didn't stop until they ran out of gas or reached Paris.

Feb. 22-28, 1945   We received news of 1st Army's long delayed attack across the Roer river after the dams were neutralized. One of them was broken by a big blockbuster bomb dropped alongside it. Later, I read that it was a special 10,000 pound bomb. As the month drew to a close, 1st Army was pushing into the industrialized Ruhr and Patton's 3rd Army (south of us) was getting ready for the dash to the Rhine. As these big events shaped up, we sat in our positions. The Germans fired enough to let us know they were still there, and annoyed us with those 75mm SP's and a few rockets occasionally. The mines and the weather were the worst thing and there were all kinds. Wooden box mines that mine detectors couldn't pick up; bouncing betsies, a steel impregnated concrete cylinder that bounded up before exploding. The little pencil mines buried on trails; when a man stepped on one, it fired a bullet into him.

Then there were the big teller mines planted wherever a vehicle might go. We had one case where a road had been used safely for several days. Then "BOOM", one of our trucks gets it. It was rough on the nerves and of course, rougher on the victims.

We managed to have some laughs once in a while. Like the time several sergeants from division visited us. We had a deactivated bouncing betsie mine at the CP on which the trip wire and latch and primer had been re-installed. Thought we'd have some fun with it. I'd show them the mine and explain its operation, pointing out the tripping mechanism, etc. After cautioning to be very careful, I'd hand it to one of our visitors, managing to fumble and drop it in the process. The trick worked perfectly and as the mine dropped, there were four non-coms trying to get out the single door at the same time. Better yet, the primer when off with a loud bang, and they thought they were dead. Well, those of us in on the joke had a good laugh, but you don't make many friends that way.

We totaled 18 killed, 21 missing, and 87 wounded in February, the lightest casualties for a month since going into combat. Of course, the weather took its toll in frost bite and sickness and accidents added a few more. However we had come a long way, learning to survive whether from the enemy or the weather.

MAR. 5, 1945   1st Army and 3rd Army were cutting thru the German defenses and rushing for the Rhine. Finally our part of the line had received orders to advance. With 3rd Bn on the left and 1st Bn on the right, our units took the high ground overlooking the Lewert river, which flowed in a narrow wooded valley across our front. Opposition was surprisingly light. We took 20 prisoners and casualties were light. The 69th Div on our right and the 87th Div on our left also started their attacks. Our artillery moved forward and the attack resumed the next day. We had also moved the CP forward into some dugouts. Our units crossed the Lewert and took the high ground overlooking the Berk river defile. They only met token resistance. Obviously the enemy had pulled out. We figured they probably occupied the strong defenses of the Zeigfred Line which was just beyond the town of Berk.

The 69th was making good progress on our north, but the 87th reported rough going and heavy casualties, mostly from mines. On March 7th, our units pushed through Berk, Kronenfeld, and Baasem till they contacted the 69th Div., which had shifted its attack southeastward. In the process, they passed through parts of the Zeigfred and found them unoccupied. So Hitler's boast that this fortified line from Switzerland to Holland would protect Germany proved as meaningless as the Atlantic Wall or the Maginot Line. So our troops took occupancy of the German bunkers and we moved our regimental HQ into Berk, Germany. In normal times, the Kyll valley must have been very picturesque but right now, it was broken buildings, and a muddy torn landscape bleak under gray skies.

MAR. 7, 1945   Berk was at the edge of the Ziegfred and after getting settled in, we examined some of the fortifications. The dragons teeth were closely space concrete pylons forming a continuous tank barrier about 50 yards deep and marching inexorably across the rolling landscape. Where a road passed thru this barrier, it was heavily mined and ditched, plus being well covered by antitank guns in strong concrete bunkers. The Germans had removed the guns when they abandoned the fortifications, but looking thru the gun embrassures showed their well placed fields of fire. The bunkers were grouped to support each other. Concrete MG pillboxes, concrete mortar pits and well constructed network of trenches would have made an infantry assault very costly. I'm sure concealed artillery positions further back offered effective support and of course, the whole area was grid-surveyed and ranged for pinpoint accuracy. I was glad the 1st and 3rd armies' breakthru had flanked these positions and made them untentable.

Later in the day we received reports that seemed too good to be true. Elements of the 9th Armored had taken a bridge over the Rhine. This turned out to be the bridge at Remagen. The 9th had first seen combat in their unsuccessful attempt to reach our 1st Bn at Winterspelt. We hoped we would be among the troops sent to exploit this fantastic stroke of luck. Although Remagen was probably only 30 miles east of us, as the crow flies, there were large pockets of Germans trapped and milling around between us and the river. I think around 120,000 were eventually taken prisoner.

Mar. 8, 1945   Went into Kronenberg on the Kyll. A sizeable town. The civilians were sullen and looked hostile, as might be expected. Before, we were in Belgium towns; this was the enemy's land. I'm sure the people were shocked to have American soldiers wandering the streets, as right up to the end, Goebbles and Hitler assured the people no enemy would set foot on German soil unless dead or a prisoner. As we drove down a narrow cobbled street, someone dumped a slop jar out of an upper window. It splattered right behind our jeep. I'm sure it was deliberately thrown at us, but no way we could find the culprit. After that we were cautious about looking up, and kept to the middle of the street.

We came to a large building that was a Herman Goring art gallery. Went inside, but any paintings had been stripped from the walls. It was an impressive structure, high ceilings, but debris littered the marble floors from shelling and air raids. I salvaged about a dozen lithographs that lay among the litter. They had Herman Goring's stamp on the back side, and I though someday they might become valuable souvenirs.

Reports came in that 1ˢᵗ Army was starting to build up a bridgehead at Remagen bridge and that the enemy was desperately committing his airforce to destroy it. You can't imagine our jubilation at having this bridgehead across the Rhine. We had expected a bloody river assault. It was the next morning I was snooping around an abandoned German ammunition dump on top of a hill. It was wooded and fog shrouded the hill top. Suddenly a terrible sound ripped thru the air, in the fog. It left me shaking with fright and all I could think of was maybe a big 14" shell; except there was no explosive aftermath. It wasn't until years later when I experienced the same sound and fright from a jet plane passing over my house at roof level, then I realized what it was. I had never heard of an jet plan least of all seen one. I read that the Germans used their new jet planes to attack the Remagen bridge and apparently one of them must have passed right over me in the fog. It felt like an earthquake.

Mar. 9-13, 1945   These were uncertain times, and a bulletin from 1ˢᵗ Army didn't help. It warned to be alert for gas attacks. Now that the Rhine had been breached, the enemy was expected to unleash the large stocks of poison gas they possessed. Of course, we had been issued gas masks as standard equipment, but these cumbersome devices were the first things we got rid of in combat. We'd tear the mask and canister out, but retain the cloth pouch to carry more useful items in. There probably wasn't a half dozen gasmasks in the company, and that was typical throughout the regiment. If a gas attack had materialized, the unfortunate soldier with one would have been hit on the head and stropped of it. Fortunately, they never used gas, though later we saw thousands of gas shells stockpiled in the ammunition dumps.

The civilians kept their drinking places closed in Berk, but rumor had it that beer was available in a small village a couple of miles away. Sgt Lucas and I decided to investigate and we hitched a ride on a weapons carrier headed that way. Passing a German girl on a bicycle too closely, the projecting bed of the truck caught her handlebar and tossed her and the bike into the ditch. We stopped and fortunately except for scrapes and dirt, she was uninjured, but she was one mad fraulein. Several other Germans came over and added their rancor. Couldn't blame her, as the bike was wrecked and at that time there were no new ones to be had. I'm ashamed to say we finally drove away, leaving her & the Germans still shouting sullenly at us.

In the village, we found the beer hall well patronized by GIs. It was after dark when we staggered out and faced a long walk back to our place. On the map I noticed we could cut the distance in half if we went cross-country. It was pitch black though and the first thing we stumbled into was a large patch of nettles. I was never aware of nettles at home, but I can assure you the German variety torment you with an unbearable itch. My friend howled and cussed as we fumbled and rolled getting out of those things. Then he started cursing me for talking him into taking this shortcut. That wasn't to be the end of the troubles, as later we fell over a bank into a stream bed. I imagine it was a four foot fall, as it jarred us both. Not too steady on our feet, we fell several more times before climbing the overhanging bank on the far side. Muddy and wet, he was really complaining now and crying that his arm was broken. It probably took us twice as long to cover that mile than it would have had going by road. It was with relief that I finally deposited him at his tent and then headed for my own. Next morning I went over to see how he was and was surprised to see him sitting in front of his tent with his arm in a splint and sling. He really had broken that arm. He'd have nothing to do with me then, or later. Even when I wrote him after the war, he didn't answer.

One night we watched strange flashes on the northern horizon. They didn't look like the glow of shellfire. Someone told us the Germans were firing their rockets before allied troops overrun the launching sites. I guess they were the big V-2 rockets, as the V-1 (bBuzz Bomb) launchers wouldn't make a big flash. A German plane dropped several bombs in our area, but caused no damage. I think it failed to drop its bombs on a raid on the Remagen bridge and just came over and unloaded them before returning to its base. Then one day we were surprised when a truck convoyunloaded two platoons of colored troops assigned to the regiment. First time we knew there were colored combat troops. Guess this was the beginning of integration. Well they joined us too late for combat.

DESTROYED GERMAN 76mm SP ASSAULT GUN

JAN.16,1945 AND FINALLY BACK TO
WHERE IT ALL STARTED DEC. 16,1944

GERMAN PRISONERS

LONG RANGE BIG GUN

TOO LARGE TO MOVE IN A HURRY, THE GERMANS DESTROYED IT

MISERY AROUND A SMALL FIRE

SCENE AROUND REGIMENTAL HQ

149

WEASEL NEGOTIATES ROUGH BACK TRAILS

MK V TANK (PANTHER)

PROPAGANDA LEAFLET

ASSAULT HOWITZER

ARMORED COMMAND CAR

FRANCE
MAR 16 – NOV 15 1945

"AND THEN HOMEBOUND"

A division with only one regiment isn't much use. Like a boxer with one arm. We received orders to prepare to leave the combat zone and regroup in the vicinity of St. Quentin, France. There, we would receive a large group of replacements and reconstitute the two regiments and two artillery battalions lost in the Battle of the Bulge (Ardennes). We were scheduled to begin our move on March 14.

The Ardennes had been a big battle that proved nothing. The German losses were put at around 82,000 casualties and 25,000 prisoners plus much of their armor. Our losses (1st and 3rd Armies) were estimated at 90,000. Far exceeding the losses in Normandy.

An Item of Interest: The Remagen bridge was built during World War I (1917) by French prisoners. It is standard practices in Europe to build in special cavities in piers and abutments for demolition (explosives). The French officer in charge of prisoners building this bridge deliberately omitted the explosives cavities, which apparently the Germans never discovered until 27 years later. As a result, their attempt to destroy the bridge failed and the Americans gained a direct path into the heart of Germany. How little that French officer could imagine the impact his actions would have.

Mar. 15, 1945   For a change we had beautiful weather as we left Berk, Germany, and traveled to St. Quentin, France. Passed thru Liège, Belgium on the way and again observed the terrible damage the V-1 and V-2 rockets had inflicted on that city. We set up camp on one of the old WWI battlefields near St Quentin. It was around here and Cambria that tanks were first used in combat (1918). We sat here nearly two weeks and were getting things pretty comfortable, when orders came for the division to move to Rennes (Brittany) where the units destroyed in the Ardennes were to be constituted. The cadres (nucleus) to form these units would be provided from the division, including survivors from the destroyed units. I was among those selected, and assigned as S-3 Sgt fro the 422nd Inf. It was from some of these survivers of the 422nd and 423rd regiments I learned details of what happened on Schnee Eifel.

This was a long trip across France, so while some of the division would go by truck, the rest of us would travel by train. This sounded great until we saw the train. It was the little 40 or 8 boxcars (40 men or 8 horses). World War I veterans at the American Legion always joked about the 40 hommes or 8 cheveau.

Apr. 1, 1945   The trip would take several days, for which each car was issued rations. No dining car on this train. In due time, a little French engine hooked on to our string of boxcars. After several shrieks of its high pitched whistle, which left it panting for breath, we jolted off amid the clatter and banging of the couplings. I guess there were about 30 of us to a boxcar (half the size of an American boxcar) which with duffle bags and gear was pretty snug. Speed was not a factor as we rolled leisurely thru the countryside. The railroads were in bad shape from five years of war usage plus being badly torn up by our air force. Every so often we passed rusting wreckage strewn in the ditches or fields by the track even the remains of several planes (B-25s) that probably had been shot down while strafing.

On slight grades, the engine would slow to a crawl and many of us would jump off and walk or jog alongside for exercise. In addition to the normal sliding door, there were several openings with hinged wood closures. I guess for ventilation when shipping horses. Several of the fellows, by crawling out these, found they could grasp the iron rungs of the ladder and climb up on the roof. Ignoring the occasional wisps of smoke and soot, it was pleasant to sit up in the breeze and watch the scenery. Certainly more pleasant than sitting in the cluttered boxcar with limited viw, so soon most of us were up on top. Everything was great until we heard some shouting from the cars ahead of us and noted a mad scrambling of bodies trying to get back down into the boxcar. We soon learned what it was all about as we rounded a curve and saw the train disappearing into a tunnel. Then it was our turn to scramble. Obviously there wasn't time for all of us to go down the ladder and swing sideways into the ventilating window, so some had to lower themselves over the edge of the roof, over the door, and trust that others in the car would drag them inside. A rather risky maneuver. Hanging on the ladder was no good either, as the tunnel appeared much too narrow for that. Thos that didn't make it had to lay flat on the roof and take the smoke, fumes, and soot as they passed thru the tunnel. They were a mess when the came out on the other side.

The roof was too nice a deal to let one tunnel discourage us, so soon we were back up on top. However, we reacted quickly to any signs of activity on the cars ahead and managed to get safely inside when other tunnel disturbed our ride. The train was sidetracked occasionally to allow others to pass. If we were in sight of some village, there were those adventuresome souls who would run over to it for wine or food. And especially if any girls were seen. Then, when the train pulled out, there was a mad exodus of GIs jumping walls and running across fields. There was even one fellow running in his long johns and carrying his bundled up uniform. Of course, one should give him the benefit of doubt. He may have just been trying to get his uniform cleaned and pressed.

It took us a half day to pass around the outskirts of Paris in a maze of railroad yards. Much of the trackage showed signs of recent replacement or repairs, however there were areas of bomb craters and twisted rails and ties. In places were neatly stacked piles of salvaged rails and ties. We passed several big junk piles of tanks, locomotives, trucks, and other war debris. Also, rows of damaged boxcars waiting for repairs. We kept watching, but never did spot the Eiffel Tower. That night we slept best we could on the floor or on duffle bags. The train sidetracked and waited several times, but luckily never near a town, or we would have lost half our compliment. Passed some pretty country next day. Tree lined canals, chateaus. Typical of GIs, we had consumed the rations for the trip the first day. We were grateful for the cheese and bread some of the fellows had gotten the day before when they visited the villages.

We arrived somewhere in the vicinity of the Rennes the next day. Never did see the city. After the usual period of waiting, trucks arrived and hauled us to some big abandoned German airfield, where we set up temporary camp in tents. We had a few days to prepare for the horde of replacements that would descent on us to form the new regiments. It was a busy time preparing camp area assignments, establishing administration, supply, communications, and mess facilities. In any time left over, we explored our new surroundings.

Apparently this had been a German airdrome used during the bombing blitz of England. It covered a huge area. Earth revetments for airplanes were scattered over a wide area. These protected the planes from strafing and bombing. Some were quite a distance from the runways. There was a group of hangers that had been bombed and burned in a mess of twisted girders and sheetmetal. Parts of wrecked German planes lay here and there as well as rusting tractors and dollies for hauling bombs. Most interesting was the little narrow gauge railroad that wound back through the woods to a big, well dispersed ammunition dump, where long stacks of bombs and rockets remained. Not too far from the dump were the smoke stained walls of a gutted manor. From the formal but weed-grown gardens, it must have been a pretty nice place.

During this period, the 3rd and 159th Inf Reg'ts and two artillery battalions joined the division, bringing it up to its normal compliment of 3 Infantry combat teams. Our new units being formed will take months before they are combat ready. The div. was put on alert as tactical reserve for the 66th Div. which held the lines around the St. Nazaire pocket about 12 miles south of us. Following Patton's 3rd army break out of the Normandy bridgehead and the subsequent taking of Cherbourg and Brest, the Germans holding the big submarine base at St. Nazaire and about 15 miles of coast were bypassed. They also controlled the Loire estuary. It was estimated they had about 12,000 combat troops plus naval personnel. They were not aggressive at this point, but posed a problem that would have to be dealt with sooner or later. The 66th Div. Suffered heavy casualties when their troopship Leopold was torpedoed outside Cherberg harbor Christmas Eve, 1944. Instead of being sent to the main front, they were diverted to St. Nazaire to recuperate. So now, our two unfortunate outfits find themselves together on a forgotten front.

Apr. 6, 1945   This was the day 6600 men arrived from the replacement depots to flesh out our cadres (422nd, 423rd Inf and 589, 590th FA). It was a mad house to process all these people, assign them to their respective units, and establish some semblance of order. Many of these unfortunates a few weeks ago had been in officers candidate schools, college training programs, air corp flight training, etc.

When the Battle of the Bulge (Ardennes) cleaned out all infantry replacements, the army curtailed most training programs and reassigned the men to combat infantry, gave them a week of infantry training, and shipped them overseas. They had not yet recovered from the shock of their changed fortunes. At least we should have the highest IQ of any infantry regiment in the army.

Among those who arrived at this time was Major Riggs, who with a portion of the 81st Engineering battalion had fought a desperate delaying action at St. Vith in December to give the 7th Armored time to set up defensive positions. When the panzers finally broke thru, he was captured. Escaping from his German prison, he joined the advancing Russians, and fought with them until able to return to our side. He assumed command of his old 81st Engineers.

The next two weeks were busy from daylight to dark, including weekends, as our newly organized units were put thru rigorous small unit training. We were also training with live ammunition, mortars, hand grenades, overhead machine gun, and artillery fire. We suffered some casualties from accidents and miscalculation which is normal in such training. April 15 was the big day, as the regiments paraded before the division staff and then formed massed ranks for formal presentation of the regimental colors. Our training would be continued until judged combat ready.

April 16, 1945   Division received new orders to establish and man prisoner of war enclosures for the hundreds of thousands of Germans surrendering to the 1st, 3rd, 7th, and 9th American Armies as they swept deeper into Germany. My regiment and the other new units were detached and assigned to the 66th Division. So, the 106th Division consisting of my old 424th Inf, plus the 3rd and 159th Inf and supporting units left for Germany. They would establish prison enclosures extending from Wesel, near the Dutch border on the Rhine, south to Manheim. Eventually other units reinforced the division to help guard and process the nearly one million prisoners. In addition, they had to care and process over a million displaced persons who were survivors of forced labor gangs and concentration camps. They faced a monumental task in face of critical shortages of food, lack of shelter, and poor sanitary conditions. Improvisation was the key. They used prisoners to build their own prison enclosures and shelters, run the mess facilities, handle the administration work, and provide medical care. Locomotives were used to provide hot water and steam. The danger of epidemic was a big concern.

However, back at Rennes, I was concerned mostly with training schedules, field problems, and logistics. Any time I found free, I continued exploration of the area. One day, several of us walked over to a nearby town we found marked on the map. I never saw a town so completely destroy as this one. The land was a level landscape of debris. No walls were standing except part of the shattered church in the middle of the town. Along the faint outlines of the streets were neatly stacked stones retrieved from the wreckage. The few trees that remained were twisted and sick from wounds. We saw a tarpaper shack with a crude "Café" sign painted on it. Entering the dim interior, we were greeted with hostile eyes from a half dozen Frenchmen dressed in rough work clothes. We didn't stay. I guess this town was bombed during Patton's sweep down thru Avranches. I can't blame the Frenchmen. If this was the price of liberation, was it worth it? I imagine all of those men had lost family members in that mess from American bombs. On another day, we drove up to see the invasion beaches on Normandy. It was much further by road than we expected. We went up thru Avranches, St. Lo, Isigny, and on to Omaha Beach, where the 1st Division landed on D-Day. A lot of debris and obstacles still sat as they were. Landing craft were half buried in sand and gravel. We wanted to drive along the coast to Caen, but time would not permit it.

April 21, 1945   We took over a sector of the line around St. Nazaire. The plan was to rotate battalions frequently so they all got combat experience. The battalion in reserve continued training. The combat experience consisted mostly in patrol activities and getting used to being shot at. This was truly a quiet front and a great way to break in new troops to combat. Not like the way we were broken in, by finding ourselves in the path of the biggest German offensive on the western front. As with new troops on the line, there was a lot of indiscriminate firing. Occasionally a patrol would get into a fight and mines (of which there were plenty) caused casualties. The Germans dropped artillery fire on our positions and rear areas once in a while to let us know they were still there. Of course, our new artillery battalions needed practice, so they fired a lot more than normal. I'm sure the Germans didn't appreciate bearing the brunt of our training. If an observer even saw a rabbit or rat, he'd call in for mortar or artillery fire.

The Germans occupied the area from St. Nazaire north to Redon, then west to Vannes. We were scattered along the east and northeast side of the pocket. The FFI (French Forces of the Interior) were active around Pontchateau and south toward the Loire river. Although they were active on our side, it seemed we treated them worse than we did the German prisoners. They were dressed in ragged clothes, wore tattered sandals, and carried a mixture of German, French, and American weapons. The only uniform appears they presented was the ever present beret and usually a cigarette hanging from the lower lip. When we'd get into one of the villages like Blain or Guemene, we'd socialize with some of them over a bottle of vin rouge. They'd usually try to trade German pistols r daggers for American cigarettes, coffee, or even our weapons. It seemed to me that our army should have equipped these people with fatigues, shoes, and standard weapons rather than let them continue operating as guerillas. Perhaps they were considered pro-communist, and that is why we officially neglected them. I don't know.

One night I checked on our messenger drivers in case I needed them. They were comfortably settled in a dry hayloft. As I was talking to them, a shell hit and exploded maybe a hundred yards away. These were some of the new men, so I told them it was probably one of ours that hit short; nothing to worry about. Shortly after I returned to the CP another single round hit. Later when I went out to get one of the drivers, the hayloft was empty. I found them nearby in a dirt floor cellar. I guess they decided my advice wasn't worth a darn. The Germans continued their nuisance firing the rest of the night, so when I was relieved , I joined them in their cellar. It was a more comfortable night than the one I spend a few days later.

I had gone into one of the villages and met three French soldiers, two of whom could speak a little English. After drinking a couple of bottles of red wine, I went with them to their barracks where we told stories, played cards, and drank Kalvados until the early hours of the morning. Finally leaving them (though I don't think they even knew I left) I had a long walk to get back to my billet. The wine had given me a terrible headache, and the Kalvados wanted to come up, and I wanted to sleep. About halfway back, I knew I wasn't going to make it, so I crawled thru the bars of a gate in a stone wall along the road and stretched out in the weeds. This was April which was cold with a full moon and a heavy dew. Later something woke me up and I became aware of a monstrous shadow standing by me breathing heavily. I though Satan had me! Then I realized it was a cow; or was it a bull? I jumped up and bolted for the gate while the creature snorted in surprise and galloped in the opposite directions. Once the excited more off, I realized I was chilled the bone, wet, and still had my headache. I gave a sigh of relief when I and my hangover finally crawled into that nice warm bedroll. I swore, "No more wine or Kalvados," but of course once recovered, I promptly forgot the vow.

May2, 1945   We received the big news that Berlin had surrendered to the Russians. With Patton in Austria, it didn't seem the war could last much longer, but still there was the threat of a German last stand in the so-called national redoubt in the Bavarian Alps. Hitler's threat, too, that new weapons would change the complex of the war. We stepped up our activities and engaged in some company sized attacks with varying success. During one of these, the Germans shelled us pretty heavily with some big stuff, probably 8" naval guns. The 423rd stirred up a hornet's nest in their probing and a battalion was committed before it was over. In the end, the lines remained pretty much as they had been. On May 7th, Germany surrendered and the war in Europe was over. However, the commander of the garrison in St. Nazaire was an ardent Nazi, and he swore to fight to the end. Negotiations under a white flag continued, while plans were made for a final assault if necessary. Our regiment was reinforced with a company of tanks. The enemy was given until 11 am on May 9th to surrender unconditionally. As zero hour approached, our troops and the 66th were poised and waiting for the barrage that would roll in ahead of us. Everything had become very quiet. At 10:45, the welcome message arrived to stand down, as St. Nazaire had surrendered. The last bastion of Nazism had fallen.

Joyful with the end of the war here, our thoughts turned to Japan, a war still to be finished. With the fanatical nature of the Japanese, an assault on the mainland was going to be costly. I had just received a letter from home telling of the death of my friend Phil Carrier with the 3rd Marines on Iwo Jima. What a shame. He had spent almost the whole war as a drill sergeant training recruits. Finally sent to the Pacific, he only lasted a matter of minutes in his first combat.

We got down into the city of St. Nazaire, mostly around the old port area. It was a maze of interconnecting waterways with concrete bunkers and sandbagged strong points. There were some big dual purpose gun batteries that could fire inland or seaward. I was glad we didn't have to take it. We saw the huge dry-dock which British commandos destroyed in 1941. They rammed a destroyer filled with explosives up onto the seaward gates. It didn't explode until the day after the attack. When it did, they say it killed 300 Germans who were examining it. Among the weapons captured were some miniature tanks called "Goliath." They were about five feet long and remotely controlled. Filled with explosives, in theory they could be maneuvered to an enemy strong point or armored vehicle and detonated. I understand they were used on Normandy but with little success. The cable that controlled them was too vulnerable to shrapnel. We didn't see the submarine pens, which was a disappointment. There did seem to be a sunken submarine by the mole (jetty), and too much debris, to be sure. I had hoped to find a Nazi flag as a souvenir, but others beat me to any of those.

May 18th, 1945   After German prisoners were sent to regular enclosures, our work here was finished and we returned to our camp south of Rennes, at St. Jacques, I think. Training continued at a slower pace and we had lots of rain and mud. May 25th, we started our trek back to Germany as part of the army of occupation. We camped at

Soisson that night and arrived in the vicinity of Luxemburg City late on May 26th. We went into the city and found a public place to take a bath. It was a rather ornate place with copper tubs sunk in tile floors,. It wasn't private baths, but at leas the men's and women's areas were separated. The GI in the tub next to me finished and got out to dry himself. There was a cord hanging down from the ceiling at each tub, so he pulled the cord, thinking it dumped the water. Instead, to his surprise and mine too, in came a woman with a long handled scrub brush and small pail. He jumped back into the tub and had a heck of a time convincing her that he didn't want his back scrubbed. I was glad he finished before I did because I probably would have done the same thing. I just had time for a small glimpse of the city. The thing that sticks in my mind was a wide bridge crossing a very deep ravine in the middle of town. Rain and an open jeep were not conductive to sightseeing.

Next day we continued into Germany by way of Trier. Of course, war damage was everywhere, but overall, Germany appeared more modern than France or England. It was the closest thing we'd seen to the USA. Even the girls looked prettier. Too bad we were not allowed to fraternize. We ended up in a camp near Mayen. General Perrin, whom we all liked, took over the command of the brigade. Training continued and we had further casualties from old mines, which would continue to kill for many years to come. I wouldn't want to be the farmer who had to plow these fields. We also had three men killed and twelve wounded by one of our mortar shells in practice.

I finally received my long-sought furlough for Paris. I spend about three days in Paris, and then traveled by train to Dijon where my father met my mother in WWI. I had some time before getting the train to nearby Beaune. I was stuck in Beaune for the night, as there was not train to Meursault until the next morning. I couldn't find a room, but I met some GIs and spent the night with them. I took a motor railcoach to Meursault and with a few inquiries, located my grandmother Rein Maurice. She was a tall thin woman and appeared to have the survived the hardships war imposed pretty well. I gave her some coffee, canned meat, and cigarettes which I had carried for the purpose. She was most pleased with the coffee and the cigarettes were tops for bartering. Meursault is noted for it s wines, and so, I was treated royally by her and her friends. My mother, who was an only child, worried constantly during the war as to her mother's welfare. Mail service was very spasmodic during the German occupation. They told me about and atrocity in a village about 10 kilometrers from Meursault. While the Germans were retreating from the south (Marseilles) the Marquis attacked a convoy in that village. The Germans rounded up 150 hostages (men, women, and children), locked them in the church, and set it on fire. Later, I read an article confirming the story. Dr. Baret, whom I met in 1928 when I visited France with my mother, drove me to Dijon. I caught a train to Metz, where I spent the nite. I hitchhiked from there to Luxemburg-Trier Comblenz, then Mayen and camp. It was quite a trip & took 11 hours.

July 16, 1945   We moved via truck convoy to Mingolsheim, Germany (near Karlsruhr on the Rhine). It rained most of the time. We went over to Coblenz, then down along the Rhine thru Worms, Mainz, and Mannhein. The damage was terrible, and in many places, just a two lane road had been bulldozed thru the rubble that covered the streets. One wondered how many bodies were decaying in that mess. It rained all the way, and the damp air had a musty odor like an old burned building. At Worms, we passed along a railroad yard, and at one place, a locomotive had been hurled clear across the street. Somewhere along the way, we crossed the river on a pontoon bridge. Nearby, the piers and upper structure of a large bridge protruded above the swiftly running water, creating mean looking whirlpools. Anyone spilled into that water would never have a chance to survive. It must have been some job for the engineers to put this pontoon bridge together and anchor it in the current. I can't imagine it being done under bombing and artillery fire. The water along the shore was littered with sunken barges and part of the bridge had crushed a small steamer against the bank.

Down toward Karlsruhr, the damage didn't seem so bad and Baden was a surprise with its rows of fancy, stuccoed pink cottages. We had pretty good billets in Mongolsheim. Our kitchen was in a building, but they served us in an alley that had been blocked off. The garbage cans were at the street end, where we'd dump our mess kits before going thru the wash line. It was embarrassing to see the kids and old people standing by the garbage cans with plates or little pails, getting the food we threw rowing away. It made one ashamed that we had more than we could eat, and yet to scrape one's leftovers into somebody else's plate just didn't seem right.

We took part in an operation named "Tallyho." The purpose was to comb the area for war criminals, ex-Nazis, firearms, radio transmitters, and black-market operations. Roadblocks were set up and house-to-house searches were conducted. Overall, I doubt the operation was very successful. These people had spent years in a police state and were experts at deception, false identities, and forged papers. They probably had a good laugh at our amateurish efforts.

Many of our units would soon be heading for the Pacific war zone, but men with the most service points were scheduled to be rotated home. This was good news for me, as I had about as many service points as anybody.

On August 3rd, I was in a contingent assigned to the 118th Infantry at Dole, France, as the first step home. About fifty of us went by truck to Karlsruhr, and there, joined by other groups, we boarded the familiar 40 and 8 boxcars for France. Another slow trip, we crossed the border at Strussberg and then down through parts of the Vosge mountains. They looked pretty rugged. My dad had marched thru this area in 1918l. We arrived in Dole early on August 5th. It looked like a soft deal, as we were assigned quarters in town and duties were to be minimal.

We shared Dole with a regiment of French Colonial troops. The Senegalese (blacks) were officered by professional looking French officers in light blue uniforms. The enlisted men wore rough brown wool uniforms with red fez caps and tassels. They were mostly tall, athletic looking fellows with regular facial features rather than the broad Negro features. We never had any trouble with them, which is unusual in a town crowded with soldiers. A week or so after we arrived, they marched out on their way to Indochina and a war that would drag out for twenty years and end up as a defeat for both France and us. Of course I didn't know that then. They made a colorful sight as they route-stepped at ease thru the streets. Colorful red hats, the blue uniforms of the officers, rifles slung, leather accoutrements creaking, and the light tinkle of mess gear and tin cups that hung from their packs. I wonder how many of them came back from the bitter struggle in Viet Nam.

I met a White Russian family. They were former aristocrats who fled the revolution to become permanent exiles in France like many others. He was quite a craftsman and carved intricate, inlaid wooden jewel boxes. I traded coffee and cigarettes for several of them which I sent home. Cigarettes were the top item on the black market. If one needed some cash, he'd stick a carton of cigarettes under his arm and stand on the street corner. In seconds there would be several prospective buyers. Twenty bucks (1,000 francs) in those days was pretty good money. Of course, we couldn't get rich as we were limited by our cigarette ration.

Besancon was a sizeable city about an hour's train ride from Dole. I made several trips there as I found it most interesting. It had been one of the key Roman fortified cities holding the border against the Germanic hordes. Many Roman works remained, including the old city gates with their huge bronze studded wooden doors and the ruins of the amphitheater. On a hill over looking the city stood the well preserved remains of a large citadel with massive stone walls, guard towers, dungeons, sally ports, and moats. The river looped around three sides of the hill, protecting it. It covered many acres which I enjoyed exploring. Riding the last train back to Dole at night was standing room only in the swaying coaches that somehow clung to the rough roadbed. My friend Monroe Roberts and I usually stood on the platform between coaches if there was room as the whipping soot breeze was better than the smoke filled crowded interiors. One night, we were continually receiving spray as we stood on the clattering platform. We assumed it was steam from the engine. Later, as we worked our way forward through the coaches, we discovered that stupid GIs had been urinating off the platform ahead of us. Better had we never discovered that.

I made it over to Meursault several times. It wasn't too convenient to get there by road or rail. It is an old, picturesque village with narrow twisting streets. Everything is build of stone, including the roofs. There are a number of big mansions surrounded by stone and wrought iron walls. Typical Burgudian architecture with turrets and colorful zigzag roof patterns was abundant. There are extensive caverns below the town used for aging and storing wine. In many of the courtyards one sees the huge wood presses for squeezing the grapes. My grandmother's friends always made me feel welcome; various wines, brandies, and cognac were always at hand. My lack of French however was really a barrier to enjoy all this. I wasn't prepared for my first French Sunday dinner. It is sort of a social event that lasts all afternoon. Between each course, wine, brandy, and other beverages are served and everyone sits and visits, preparing for the next course. Or course, I couldn't partake in the conversation. Also I ate too much at the first couple of courses and drank too much between them. So by 5 pm, I was rather miserable with too much of both. I floated back to Dole that night. There certainly was no evidence of a food shortage that day.

Septembers 31, 1945   It had been a pleasant August and September, warm and lazy. But we wanted to get home, no spend another winter in Europe. I was glad when order arrived moving us another step in the right direction. I ended up in a place called Camp Norfolk, near Soissons. It was somewhere between Chalons and Troyes, Frances. It was a lousy camp and the weather had turned cool. The army had organized many trips and other activities to assuage the impatience of GIs longing to go home. A soldier could even go to college if he was willing to stay another six months or year. It was really a wonderful opportunity, but most of us were too dumb to take it. At any rate, I signed up for a trip to Switzerland. The seven day trip took us thru Basel, Bern, Spiez, Interlocken, and Brig. It was a great trip, but it was cold with snow in many places. Back at camp, time dragged and we welcomed an assignment one day to drive a batch of vehicles to a storage depot. It was rather an amazing sight to see maybe a hundred acres of tanks, trucks, bulldozers, jeeps, and artillery pieces parked bumper to bumper and hubcap to hubcap. They probably sat there and slowly settled into the mud. Everybody wanted a jeep after the war, but most of the rusted away other there. On the way, we passed an aircraft disposal area. The planes were parked with noses in the ground and tail in the air so they could be jammed closer together. What a waste war is.

October 19, 1945   I was ordered to report to 2nd replacement depot at Namur, Belgium, via Rheims. Nine weeks ago I thought I was on my way home, and I hadn't even reached a port of embarkation yet. I spent the night at Rheims and walked over to see the famous cathedral. I was surprised to note that after all these centuries, stonemasons were still working on the structure. I slept on the barrack bags that night, waiting for the train to carry us to Namur. I was sick of camps, but surely the next move would get me to Antwerp or Le Havre. I marked off the days on my calendar and went into Brussels one weekend. Fish and chips (french fries) are a popular snack here. I guess they take the place of our hot dog. They sell them from little stand or two wheeled carts along the street. The only excitement we ran into was a fancy bar, or rather café. It was called the "crystal palace" as there were big mirrors all round the walls and glass chandeliers. It was filled with soldiers like every place else. Somewhere in the crowd, an argument started and a chair flew, shattering one of the big mirrors. After that, a bedlam of curse and shattering glass began. We got out and just made it safely across the street when the first jeepload of MPs rolled up and waded in with billy clubs swinging. I had no intention of getting picked up and ending in the guardhouse when I was this close to going home.

I have to mention the fellow in camp who had a duffle bag full of French and Belgian francs. All the bills I saw were large denominations. I guess he was in quartermasters and made it in the black market. I never thought he would get that loot past the inspection before we were allowed to board ship, somehow he made it. Perhaps some inspecting officer was a little richer for the oversight. In any event, while most of us were going home broke, this fellow found his fortune in Europe.

November 1, 1945 Finally, after several false hopes, the day we were looking for arrived. First there were inspections to see we carried no contraband, then physicals to make sure we would be acceptable back in the states. After that, we were transported to some dock area in Antwerp and joined the endless line of burdened figures filing into a large troopship, a converted liberty ship, I think. There were tiers of pipe frame bunks stacked five high, filling the hold. There was only about eighteen inches of headroom between bunks, so all one could do was lay flat. The top bunk had headroom, but one had better not fall out of it. The hold was wall-to-wall and floor-to-ceiling humanity. The mess facilities were about like the Aquatania, tables with curbs that one stood at. Latrines were quite primitive. It was far from first class, but who cared? We were on our way to good old USA.

We pulled out early the next morning with two other troopships, but only a few observed our passage down the Shelt estuary. We passed Walcheren Island which the Germans had fortified and held tenaciously to deny the allies use of the port of Antwerp. The Germans blew the dikes and flooded much of it. The trip thru the English Channel was uneventful as we settled down to boredom, broken only by the card games and crap shooting that never stopped for the next two weeks. As we wallowed out slowly into the Atlantic, small land birds accompanied us for several days. They'd sit on the rigging or flit about on the deck. Then they gradually disappeared. I don't know if they made it back to land or got swallowed by the sea.

Somewhere south of Iceland, a North Atlantic hurricane hit us and the next five days were terrible. A good share of us were soon seasick and those on the lower bucks were unintentional victims of those on the upper bunks. There would have been some bad fights, except nobody was in condition to fight. It isn't pleasant to say, but vomit flowed back and forth across the narrow aisles and under the bunks, saturating anything on the floor. Efforts to keep it mopped up were futile. So many of those who survived seasickness fell victim to the sour stench. Even so, games continued, but with buckets placed strategically handy. It took a strong stomach though, to stay in the big crap game at the forward bulkhead. There, the deck would rise twenty feet and suddenly drop out from under you. But, if you were thirty bucks in the hole or had a hot streak going, you took your turn at the bucket and got back to the game.

The second day of the storm, a huge white owl landed on a cross member of the mast. He became a topic of interest to take our minds off our misery. Where had he come from, how did he find the ship in this storm, how long can he hang on in that wind and without food? Those coming back from their brief turn on the upper deck would describe how the wind buffeted him and whipped his feathers about. He hung on for two days and then he was gone. We figured he probably decided to take a chance and fly while he still had a few feather left. The wind was blowing south off Newfoundland at the time, so he probably was swept into the open Atlantic. The storm lasted five days, but to most of us, it seemed a lifetime. Even when it abated, the waves remained and maybe the ship didn't roll quite as far each time. I remember when I finally recovered enough to try and get some food down. I took one look at the spilled slop that oozed slowly back and forth between the curbs of the table and I was sick for another day.

November 15, 1945 We finally reached the port of Boston after two miserable weeks. I'd had enough ocean to last me a lifetime. From then on, I wanted both feet on solid ground. No wonder half the early emigrants crossing the ocean in little sailing vessels perish. In port, we heard that a hatch cover structure on the troopship ahead of us collapses in that storm. It crashed down into the bunk area below, several were killed, and a number were injured. Flexing of the hull in those massive waves caused the accident.

We went by train to Indiantown Gap Military Reservation in eastern Pennsylvania. By strange coincidence, out of the hundreds of barracks, I was assigned to one right next to the one I occupied when I started service in early 1941. That was really completing the circle. This was the old 1st Battalion area of the 112th Infantry. Looking at the nice paved streets and grassy quadrangles, my memory flooded back to the bleak, cold, unfinished camp it was then. At night, after training, we had special details hauling slate from the nearby mines to build sidewalks and parking areas to get out of the mud. We spent three days at Indiantown dragging thru more inspections, physicals, and paperwork before finally receiving our mustering out pay and discharge.

Later I learned, to my disgust, had I remained with the 106th Division, I would have been a civilian about six weeks earlier. When the Atomic Bomb ended the war with Japan prematurely, that outfit was sent home and deactivated in early October.

November 18, 1945This is it! I was a civilian again, and proud to have been part of the great adventure. I was lucky to have come thru unscathed. America had gone into the war a sleeping giant, awakened by Pearl Harbor. There was probably no time before or since that we would be more united in purpose or spirit. We merged from the war the most powerful nation on Earth in the new atomic age. THE FUTURE LOOKED BRIGHT. It felt good to be heading home. Yet, I was perhaps a little disappointed that there would be no bands or victory parade to welcome the conquering hero home. Now I had a wife to collect, a job to find, and the rest of my life to live.

Letters Home

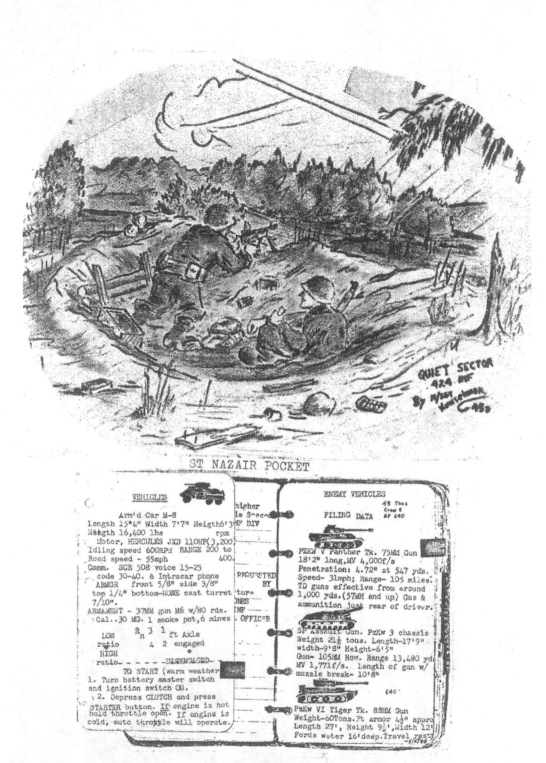

ST NAZAIR POCKET

MY NOTEBOOK

SLOW TRAIN ACROSS FRANCE

CANAL BARGE

A QUIET SECTOR

LITTLE BOYS IN SKIRTS

SENEGALIS AT DOLE FRANCE

NORTH SEA

ENGLAND

London •

HOLLAND

Antwerp •

BEL.

Namur •

GERMANY

To Boston
NOV.

Rennes •

Paris

St. Q.

Mayen

L'UX.

Mainz

St Nazaire
Pocket

APR 1-2

MAY 25-27

Manheim

Nantes •

SEP 30

AUG 3

Karlsruhr

ATLANTIC

Meursault

Dole

SWI.

FRANCE

OFFICIAL TRAVEL

FURLOUGHS

OLD SOLDIERS NEVER DIE
THEY JUST FADE AWAY.

1945-2009

I resumed civilian life in Meadville, PA, employed as a draftsman and for a time by the Postal Service. During those years I designed and built two houses. However, twelve (12) years in NW Pennsylvania was too much for my southern wife. Gray skies and deep snow from Thanksgiving to Easter. I came home one day to an empty house and a note saying my wife was taking the children home to Arkansas. Our marriage was on thin ice.

I phoned a team that was recruiting engineering personnel for government Facilities in Oak Ridge, TN., and was offered a job. I called Lois and asked "If East Tennessee sounded like neutral territory to settle in?" She happily approved. Together we visited the area and I interviewed at the National Laboratory. It looked like challenging work and a great place to raise a family. We have lived here happily ever after on our secluded hilltop five acres after retiring form O.R.N.L Engineering Dept., I continued my architectural work for another twenty (20) years.

" I praise the LORD for he has protected and blessed me all the days of my life."

Maurice Kunselman

<u>Military History</u>   M.H. Kunselamn (Bill)
                                          20-310-714

B Co. 112th Inf., 28th Division   Indiantown Gap, Penn.   Feb. 1941
                                       Carolina Maneuvers
HQ Co. "   "   "   "   "
                                       Camp Beauregard, LA   1942
HQ Co. Tank Destroyer School   Camp Hood, Texas   1942
HQ Co. 2nd Tank Destroyer Brigade   Camp Hood, Texas
                                       Tennessee Maneuvers   1943
HQ Co. TD Sect., 2nd Army HQ   Memphis, TN   1943
HQ Co. 414th Inf., 104th Division   Camp Carson, Colorado   1944
HQ Co. 424th Inf., 106th Division   Camp Atterbury, Ind.   1944
                                       European Theater
HQ Co. 423rd Inf., 106th Division   France – Germany   1945
EQ. Co. 118th Inf., 30th Division   Dole, France   1945
(X Assigned to Ser. Co.)

                                       Discharged at Indiantown Gap   Nov.   1945

Campaigns

Ardennes   (Battle of the Bulge)

Rhineland

Central Europe

Northern France

Metals

Expert Infantry Badge

Combat Infantry Badge

American Defense Zone

European Theater of Operations

Victory Metal

Occupation of Germany

Good Conduct Metal

Decorations

Belgium Croix De Guerre (Unit Citation)

Bronze Star

COMMONLY USED ABBREVATIONS

HQ	Headquarters	Inf	Infantry
CP	Command Post	Art	Artillery
Gen	General	Arm	Armored
Col	Colonel	Eng	Engineer
Maj	Major	Cav	Cavalry
Capt	Captain	TD	Tank Destroyer
Lt	Lieutenant	QM	Quarter Master
M/Sgt	Master Sargent	AAA	Anti Aircraft
1st/Sgt	First Sargent	VG	German In
T/Sgt	Technical Sargent	PZ	German Armor
S/Sgt	Staff Sargent	Flak	German AAA
Sgt	Sargent	C.O.	Commanding Officer
Cpl	Corporal	Ex	Executive Officer
Pvt	Private	S-1	Ajutant
Div	Division	S-2	Intelligence
Regt	Regiment App 3000 Men	S-3	Operations
Bn	Battalion App 800 Men	MLR	Main Line Resistance
Co	Company App 170 Men	GI	American Soldier
Plt	Platoon App 48 Men	MG	Machine Gun
Corp	Three or more Division	O.P.	Observation Post
CCB	Armored Combat Team	S.P.	German Assault Gun
Sqd	Cavalry Battalion		(Self Propelled)

BATTLE CASUALTIES ONLY, ALL DIVISIONS

4th	Infantry	22,454	94th	Infantry	5,607
29th	Infantry	20,111	87th	Infantry	5,555
9th	Infantry	18,631	6th	Armored	5,526
90th	Infantry	18,460	102nd	Infantry	4,867
30th	Infantry	17,691	100th	Infantry	4,790
28th	Infantry	15,904	10th	Armored	4,697
35th	Infantry	15,406	63rd	Infantry	4.547
83rd	Infantry	15,248	103rd	Infantry	4,543
2nd	Infantry	15,066	70th	Infantry	3,966
1st	Infantry	15,003	75th	Infantry	3,954
79th	Infantry	14,875	9th	Armored	3,952
80th	Infantry	14,480	42nd	Infantry	3,598
8th	Infantry	13,458	5th	Armored	3,554
3rd	Infantry	13,101	12th	Armored	3,436
5th	Infantry	12,475	11th	Armored	3,216
101st	Infantry	11,468	17th	Infantry	3,166
36th	Infantry	11,258	76th	Infantry	3,126
45th	Infantry	10,458	14th	Infantry	2,896
3rd	Infantry	10,105	69th	Infantry	1,556
26th	Infantry	9,956	8th	Infantry	1,313
106th	Infantry	8,163	66th	Infantry	1,098
78th	Infantry	7,890	65th	Infantry	1,052
104th	Infantry	7,011	89th	Infantry	1.006
2nd	Armored	6,751	97th	Infantry	934
84th	Infantry	6,561	71st	Infantry	788
95th	Infantry	6,370	86th	Infantry	760
7th	Armored	6,150	13th	Armored	493
44th	Infantry	6,111	82nd	Infantry	456
99th	Infantry	6,103	20th	Armored	76
4th	Armored	5,988	16th	Armored	12

82 & 101 AB Divisions Not Shown